CANTERBURY SCHOOL

The First Ninety Years
1915–2005

COMPILED BY

Kathy Bolster

ISBN 1-933002-18-2

PublishingWorks
60 Winter Street
Exeter, New Hampshire 03833

(603) 778–9883

www.publishingworks.com

Acknowledgments

The trouble with writing a history of Canterbury is that it keeps happening. Although I am seldom at school for dinner, whenever I do attend and sit with the senior faculty, stories about "the old days" inevitably come up. At the Third Form orientation field day recently, Marc Vanasse '73 regaled the faculty present with stories of field days from a decade ago. Events were announced through a loudspeaker in one of Sheehan House's upper-floor dorm rooms, interspersed with demo tapes made by Rod Clarke '46 for commercial work. In December 2004, as I was beginning proofing work, Canterbury received news of the passing of James Moore, which had to be incorporated into the rough draft. One story or reminiscence always seems to lead to another.

Then, too, there are some omissions. Distance and health in one case, and distance and marriage in another, prevented me from interviewing some longtime faculty members. There are more boxes of Sheehan correspondence that should be sorted and read. On one particularly bad afternoon, I realized that my tape recorder was not operating during part of my interview with Señora Gilda Martin. On another day, Mr. Jules Viau stopped by to discuss how I would interview him. The conversation grew into a lengthy reminiscence, but, caught off guard, I did not have my recording equipment operating and had to rely on hastily scribbled notes. To all those people whose stories are so important to a thorough history of Canterbury, and whose stories are not here, I apologize. For all the stories that, for one reason or another, did not make it into this book, I hope that a future historian will correct my errors and omissions for a centennial edition.

More people have given generously of their time, money, and expertise than were possible to include in this book. Canterbury could not have survived and prospered over these last ninety years without the ongoing support from its board members, faculty, parents, friends, and alumni. Your efforts are appreciated and held dear.

This history could not have been written without access to the School's archives, especially THE TABARDS, which are the single best source of Canterbury news and provide a student perspective of Canterbury School. I lay a charge on future Cantuarians to regularly produce and archive a quality student newspaper. Future generations will thank you. I append a plea for the general collection, preservation, and organization of the School's archives. Discerning the relationship between Dr. Hume and Mr. Havemeyer would not have been possible *without the correspondence preserved in the archives. My thanks to Algis Stankus-Saulaitis, librarian, for his assistance in the archives.*

Several people have given invaluable assistance. I am indebted to Edward Mack and Andrew Smith '59; parts of the earlier histories they wrote are interwoven verbatim into this history, especially Mr. Mack's account of prep school education in America and the founding of Canterbury School. Marc Vanasse proofread early drafts and contributed some anecdotes. Certainly I relied heavily on his PALLIUM *articles. Mr. Rod Clarke, Señora Gilda Martin, Mr. Jean Hebert, Mr. Jules Viau, and Mr. JP Mandler gave generously of their time to tell me their stories. Having just published her own book, Mrs. Lou Mandler kindly offered advice on how to organize the history. Many current faculty members responded to e-mail queries to verify dates or names. Bryan Kiefer acted as overseer to the whole project and gently kept me on task. I offer very special thank-you's to Stephen Hume '43 and David Hume '45, who spearheaded this project and provided me with wonderful stories and pictures of their father, Nelson Hume.*

Of course, my family deserves my thanks, especially my husband, John. He walked miles with me throughout our neighborhood, offered advice when it was solicited, and just listened when it was necessary.

Throughout my research for this book, I was struck over and over by the fact that although the outward trappings of the school have changed a great deal over the years, the school's mission remains essentially the same. For the last sixteen years, Mr. Tom Sheehy has guided the young men and women of Canterbury to take their place as moral leaders in a secular world. Canterbury's community, based on Catholic values, has prepared our students well to serve and to lead in the larger global neighborhood.

CANTUARIA FLOREAT.

—*Cathy Bolster*

CONTENTS

1

THE HUME YEARS

Nelson Hume, First Headmaster

The American preparatory school has its roots firmly planted in New England. Its birth certificate may be found in the act of the General Court of the Massachusetts Bay Colony, which in 1647 decreed that every town of fifty families must provide a schoolmaster and be responsible for his salary. At the same time it also decreed that every town of one hundred families should establish a "grammar" school. The fact that these educational dictates were designed for the sole purpose of ensuring a continual supply of ministers for Puritan pulpits does not gainsay their importance. They established a mold and a pattern for later public school education throughout the whole of the United States as new territories were developed and new states were admitted to the Union.

Some twenty-seven or more of these "grammar" schools were established in and about Boston to prepare boys for Harvard. Some were scattered throughout the rest of Massachusetts and into Connecticut after the founding of Yale in 1701.

In 1763, Lieutenant Governor Dummer of Massachusetts bequeathed his farm and his fortune for the founding of a boarding academy at South Byfield. Samuel Phillips, himself a graduate of Governor Dummer's school, established a similar one at Andover in Massachusetts, and three years later one at Exeter, in New Hampshire, both bearing his name. But these schools were comparatively early. The Methodists established Wesleyan Academy at Wilbraham, in Massachusetts, in 1817, but it was nearly a hundred years after Samuel Phillips's day when St. Paul's appeared in 1856, to be followed by St. Mark's in 1865 and Groton in 1884. It would seem that the full flowering of the modern preparatory school began with the turn of the twentieth century. Hotchkiss, Lawrenceville, and Taft all date from the 1890s.

Deerfield, as a crossroads academy (so-called because it was situated at a crossroads to accommodate several communities), was established as Dickinson Academy in 1797, and began its later expansion, under Mr. Frank Boyden, into one of the largest boarding schools in the country by 1922. Father Sill, according to legend, cooked the first meal for his dozen or so boys at Kent in 1906. Thus, the stage was set for the founding of Canterbury School.

The time and the timing of Canterbury's founding is significant. By 1914, several Catholic immigrants or their sons had acquired considerable wealth. The Havemeyers had made a fortune in sugar; Thomas Fortune Ryan, at his death in 1928, had amassed the second-greatest fortune in United States history by speculating on the stock market and other enterprises.[1] John Mackay, and his son Clarence, had made millions in western silver, and Nicholas and James Cox Brady were powers in the utility field. It is interesting to note that most of this accumulation of wealth took place in New York or made its influence felt from that metropolis. Since the days of the Dutch, New York had always been a tolerant city, and its large Catholic population consisted of the two prominent immigrant peoples of the time: the Germans and the Irish. In this setting, for the first time in America, an example of a purely Catholic social idea was to be activated by a group economically strong enough to wield power and influence.

The idea for Canterbury School originated with two men. In 1914, Henry Osborne Havemeyer, descendant of the prominent New York family that had made a fortune in sugar refining, was looking for a school that would prepare his son for Yale College while at the same time providing him with a Catholic religious education. He believed that the best college preparatory education was then being offered at schools such as Groton, St. Mark's, and St. Paul's. Because each of those schools was an Episcopalian church school with a strict and sometime militant emphasis on religion in their curricula, he considered them unsuitable for the training of his son as a Catholic. On the other hand, he felt just as strongly that if fortified with a sound Catholic secondary education, it was desirable for a Catholic student to attend a non-Catholic college. As a matter of conscience, the schools conducted by the Jesuits, Dominicans, and other teaching orders would not prepare boys to enter non-Catholic colleges, and Harvard, Yale, and Princeton refused to accept boys from such schools unless they had passed the examinations of the College Entrance Examination Board. This was a stalemate from which neither side would move. So, from its inception, Canterbury was not to be militant; rather, it was to be strict in the matter of Catholic teaching.

Nelson Hume, a successful Catholic schoolmaster who had recently resigned as associate headmaster of the Newman School in Hackensack, New Jersey, had reached similar conclusions regarding preparatory schools through his own studies and experiences as a teacher. He was born in New York City, in January 1881, the son of Hattie Kean and Thomas Joseph Hume. His father was part owner of a gentleman's tailoring establishment and a cloth merchant. Nelson graduated from The College of St. Francis Xavier at 16th Street in New York City in 1900. During his student years, he had for a time considered the priesthood, but upon graduation became a teacher at the Loyola School in Manhattan. He remained there for one year. At the same time, he took courses at Xavier for his Master of Arts degree, which the college awarded him in 1901.[2, 3]

Nelson opened his first school, the Hume School, in New Rochelle in 1907, facilitated by the fact that his family had acquired a large house in New Rochelle with extra rooms and a carriage barn that could be used for the school. The school was a success from the beginning. It grew to an enrollment of seventy, of whom a number were boarding students. Significant for the future development of Canterbury was the fact that among the first students at the Hume School were two nephews of Henry Havemeyer, sons of Mr. Ned Potter.[4]

Several years later, with the expectation that he might soon thereafter become headmaster of the combined institutions, Nelson Hume agreed to a merger of his small school in New Rochelle with the larger Newman School in Hackensack, with the understanding that Jesse Albert Locke, the head, would soon retire, and that Hume would replace him. Hume went to the Newman School as associate headmaster.

Newman School appeared to thrive under the merger. So pleased was the headmaster that there seemed to be no immediate push to have Hume take his place. Meanwhile, as was perhaps inevitable, Hume's strong personality—held to a subordinate position—clashed on policy matters with Mr. Locke, and Mr. Hume resigned from the Newman faculty at the end of the 1914 school year. At least two masters followed Nelson Hume to Canterbury, causing Locke to feel bitter. Locke, and several of his supporters, wrote letters to prospective Canterbury backers and parents trying to discredit Hume. Later, in 1915, the Newman School was the scene of a scandal relating to a bonfire held there. The fire got out of control, and firemen were called to extinguish the blaze and protect a neighboring residence. The students attacked the firemen, injuring several, including the chief. Two boys were arrested, but released into the custody of the school authorities.[5] The Canterbury trustees, particularly Clarence Mackay, felt they had rightly supported Nelson Hume against his detractors, and they discounted Locke after news of the scandal reached them.

Immediately after leaving Newman, Nelson Hume began his second venture in business with the WP Nelson Company of Chicago.[6] It was at this time that Monsignor P. J. McCloskey of Fordham came to him with a proposal that Nelson accept a position as tutor for the son of Henry Havemeyer. Instead of accepting the job, he recommended his younger brother, Alexander (often called Alec), who went to Newport with the Havemeyer family in the summer of 1914. Later, Nelson matriculated at Georgetown University in Washington, D.C., for studies which in 1915 earned him the degree of Doctor of Philosophy.[7]

As the summer ended, Mr. Havemeyer broached his idea of a new Catholic secondary school to Alec, who agreed to discuss the project with his brother Nelson. Later in the fall of 1914, at Alec's suggestion, Mr. Havemeyer met with Nelson and reiterated his interest. They agreed that Nelson Hume would call on several other families who might be interested in supporting such a school.

Among those first interviewed by Nelson Hume and then by Mr. Havemeyer were Ernest Iselin of Newport and Allan A. Ryan of New York. They and others were favorably disposed to the idea, but definite financial commitments were not made until Clarence Hungerford Mackay joined the group. Henry Havemeyer provided the letter of introduction from Dr. Hume to Mr. Mackay. Clarence Mackay was head of the Postal Telegraph Company and the son of John William Mackay, who had made a great fortune in western mining. Havemeyer and Hume hoped that with Clarence Mackay's backing, the needed capital would be raised in short order.

Nelson Hume was encouraged to begin searching the Northeast for a possible site for the school. He wanted a location that was reasonably close to New York City, but sufficiently removed to ensure a separate identity and independent development of the school. While searching for just the right place, he drove many miles through the towns of northwestern Connecticut. He had almost concluded that the town of Litchfield would be an ideal place when he learned that the site and buildings of the recently closed Ingleside School in New Milford were for sale. He was immediately enthusiastic about the possibilities of the New Milford location, all the more so when he found that Weantinaug Hall (the largest building on the site) and 12 acres were available for $25,000. Discovering this parcel made it possible for him to provide concrete form to the project. He drew up a prospectus, which he presented at a meeting attended by Mr. Havemeyer, Mr. Iselin, Mr. Ryan, and a group of their friends in New York City on Tuesday, January 12, 1915.[8]

He proposed that a corporation be organized with authorized capital of $100,000 to operate a school to be opened in New Milford on September 15, 1915. He stated that no more than $24,000 would be needed at the outset: $18,000 for the down payment on the purchase price of the land and buildings, and $6,000 for start-up expenses. He was confident that tuition fees would cover the remainder of the expenses for the first years, and yield a modest profit. He believed this could be accomplished with an enrollment as small as thirty boys, but he also believed that the initial enrollment would be not less than forty.[9] Even at the time he was presenting this prospectus for opening the school, Hume foresaw the expansion of the school to an enrollment of 150, and recommended the acquisition of the entire Ingleside plant.

Because those first contacted were unwilling to pledge tangible financial support until a broader group had shown interest, Dr. Hume was compelled to scale down his proposal. After a meeting with Mr. Iselin in January of 1915, Dr. Hume wrote to Mr. Havemeyer:

> He is interested in the school and thinks it will be a success; that he will try to get others interested; that he expects to send his boy to the school when he is old enough; that he will be glad to be consulted, to be used as a reference, to recommend boys to the school and the school to parents— everything, in fact, but to have his name down as a trustee or to invest any money.[10]

By arranging for a lease of Weantinaug Hall and its immediate property at $1,500 a year, with an option at the original price later, Dr. Hume was able to demonstrate, at least to his own satisfaction, that the school could be opened with no more than $10,000 of working capital.[11] Dr. Hume was so confident of the success of this modified proposal that he wrote to Mr. Havemeyer, "A few Catholic men now have it in their power to start a school that will be successful and creditable. It all depends on raising that initial $10,000. If this will get that, I can assure them of the rest."[12]

Dr. Hume presented this modified proposition to Mr. Clarence Mackay at the decisive meeting in Mr. Mackay's office in New York City on St. Patrick's Day, 1915. The meeting was a success. The following day Mackay reported to Havemeyer that he was very impressed with Hume's general ideas on education. Mr. Mackay told Havemeyer, "Mr. Hume is an enthusiast on his subject and if energy counts for anything, I should judge that he would make the proposition a go."[13] Hume had a second meeting with Mackay on April 18, 1915, where Mr. Mackay agreed to contribute as much of the initial $10,000 as would be necessary to open the school in the fall.

With this backing by Mr. Mackay, Nelson Hume moved rapidly to bring the school organization into being. A corporation was organized under the laws of the State of Delaware, empowered to own and operate a school for boys. Its first Board of Trustees consisted of Dr. Hume (6 shares), Mr. Havemeyer (15 shares; Henry Junior also purchased 15 shares), Mr. Mackay (60 shares), Conde B. Pallen, editor of the *Catholic Encyclopedia* (3 shares), and George Cabot Ward (3 shares).[14] Joining with them under the Delaware charter were John D. Ryan (50 shares), James A. Farrell (50 shares), and James H. Ward (25 shares). However, this was just the beginning; money had to be provided for the purchase of school property, and it came from James A. Farrell ($10,000), Clarence H. Mackay ($5,000), Allan A. Ryan[15] ($5,000), and Thomas C. Dennehy ($2,500). By July 1, Allan Ryan had joined the original group and purchased 35 shares of the school's corporation.

Dr. Hume even had the name and seal ready for the organizational meeting of the trustees. He wished to name the school Canterbury, after his baptismal saint, Edmund of Canterbury.[16] The traditions of Catholic education made the choice of this name an appropriate one. Another saint, Saint Dunstan, well known for his devotion to learning, retired to Canterbury, England, where he spent the remainder of his life as a teacher and protector of boys. Veneration of St. Dunstan at Canterbury flourished for eight hundred years, until the bitter struggles of the Reformation.[17] Havemeyer and Mackay readily approved the name Canterbury, which was used on May 1, 1915, when it was announced that the school would open in September. Hume then wrote to Havemeyer: "Now that I am on the verge of realizing my hopes and of seeing my dreams come true, I cannot refrain from telling you how much I appreciate all you have done to help me."

Dr. Hume began immediately to assemble a faculty, and by the end of June had signed contracts for a workable nucleus. An office for the school was opened at 18 East 41st Street in New York City. Interest in the school was increasing. Dr. Hume petitioned Mr. Havemeyer to release Alexander from his duties as young Henry's tutor as soon as possible, so that Alec could help Dr. Hume in readying the school for opening.[18] Mr. Havemeyer declined, stating that he would have need of Alexander. As a matter of fact, Havemeyer wrote to Hume, "I do not see how we could very well dispense with his services much before Sept. 15th, as Henry needs someone to keep him in line."[19]

Now came the decisive task of enrolling the first students to attend Canterbury. A meeting of the trustees was held on July 7, 1915, to establish admission standards. Dr. Hume presented a carefully prepared memorandum. To begin with, Hume stated that Canterbury was faced with two outstanding problems. The first: owing to the fact that the first students in a new school were usually those boys who were not doing well at other places, Canterbury should be careful about "admitting boys who might find it difficult to live up to the standards set by the school or who might attempt to set up standards of their own."[20]

The second problem was "making the school too much a school of one class of people or one section of the country by which it might become narrow, lifeless, un-American and what is called 'snobbish.' " He said he had a great affection for the boys from the West, who enjoyed a much more vigorous democracy than did the boys in the East, and he thought it would be good to bring them together.[21] A potential backer, Mr. Purcell, wrote to Dr. Hume that "unless the West were well represented, the school might be dominated by Eastern influences and thus made somewhat uncomfortable or unattractive to people from other parts of the country."[22] Mr. Purcell wrote in response to Dr. Hume, petitioning Mr. Purcell to become a subscriber to the school.

At the outset, however, Dr. Hume's high standards were administered with some flexibility. The trustees' recommendations were necessarily given great weight in the initial acceptances, and a special effort was made to bring together a group of well-mannered boys.

With his brusque manner and outward toughness, Dr. Hume would not have been judged a sentimental lover of humanity; nonetheless, he had a very special regard for boys. He considered them his adopted sons, and as such, wanted them to be the best of men. He bore down on them heavily as a disciplinarian, but at the same time, sought to bail them out of their difficulties, defending them fiercely against an ofttimes-hostile world. A distinct extrovert, he had a natural bent for theatrics, a commanding voice, and an utter domination of a class that inspired a mixture of fear, respect, admiration, and amusement. As a teacher, Dr. Hume possessed both powerful authority and boundless enthusiasm.

Dr. Hume made it explicit in the first school bulletin that Canterbury would not tolerate poor scholastic work or a failure on the part of any student to live up to the high academic standards he intended to set for the school. He was determined that even though it was a new institution, the school would not become a haven for boys rejected by the older, more established schools. It was no easy task to assemble forty boys who could meet Dr. Hume's high standards. Both he and the trustees experienced many moments of doubt and discouragement during the summer of 1915.

Dr. Hume vigorously campaigned among families with potential students. Mr. Havemeyer believed Dr. Hume's spirited personality would help attract candidates to Canterbury, and wrote to Dr. Hume: "It . . . would be most desirable that they may know in the first place what a live wire you are, and at the same time for the effect it will have in bringing others to decide immediately where they propose to send their boys."[23] Hume sent letters to many parts of the country, but for practical reasons, he concentrated on the East. A letter sent to Mrs. Winslow, sister to Mr. Havemeyer, is typical. In it, he stressed the opportunities for physical training and the sturdy outdoor life he planned for Canterbury. He also emphasized his plans for making the school a place of pervading Catholic culture, rather than merely a source of catechistic training. "Having been a Canterbury boy," he wrote, "will be for a Catholic young man at college or in business, an anchor to windward."[24]

Although it was always understood that Henry Havemeyer's son, Henry Jr., would attend Canterbury, the first boy to officially enroll at Canterbury was Cyril Clemens, Mark Twain's nephew. Cyril's enrollment occurred on September 6, 1915. Cyril Clemens had previously attended Newman School. Mr. Havemeyer's son, Henry, was enrolled on September 8. A trip to the cities of the Midwest netted only two boys, Joseph Graham and Joseph Kelley. However, Dr. Hume was enthusiastically received in the Catholic circles of those cities, which gave him and Mr. Havemeyer renewed hopes that wider support for the school, both in students and in funds, would be forthcoming. As Hume expressed it to Havemeyer, "[A]t least we have put ourselves in a position to secure a large investment of funds, which, after all, is the next best thing to securing a large number of boys."[25]

Canterbury School opened on September 22, 1915, with an enrollment of sixteen boys. The charter members of the School were: Cyril Clemens,[26] John Crimmins, James A. Farrell Jr., Joseph Graham, Henry O. Havemeyer Jr., Cyril Hume (Nelson's youngest brother[27]), Joseph Kelley, Peter Maloney, Nicholas Nelson, Richard and Swithin Nichols, Thomas Pallen, Allan and Theodore Ryan[29], George Saportas, and Charles Ward. In the middle of October, Edward Carmody of Waterbury entered the school along with Lambert Borden, whose family in Lakeville brought him over the hill and enrolled him one day.[30] Two more boys joined at midterm—Charles Martin[31] and Grosvenor Fessenden[32]. However, the eighteen enrolled in the fall of 1915 are generally given the distinction of being Canterbury's charter students.

So it was that in the fall of 1915, Canterbury School and all its future interests were committed to the town of New Milford in the Litchfield Hills of Connecticut. The school was situated on Town Hill, rich in the history of the town since its founding in 1707. In fact, the original settlers built their first houses on the hill. The first well in town was dug for the preacher, on the site of Hickory Hearth. The land on Town Hill was later turned over to the farmers to use for grazing. When Nelson Hume cleared a stone wall from the land in front of the chapel that ran up the Hill, he found an English coin dating back to 1711, which attested to the early use of that land. Roger Sherman—New Milford's most celebrated settler, and signer and co-author of the Declaration of Independence—used much of the Town Hill land to graze his cattle.

Aspetuck Avenue, which runs along the spine of the hill, was originally the Wellsville Road and served as a link in the post road system,[33] as well as the farmers' main link with Wellsville on the other side of the hill. The milepost still stands near the chapel and records the distances to New York and New Milford.[34] It was extremely difficult to use this road in winter. In 1850, the townspeople finally succeeded in persuading the government to provide funds for a road around the Hill on the path that the farmers had forged themselves. This new road then became Wellsville Avenue, and the old road was renamed. For more than one hundred years it was not used beyond the site of the school.

Mrs. William Black, widow of one of the partners of Black, Starr and Frost, had opened the Ingleside School for Girls in 1892 at the foot of Town Hill. The main building of that school stood on the site once occupied by the former St. Francis Xavier parochial school. The Ingleside School expanded up the hill, most of which was also owned by Mrs. Black and her family, the Sanfords. The headmistress resided at the impressive Hickory Hearth, which was much larger than its white clapboard successor and was constructed in the shingle style.

The Ingleside School prospered. In 1901, Mrs. Black decided to open a boys' side to Ingleside, and for that purpose erected Weantinaug Hall. The large half-timbered building occupied the site of what is now a parking lot in front of Sheehan House. At the same time, she purchased a small building from the defunct Adelphic Institute, which had closed in 1880, and had the building dragged from its original site on Chicken Hill[35] to its present position on the campus. That building, greatly renovated and expanded, is now the Chaplain's Residence, and is the oldest building on campus. Mrs. Black first used it as a residence for the servants of Weantinaug Hall. It has seen more varied use than any other building on campus.[36]

The boys' school venture was abandoned in 1904. Weantinaug Hall became the postgraduate department—or finishing school—for the Ingleside girls. It flourished in this capacity for close to ten years, during which time the alumnae of Ingleside built the Bungalow that stood on the foundation of the present Carter House. The Bungalow served as an alumnae house for the returning girls, and many of the classes sponsored rooms that they furnished and decorated for their own use.

When Mrs. Black died in 1910, Ingleside School died with her. Although her niece, Miss Jennie Daniels Pell, tried to operate the school after Mrs. Black's death, she was unable to make the venture successful, and the school closed in 1914.[37] Mrs. Black's executors immediately put the buildings and grounds on the market. Thus, the stage was set for the arrival of Nelson Hume. The timing of events was fortuitous. Nelson Hume was presented with a school whose facilities were only fifteen years old, and whose premises had been vacated for only a year. In addition, the estate was eager to get the unwieldy Weantinaug Hall off its hands. Only a headmaster in search of a school would have been interested in such an oddly placed edifice.

Hume was able to persuade the trustees of the newly organized Canterbury School to lease both Weantinaug Hall and the alumnae Bungalow, so that from its beginning, Canterbury was in possession of all of the properties that had constituted the Ingleside Postgraduate School. The lease included the soccer field that had been the scene of the first game of girls' field hockey ever played in the United States. The lease also covered the land as far north as Duffy House, on a line that followed a stone wall up the Chapel Hill. On Saturday, June 19, 1915, Dr. Hume went to New Milford and took formal possession of the grounds and buildings. The keys to the buildings were handed to him by Mr. William Black Pell, executor of the estate of Sarah S. Black as representative of all the executors of the estate.[38]

The original Weantinaug Hall was the heart of the school, and incorporated the dining hall, kitchen, classrooms, and living quarters for the boys and faculty. Its excellent design guaranteed that every bit of floor space was used. It became the Main House of Canterbury. On its third floor were the headmaster's apartment and quarters for servants. The second floor comprised boys' rooms, classrooms, the infirmary, and the infirmarian's apartment. The first floor held more classrooms, the kitchen, dining room, and common room, as well as the school's office.

The Bungalow,[39] which had been built in 1906, had its own distinctive atmosphere, with its brown-shingled exterior and white porch. It was built as a club or lodge rather than an institutional building, and had a warm atmosphere. Inside was a single large living room that reached up two stories, which Dr. Hume divided in half to provide a study area at one end. Around the top of the room ran a balcony that opened into the large sleeping rooms. The third story held several large double rooms. After some casual use, including service as temporary quarters for the chapel, the Bungalow became the living quarters for the boys of the lower school. However, the upper-form boys soon discovered the amenities of living in the Bungalow, and persuaded the headmaster to assign them to it. For years thereafter, the Sixth Formers lived in the single rooms on the second floor, and the Fifth filled out the third floor. All the teas for visiting groups were held in the Bungalow, as well as the dances, lectures, and plays, for which the Bungalow seemed well suited.

For the first faculty of Canterbury, Dr. Hume drew heavily upon his own associations. His brother, Alec, was engaged as assistant headmaster and placed in charge of studies in the lower school. He had attended St. Francis Xavier College (which later merged with Fordham), and then had taught six years at the Hume School and one year at the Newman School. For the two years before his appointment at Canterbury, he had been employed as the summer tutor of Henry Havemeyer Jr. Alec Hume was Nelson's right-hand man.

Alec—or Al, as Dr. Hume always called him[40] —was a cheerful bachelor, a friendly type who liked the boys and who, in turn, was well liked (even though they did tease him a great deal). He exercised general control of the business management of the plant, ordering supplies such as coal and handling the school's insurance, as well as doing his share of teaching. He was on the permissive side; no boy in his classes ever failed if he sat up straight, asked no silly questions, and otherwise behaved himself. Alec liked bridge, golf, good food, and beverages, and most of the finer things in life. When declining another year of tutoring Henry

Jr., Alexander wrote, "For nearly four years now, I have had a constant state of responsibility for boys placed upon me and I feel the need of a complete rest from this strain in order to be in proper condition for my duties at the school next fall."[41]

In 1918, in a nod of confidence for his work, Alec was elected as a member of the Board of Directors. It was an honor that he wished to decline, saying, "I feel a little out of place to be a member of the same board that such important men are on, and I do not see how I can qualify to become a director as I am not a stockholder."[42] Alexander served on the board for less than six months and then happily resigned his position to Mr. John T. King.[43]

Maximillian von der Porten was by far the most distinguished scholar on the faculty. He was a doctor of languages and had studied at the Sorbonne, the University of Vienna, and Heidelberg, and had formerly taught at the Hume School. He taught a mixture of modern languages and European history. Next to Nelson Hume, Dr. von der Porten was the most colorful personality in the school. He was an enthusiastic liberal and would side with the students in their disputes with the headmaster. This apparent division of loyalty eventually led to a split with Hume, and von der Porten left Canterbury in the early 1920s.

The professor of history and the classics was Patrick Downing, who had been educated as a Jesuit Scholastic but had turned to teaching. He had served on the faculty of the Newman School, where he taught for five years before coming to Canterbury. Subsequently, James J. McCarthy succeeded to the Latin post, and in 1919 published his own book of Latin rules of syntax. Frank Rooney, the mathematics teacher, was also late of the seminary and had taught at Newman.

Dr. Hume was a staunch supporter of the "sports for all" policy. He felt that being outdoors was therapeutic, and blamed any illness in the School on the fact that the boys had not been able to spend as much time outside as he would have liked. Although he had brought soccer to the Hume School in New Rochelle, he could see that the new Canterbury School could not, in its first years, support two sports in any season. He therefore chose football as the fall sport. No more than nine boys were large enough to sustain a team for the opening fall term. The team played several pickup games with The Gunnery and Salisbury, in which they were soundly defeated, but they did manage to win a few games with local high school teams.

Dr. Hume hoped to have a full-time athletic director at the outset, but the trustees did not consider the cost to be justified during the first years of the School. To fill the gap, the headmaster required Dr. Barker, the school physician, to come to the School daily to supervise exercise for the boys and keep detailed charts on their growth. Dr. Barker was reluctant to spend his afternoons doing calisthenics with eighteen adolescents, but Dr. Hume made it clear that his job depended on it.

From the beginning it was Dr. Hume's policy to provide the best possible fare in the Main House dining room. The boys were required to dress in dark suits, patent leather pumps (slip-on shoes for formal wear), and Eton collars for the younger students. The boys went directly from chapel to the evening meal, which was served at 7:00 P.M. The dining room must have been a very civilized place. The dining-room chairs were high-backed and sturdy, and had leather seats. There were tureens for soup, and the silver was substantial. Conversation had to be fitting, decorous, and cheerful. The pace of meals was leisurely, as befits civilized humans. The food was excellent, and parents used to send prize beef and partridge, potatoes (from the Northern Pacific Railroad, "the Route of the Great Big Baked Potato"), and fresh asparagus (all vegetables were fresh) as gifts for the School.[44] At one point, crops were even planted on some of the grounds. In 1917, Dr.

Hume plowed under two acres of land to plant twenty-five bushels of seed potatoes.[45] The daily dinners were full-course meals, served in the early years by maids who also worked in the kitchen. Later, Filipino waiters took over the service. There was quantity as well as quality in the food. Here is a description of a typical Thanksgiving meal from an issue of *The Tabard* (1926):

> This delicious repast commenced with grapefruit accompanied by olives, celery, and nuts. This opening course was followed by ox-tail soup, and then, the soup finished, the main course was put on the table. This course consisted of delicious turkey, dressing, gravy, mashed potatoes, green peas, and cranberry sauce. This course finished, salad and cheese were served before pumpkin and mince pie was placed on the table as a desert [sic]. After this course was finished, those boys who desired coffee and cigarettes remained at their places, while those who had satisfied their appetites departed. This delicious meal, accompanied by cider, candy, nuts, and raisins, was indeed a repast to remember.[46]

Mr. Mack, one of the first schoolmasters, vowed that at one sitting, Ben Halsey[47] was allowed to eat twenty-one lamb chops. Canterbury's food costs were higher than other schools' because "our boys demand second helpings of a great many things that other schools do not allow second helpings of."[48] During the Depression, when it became absolutely necessary to reduce costs, Dr. Hume wrote, "Another way in which we can reduce the cost per meal is to be more positive in budgeting our outlay . . . [our head of dining services] did not absolutely know [what] good meals we would require nor how much the boys would eat."[49]

Dr. Hume was justifiably proud of Canterbury's dining room. He even excused the masters from fasting during Lent on the grounds that their jobs warranted the exemptions usually given to laborers. He also established a rotating seating plan using name cards, so that each boy had the experience of eating with each master, including the headmaster. "The cards [were] shuffled. The headmaster quickly [dealt] out groups of six, at the same time calling out in rapid succession six boys' names."[50] When the noise in the dining room became too much for intra-table conversation, a rap on a water tumbler would bring the tumult to a hush with dramatic suddenness.

Originally the kitchen was in the charge of Marie Hume, the headmaster's eldest sister. She had an encyclopedic knowledge of the inner workings of a household, and was well suited for her duties at the School. These responsibilities included overseeing the kitchen and the preparation and serving of meals, together with supervising the general housework and the running of the infirmary. She made the menus, ordered food and supplies, and hired the kitchen help. Under her direction the cuisine at Canterbury became popular folklore, spoken of in awed whispers.[51] Marie remained in service to the school until failing health forced her to retire in the summer of 1941. At that time, Marie purchased a small cottage close to Canterbury, where she was joined by her sister Constance, who helped take care of her.[52]

In the late 1920s, when the task became too much for Marie, Dr. Hume hired the MacDermott[53] Group to take over the catering duties, under the headmaster's close supervision. In 1929, they assumed full responsibility for food at Canterbury. Their success with Dr. Hume, and their ability to provide the excellent meals he required, came to the attention of other schools and institutions. Soon MacDermott became the leading school caterer in Connecticut. Dr. Hume's concern for the food at Canterbury prevailed throughout his tenure as headmaster. Even after he had delegated the responsibility to the MacDermott Company, Dr. Hume remained the final judge of the food's quality. More than once, a meal was stopped in mid-course with the tapping of a glass and Dr.

Hume's voice proclaiming, "The waiters will remove the soup."[54]

The daily schedule was a long one and, as a result, Dr. Hume instituted a break for tea in the afternoon, between sports and the early evening study hall and chapel. The daily teas were held in the library, and consisted of two large cookies and tea with milk. While these daily teas were formidable affairs, they did not compare with the spreads provided for visiting teams. Long after opponents had graduated from neighboring schools, they remembered the Canterbury teas—the single most outstanding thing for which Canterbury became famous in the early years. As the school grew, so did the teas, and with the addition of the other dormitories, the main tea was divided so that each house played host to its own members.

The School's colors were chosen in connection with the purchase of hatbands in September 1915. Mr. Havemeyer wrote, "Canterbury to me implies cardinal red, but it would be my desire that the colors be navy blue and white, which are quite quiet and refined, not ostentatious as reds always appear to me."[55] His inclination toward blue was probably influenced by his affinity for Yale; however, Hume acted independently to pick navy blue and Columbia blue. This combination he found especially pleasing to his own eye, and his choice was abetted by the fact that these colors were also those of the Blessed Virgin Mary.[56]

When it came to the selection of a School motto, Dr. Hume made the choice. Because he believed that his prayers to St. Jude had had some efficacy in the establishment of Canterbury, he found, in the Introduction to the Epistle of Jude, the Apostle, these words:

> *Beloved, when I gave all diligence to write unto you of the common salvation, it was needful for me to write unto you, and exhort you that ye should earnestly contend for the faith which was once delivered unto the saints.*[57]

Thus, *Supercertari semel traditae sanctis fidei*—to fight valiantly for the faith once delivered to the saints—became the expression of Canterbury's mission.

Organizing the school and piloting it through the treacherous waters of the first year involved countless decisions about small details, all of which warranted Dr. Hume's personal attention. While the trustees kept a careful hold on the purse strings, Dr. Hume became quite adept at convincing Mr. Mackay and the other trustees that a particular expenditure should be made. His first decision was regarding the employment of John G. Weckerle as janitor and groundsman, who, he assured the trustees, had a "good character for efficiency, sobriety and diligence."[58] Mr. Mackay, especially, was a strong advocate of advancing faculty salaries. Mackay felt the faculty should ". . . be composed of as good men as we can get, and consequently good men for the right positions have to be paid, and rather more these days than before."[59]

Another undertaking was to transform the small building, once used as quarters for the staff of Weantinaug Hall, into the Canterbury School chapel.[60] The trustees rejected his first plan for this transformation, but a revised plan went through without trouble. A real debate then arose over paving the roads on the school property. Hume desired the best macadam, similar to what was used to pave the roadways on Newport estates. The cost was estimated at $900. Havemeyer exploded, writing to Dr. Hume, "You can pave a hell of a lot of road for $900."[61] A further disquisition by Dr. Hume on the long-term value of the quality of road he wanted convinced Mr. Mackay, who in turn convinced Mr. Havemeyer.

Differences between Dr. Hume and the trustees during the early years were almost always related to money matters, and arose inevitably from two opposing views on the school's future. Nelson

Hume was supremely confident from the outset that the school would succeed. Thus, all of his preparations, including the expensive roads, were made as permanent improvements, the cost of which would be amortized over many years of use. Some trustees, Havemeyer among them, considered the road-paving project to be a very precarious one. Their caution dictated very tentative expenditures until it became clear that the school would survive.

In most matters, through the force of his personality as much as the logic of his proposals, Dr. Hume's confidence in the future prevailed. Had it not been for his constantly pushing the trustees for a deeper commitment and for more improvements to their original investment, the school might well have died in the first few years. Hume knew exactly what he wanted and when he wanted it. He would carry on almost endless negotiations on a proposal, no matter how flatly Havemeyer had turned it down. Havemeyer questioned all expenditures, large and small, including the Tiffany stationery that Dr. Hume once used in a letter to Mr. Havemeyer, but Nelson's reasons for the expenditures were generally sound and forward-thinking.[62]

The families of the first boys at the school shared the sense of adventure in the project and "pitched in" in many ways. Mrs. Havemeyer sent up a phonograph. Soon both study and sleep were interrupted by the sounds of jazz wafting through the Bungalow, until it was limited to three-quarters of an hour every day after lunch.[63] Mrs. James A. Farrell gave the first twenty-five books for the library.[64] Cyril Clemens of Second Form gave a complete set of Mark Twain.[65] Several years later, Mr. Michael J. Meehan donated three "superheterodyne" radios for the boys. These radios were encased in lowboy cabinets of finished walnut.[66]

By mid-October of 1915, a golf course was being laid out at the request of and through the generosity of the Havemeyers. "In order to establish some sort of system on the course, a chart was

placed on the bulletin-board before the eyes of the waiting multi-
tude. This chart, when first viewed, [appeared] to be nothing but
a very intricate and cunningly constructed maze."[67] The golf
course covered a large portion of the grounds, and grew as the
school acquired more land; eventually, it became a par-three, nine-
hole course. Golf was a major pastime of the boys during those
years, rivaled only by trapshooting. The trapshooting grounds were
behind North House, pointing north, and the sport continued
through the First World War. The traps were set on the edge of the
old football field, immediately west of the Main House. The clay
pigeons flew westward, toward the valley, set on and triggered from
the traps by the mechanically dexterous boys from the Lower
School.[68]

Dr. Hume was faced with a number of discipline problems
during the first year. He blamed this on the fact that because of
continuously bad weather, the boys were unable to get outside for
hockey and coasting, and facilities for indoor recreation were not
yet completed.[69] Dr. Hume's remedy for all ills was to lead the
boys on a "Saturday afternoon tramp" through the woods and
neighboring fields. As a matter of fact, he purposely held back
the opening of a much-talked-about bowling alley in hopes that
the weather would break before he would have to provide indoor
entertainment.[70] One such tramp was to Green's Pond,[71] "at least
six miles along winding roads, over steep hills, and through deep
woods." For their rations, they received "six large sandwiches of
different sorts, two eggs and a piece of cake, besides an orange
held in the hand."[72]

Henry Havemeyer Jr. was prone to colds. Havemeyer often
worried about the care his son, Henry Jr., received, when he
was not worrying about school expenditures. Mr. Havemeyer
was especially worried about all the time the boys spent outdoors. At one point, Dr. Hume was forced to write this reassur-

ance to Havemeyer:

> I note your comment in regard to paying attention to
> what the boys wear and changing their clothes . . . The fact
> that Henry did not put on his winter underwear may be
> explained on the ground that it may not have occurred to
> my brother that the weather had become cold enough yet to
> require this change. As a matter of fact, we give an unusual
> amount of care to this very point, and when the boys go out-
> doors, they must always report to the master in charge for the
> day, and he sees that they are properly equipped. You may
> rest assured that we give particular attention to Henry. [73]

The thing that saved Canterbury in any winter, according to
Hume, was the hockey season. Hockey was Nelson Hume's great
love, and he personally coached the team. The school thus made
up for some of its ignominious defeats in football and actually
became quite a hockey power during those first years. During the
early years, the players used the natural pond on the Pell property,
north of the school.

Outdoor activities in the spring consisted chiefly of extended
hikes in the woods and baseball,[74] which, like hockey, enjoyed the
headmaster's special patronage. As the weather became milder, it
was possible to take the entire school on overnight camping trips.
These exciting adventures, however, were limited to the early
years. By the mid-1920s, both in size and inclination, the school
had outgrown them.

The study hall was the forum for briefings and morale boost-
ers by the headmaster, although he reserved most of the latter for
the chapel. "Only the French word *longueur* captures the fine shading needed to describe the erosion of spirit that gradually occurs
in a group of hard-driven boys during the long New England
winter."[75] The headmaster could always sense this restlessness,
and defuse it with a quiet talk during which he held his right index
finger pointing upward and unmoving while nodding his head for

emphasis. Nelson was always true to himself, and did things his way—even down to small details of fashion or hairstyle.[76] Early pictures frequently show Nelson's hair parted on the opposite side from those around him.

It was common for the boys to gather in the living room to listen to the headmaster playing piano while waiting for dinner to be announced. Much later, Edward Carmody would write to May Hume, wife of Nelson:

> I did enjoy it [the piano] but that was not, as Penrod used to say, 'the main and simple reason' for my attention. There was no better way to get a reading on the Headmaster's outlook on life at that particular moment. If someone had done something absolutely outrageous he played Chopin smolderingly. If my conscience was clear I hugged myself and waited for the drama to unfold. If everyone had done what he was supposed to have done, just as a Canterbury boy should have done it, we heard Mendelssohn—sweet Mendelssohn.[77]

The tuition at this time (including room and board) for the upper school was $1,000, payable in two installments; for the lower school, it was $800. Expenses during the first year far exceeded the budget, so that money had to be borrowed early in January 1916. The final deficit for the first year was $30,000. Messrs. Mackay, Ward, Ryan, and Havemeyer advanced working funds to keep the school going. Despite the deficit, Dr. Hume had proved his point. A new school—Roman Catholic, but in pattern like the older Episcopalian church schools of the East—could be established and made to function in a single year. Individual trustees began advancing their own funds in growing confidence that Dr. Hume was succeeding.

As a result of a trip through the West, the headmaster was able to plan for an enrollment of forty boys for the second year. To meet the increase, it was necessary to remodel the Bungalow as an upper-school residence, and to enlarge the dining room in the Main House. The basement in the Main House was also renovated to provide living quarters for employees, so that the entire third floor could be used for students. An epidemic of infantile paralysis, or polio, in the summer and early fall of 1916 caused postponement of Canterbury's opening until October 1, but by that time, all alterations had been completed.[78]

In a memorandum sent to the parents before the opening of the second year, Dr. Hume announced that a special parlor car[79] would take the boys from New York to New Milford. He outlined exactly what the boys were to bring and what they were not to bring. The school provided bed linen, towels, napkins, and blankets. Each boy was required to have "two dark suits for wear in the evening and on Sundays, also a corduroy suit for the younger boys." It was "preferred that the younger boys wear Eton collars in the evenings and Sundays." In addition, the boys were to bring a pair of high Arctic overshoes, rubbers, and a pair of formal patent leather shoes. During World War I, each of the older boys was required to have a pair of army shoes that could be purchased at the school. All sweaters and athletic supplies had to be uniform, and therefore were to be purchased at the school store.

In December 1916, the first volume of *The Quill* was issued. Although there had been several earlier "corridor" publications put out privately by the boys,[80] *The Quill* was the first official Canterbury publication. Dr. Hume had established *The Quill* at his own school in New Rochelle, and had then carried it to Newman, where several volumes were published. *The Quill* functioned as a chronicle of happenings at school, as well as a forum for the creative talents of the literary-minded.

With Cyril Hume as editor, the quarterly burst upon the scene with glimpses of school life and a record of significant school events, called the "Canterbury Tales" section. There was a review of the preceding athletic season complete with pictures and details of each game. The bulk of the quarterly was filled with the best essays from Dr. Hume's English classes. These essays lent a lofty tone to *The Quill*, and provided the basis for its continuation as a scholarly magazine when *The Tabard* came on the scene in 1919 to take over most of the news reporting. By 1923, only a few short years after graduating from Canterbury, Cyril Hume published a novel, *Wife of the Centaur*.[81] A later *Canterbury Quarterly* contributor, Edward Ryan, was presumptuous enough, albeit favorably, to review Cyril's book in the December 1923 issue.[82]

The Quill first exhibited a literary taste among Canterbury students that continued until the Second World War. Canterbury boys enjoyed reading humorous columns in school publications, and there was a succession of exceptionally competent writers of those columns. Beginning with the "Canterbury Tales" up through the "Gleams and Glooms" of *The Tabard*, these columns kept an anecdotal record of the lively things that happened at the school and, on the side, dispensed a special brand of Canterbury wisdom. The models for these Canterbury columns were no less than the famous columns of the old *New York World*. *The World* was Dr. Hume's favorite paper. He would often devote an entire session of his English class to reading the columns as examples of modern prose. "Impressions," which appeared for many years in *The Tabard*, was probably the greatest Canterbury example of this kind of newspaper entertainment. Sometimes the best of the "Impressions," or even original quips, were sent to the World. The boy who authored a piece that was accepted would receive Dr. Hume's highest reward—cancellation of all days "on bounds" (which meant being confined to the campus for a day or days). The genius of this particular system of discipline lay in the fact that if a boy went through a school term with no days on bounds, he was rewarded with extra days of vacation.

One of the best examples of early Canterbury literature is the editorial in *The Quill*, written by Gilbert King, commenting on the establishment of *The Tabard*:

> So, one wintry Wednesday, a holiday to be sure, four boys, four cans of beans, and one frying pan set forth for regions unknown. That they soon found a convenient cave-like cleft in the rocks on the side of a mountain is good evidence that a strong biting wind and empty stomachs, and the prospect of lukewarm beans, and, well, perhaps pure laziness, were all fatal precursors of this momentous occasion. There is apparently no logical reason why fate should have chosen this day and, most of all, this unfortunate group of soon-to-be journalists.
>
> . . . The meal finished, the party proceeded to recline on full stomachs and such soft rocks as could be conveniently found and to discuss the weighty problems that confronted the world at that moment. . . . It was only natural that, as the conversation became more involved and the problems more momentous, a weekly paper should be suggested.

A story printed in 1923 discussed how *The Tabard* was named. The newspaper takes its name from the inn made famous by Chaucer's *Canterbury Tales*; also, a tabard is the official garment of a herald.[83]

In 1923 the name of *The Quill* was changed to *The Canterbury Quarterly*. The new publication made an impressive appearance in its colors of Canterbury blue, with the contents printed on the cover in accordance with the best form of the day for magazines with an intellectual appeal. From the beginning, *The Quarterly* carried many pages of national advertising, and soon became the rich uncle of *The Tabard*. Under a succession of canny business managers, it waxed increasingly prosperous.

The Tabard and *The Quill* were the prime sources of extracurricular activity. *The Tabard* provided weekly news about visitors, alumni, sports, and other items of interest. The first issue of March 3, 1919, listed John Hughes as editor, Allan A. Ryan and James A.

Farrell as associate editors, Joseph Lilly as business manager, Thomas Dennehy as assistant business manager, and Gilbert King in charge of athletics. Competition for posts on these publications was as intense as that on the athletic fields. There was a strict system of "heeling" for appointments on both papers.

"Heeling" was the competition among the boys for places on the staff of *The Tabard* or *Quill,* as either writers or members of the business staff. The current editors wrote the regulations for heeling, and specified the relationship between the heelers and the staff, and the number of boys eligible from each form.[84] Sometimes the heelers were the butt of practical jokes. One of their jobs was to go around the dining room taking down the names of the people who had visited the school during the past week for *The Tabard.* Each boy who was asked for a visitor's name would manufacture a visitor for the benefit of the new heeler. The heeler was called back time after time to take down another imaginary name from another imaginary town. Even the masters joined in the fun.[85] Heelers were judged on their success in handling a story, writing its headline, and setting type at the offices of the *New Milford Times.*[86]

By 1936, *The Tabard* offered special journalism classes, including instruction in writing headlines and proofreading galleys. The headmaster exercised strict supervision over the copy, meticulously reviewing each printed page with the faculty advisor and the current board of editors.[87]

By 1920, the circulation of *The Tabard* was more than 300. The publication had taken up offices in the Bungalow, and proved itself financially solvent thanks to the vigorous business managers, who were able to place many New York advertisements in the paper. It was remarkable that the paper appeared without interruption every Monday, from the first issue in 1919 until the Second World War put a ration on paper.

Not long after its founding, *The Tabard* began to function somewhat as a yearbook. The final issue of the year—the "Graduation Number," as it was called—was much enlarged to include photos and biographies of the graduating class, together with a general résumé of all the year's activities—academic, athletic, and social. This continued until the arrival of Mr. Sheehan, when a full-scope yearbook began to appear annually.

The "Graduation Number" of *The Tabard* provided long-lasting memories for many an editor and staff member. In the earlier days of the School, graduation exercises began with the graduation dance on Friday evening. The actual granting of diplomas and prizes took place on Saturday, before noon. The last baseball game of the year was played on Saturday afternoon, and the school year ended on Sunday morning with High Mass and the graduation sermon. Although the "Graduation Number" had been in preparation for some weeks, the final printing was done on the same Friday night of the graduation dance. This meant that the editor and staff members had to shed their evening wear for working clothes, dash downtown to the *New Milford Times* establishment, and work most of the night getting out the special issue, which, according to the proud boast of the staff, was always on the chapel steps for distribution as the guests emerged after Mass. The first graduating class in Canterbury's history consisted of four students: Cyril Hume, George McLaughlin, Swithin Nichols, and Arthur O'Gorman. His Eminence John Cardinal Farley, under whose patronage the school opened, telegraphed that he would be present at the graduation exercises on Saturday, June 8, 1918, but took sick and could not attend.[88]

By the end of the second year, the development of Dr. Hume's discipline standards was well under way. Years later, students would recall one boy who was so bold as to catapult a ball of butter to the dining-room ceiling, right under the good doctor's nose. The offending student had to stand up and apologize to the assembly[89].

Dr. Hume dismissed one boy because of his bad attitude and his failure to make the school's standards his own.[90] The dispute was precipitated by the boy's refusal to take a bath once a week. Another early dispute arose between Dr. Hume and three masters. The dispute centered on the refusal of one master to comply with Hume's authority. The master was supported in his decision by two other masters, since the three were business associates in a small venture outside Canterbury. The master was summarily fired, and his dismissal was announced to the boys at chapel the same evening.[91] Dr. Hume said, "You know, when a master is insubordinate, he has to be sent away just like a boy who is disobedient." The other two masters resigned at the end of the school year. In each such case appealed before the Board, the Board sustained Dr. Hume. Dr. Hume strongly believed that the faculty should act as one unit; any separation into cliques he considered as "one of the most harmful and difficult conditions that can arise in a school if it comes to the knowledge of the boys."[92]

While from Dr. Hume's point of view the school was sensationally successful during the first two years, the more cautious members of the Board of Trustees, such as Mr. Havemeyer, still hesitated to proceed much further while the project was operating on such a shoestring. The essential buildings of the school were still held only under a lease, and there was a crying need for increased working capital. Although the Board as a whole hesitated, one member—James A. Farrell, then one of the younger luminaries of United States Steel, who later became president of the corporation—was quietly making plans on his own to acquire land adjoining that covered by the school's lease. In June 1917, he purchased the 12-acre lot north of the school property. Later that summer he purchased the Windmill lot east of the Bungalow. It can be said that Mr. Farrell's confidence and vision at this time was in many ways instrumental in ensuring the future success of the School. Mr.

Farrell also promoted the establishment of a Foundation Fund for Canterbury School on December 17, 1917, to encourage more generous gifts that could be classified as charitable contributions. The response to the creation of the charitable foundation was immediate and substantial. By January 19, 1918, the School had accumulated $43,200 through gifts to the Foundation, which enabled it on that date to purchase the buildings and immediately surrounding acres of the Black estate.

Mr. Farrell was also the prime mover on the Board of Trustees behind the plan to transform the school corporation itself from a business corporation, organized under the laws of Delaware, to a nonprofit corporation under the laws of the State of Connecticut. He felt that such a reorganization of the school's corporate setup would not only ensure the charitable character of all future contributions to the School, but would also alleviate Dr. Hume's concern about his own future. This is because the reorganization would allow Dr. Hume to be paid a fixed salary as headmaster, without regard to the profit derived from school operations.[93]

Strange as it now seems, and despite the deep interest in the true purpose of the school, Canterbury was originally conceived both by Dr. Hume and the original Board members as essentially a money-making proposition. All of Dr. Hume's original solicitations consisted primarily of justifying an investment that would yield dividends. Many of the earlier schools in America had in fact been proprietary, and it is doubtful that Dr. Hume could have raised the original capital on any other basis. In fact, even in 1918, most of the trustees hesitated to launch the complete corporate transformation urged by Mr. Farrell. Finally, however, his views did prevail.

The Board had soon retained Terence F. Carmody of Waterbury, one of the leaders of the Connecticut Bar, to undertake the reorganization task.[94] He had previously drawn up the

papers for the establishment of the Foundation, and fully understood Mr. Farrell's objective. His eldest son was already enrolled in
the school. Thus began another family association that was to
mean much to Canterbury's future. T. F. Carmody served as a
trustee of the school from this time forward, until his death in July
1943.[95]

World War I and the 1920s

World War I was taken fairly well in stride at Canterbury. War
measures taken in the fall of 1918 were a portent of what might
have been expected, had not the Central Powers collapsed so pre-
cipitously. Coal rationing came into effect; streetlights were
dimmed, and store windows were darkened to save coal. Alec
Hume had occasion to write to Mr. Havemeyer regarding the coal
situation: "Pea coal is the only kind they had to sell, and they had
very little of that. . . . I consider this a rather serious situation."[96]
Canterbury's coal requirements were fifty tons of stove coal and
two hundred tons of nut coal.[97] As early as 1917, some foods were
scarce, particularly potatoes, causing the author of the
"Canterbury Tales" in *The Quill* to write, "Although potatoes are
generally a commonplace and ordinary dish, they are hard to do
without. This the boys realized after they had been deprived of
them for a few weeks, because of their scarcity and high price in
the neighboring country."[98] They also had to endure power out-
ages, as reported in *The Tabard*: "On certain nights, all local power
was shut off in order to provide more current for the nearby muni-
tions plants."[99]

During the war, the headmaster organized the Canterbury
Corps of Cadets, fully outfitted with army-style uniforms, hats,
and wooden guns. Mr. Havemeyer would have preferred sailor
suits as "more becoming and 75 cents cheaper."[100] The Sixth

Formers served as officers and the Fifth Formers as sergeants. The corps marched in a War Bond Parade in the village shortly after school opened. Their enthusiasm made up for any deficiencies they may have had in close-order drill.[101]

Both the false armistice and the real event on November 11, 1918, were celebrated with great gusto at the school. The school truck was decked out in colors and run through the streets of New Milford on each occasion. Even after the Armistice, the corps continued to drill, and gave a number of creditable reviews for visiting dignitaries. Ultimately, with the war ended, both the headmaster and the students returned their primary focus to sports. On April 2, 1919, the Student Council voted that in view of the world situation, the Canterbury Corps should be disbanded, since there no longer seemed to be any need of it.

The enrollment at the beginning of the fall term in 1918 had reached fifty. It was clear that the existing facilities would soon be inadequate. Dr. Hume's idea was to increase the tuition to $1,200, and to endeavor to purchase the Hickory Hearth property adjacent to the school. The Board, however, turned down the purchase at that time. Hickory Hearth did not become a part of Canterbury's campus until sixty-seven years later. In 1918, Dr. Hume had acquired additional property to the north of the School. This property had no buildings, and was used at first by the newly organized Gun Club of the School, which soon became one of the best such clubs in the area.[102] Dr. Hume was himself a member of the Gun Club, and in 1919, the boys in Middle House presented him with a twelve-gauge Parker shotgun, suitable for trap-shooting and in the field.[103]

The development of Canterbury consisted of more than the direction of Dr. Hume, more than the acquisition of land and buildings—more, even, than the beginnings of tradition. Each new year brought new personalities to the school, both in the faculty and in the student body. The flowering of Canterbury was most evident in this growing family of personalities.

Save the School's headmaster, the dominant personality of the growing Canterbury was Philip H. Brodie. Philip Brodie was a native of Arkansas, a graduate of Van Buren High School, and in 1913, while in attendance at the University of Arkansas, was awarded a Rhodes Scholarship. He enrolled at Worcester College, Oxford, and graduated with the degree of Master of Arts in 1917. He was commissioned a second lieutenant at the outbreak of hostilities with Germany, and saw service at the Mexican border. He acquired most of his teaching experience at Van Buren High School and at the St. Louis Country Day School. While at the University of Arkansas, he coached the local high school football team.[104]

Although the title was never officially conferred upon him, Mr. Brodie was, to all intents and purposes, the assistant headmaster. He taught Latin with thoroughness and an unrelenting demand for accuracy and precision. His classes became models of these exacting standards. Although never one to insult or belittle a student, he wouldn't hesitate to "read him out in lavender" for shoddy work or bad behavior.[105] He attended to the complicated and often difficult task of arranging schedules for classes as well as individual students. He was the czar of the dining room at breakfast, when his eagle eye would detect the large hand of the clock at exactly two minutes before 7:30. Soon, the wailing banshee cry of "All in!" would reverberate through the Berkshire Hills, as records for the 100-yard dash were broken repeatedly to avoid the day "on bounds" that a second's tardiness was sure to entail. Years later, when on campus to attend a Hume Society Dinner, Sargent Shriver '34 still recalled Mr. Brodie and his stopwatch, standing guard at the North House dining-room door.[106]

After the death of Alexander Hume, Mr. Brodie was always in

charge of affairs when Dr. Hume had to be absent. With Mr. Edwin Lindman and Mr. Mack, he was a College Board reader for many years. In later years, Mr. Hebert would say of Mr. Brodie, "He had perfect disciplinary control, yet he never raised his voice. He was an excellent teacher, coach, and dorm master. He was the consummate schoolman . . . for Phil Brodie, Canterbury School came first, nothing else."[107]

In addition to his scholastic services to the school, Mr. Brodie acted as director of athletics, and successfully coached football, baseball, swimming, and track over a period of many years. His football teams were well conditioned, well drilled, and schooled in reliable defense. Once during a football game, so the story goes, a student went down, bleeding profusely. Phil said, in his inimitable Arkansas drawl, "Drag him over to the side of the field, boys. We can't scrimmage with him in our way like that."[108] Of course, after practice, the first one down to the infirmary to check on the boy's condition was Phil. In later years, during an interview about Shriver's work in the Peace Corps, he was asked about his Canterbury memories. Once again, Shriver remembered Phil Brodie and the Canterbury faculty.

> I remember the faculty very vividly. Mr. Brodie, Mr. Mack, Mr. Maloney, Dr. Hume himself. They truly had vocations. Brodie . . . was an extraordinary teacher of Latin. He was a strict disciplinarian. But his most important qual-ity was that he truly loved the students and the school . . . [T]he same can be said of men like Mack, who played the organ in the chapel, taught history, and wrote music. Overall, there was an incredible bond of compassion . . . It was very academic, very religious, very warm, and person-al.[109]

Mr. Brodie was a personality in his own right. He never quite lost his southern drawl, and certainly never his gentility or his adherence to strict social protocol. He was adamant in his resistance to any breakdown of formality, whether it was at tea or on the athletic field. Once after he retired, Mr. Brodie called longtime faculty member Jean Hebert to play golf one day at Waramaug Country Club. Mr. Hebert said even after working with Phil Brodie for years, he couldn't bring himself to call him "Phil."

Once, during Walter Sheehan's administration, Jules Viau came down to dinner wearing a sweater under his jacket. Mr. Brodie met him in the dining room and said, "Sir, gentlemen do not wear sweaters to dinner." Phil Brodie functioned, wholly without self-consciousness, as just about the best public relations promoter the School could have employed. He had a silent contempt for ostentation and insincerity. His favorite pastimes were bridge and golf. He was loved, honored, and respected by generations of Canterbury boys, by the men and women of the faculty, and by all those who had any connection with the institution. He retired in 1956, full of memories and honors, and became the familiar "Mr. Chips" about the School. His only son, Philip, graduated from Canterbury in 1937 as the first faculty child to graduate. After the death of his wife, Sarah Miller Brodie, in 1961, he lived alone next to the campus, and died on October 22, 1975.[110]

In the fall of 1919 the Blessed Sacrament was installed permanently on the campus of Canterbury through the permission of Bishop John J. Nilan of the Hartford Diocese, who had visited the school the prior spring. In a Mass and ceremony, Father Joseph King, pastor of St. Francis Xavier Church in the village, brought the Sacrament to the chapel on September 26. Because Father King had no assistant at St. Francis, he could not take on the duties of a regular chaplain at the school, and the Jesuits from Tarrytown[111] continued for some time as the school's spiritual directors.

When the influenza epidemic hit in 1918, Dr. Hume took it in stride. He quarantined the students and placed the school under the protection of St. Michael the Archangel. The result was that Canterbury was completely spared. The devotion to St. Michael, not only as the protector of Christ in his youth, but as the deliverer of Canterbury, continued after the epidemic. Specific mention of St. Michael still remains in the school prayers,[113] and in the west window of the Chapel of Our Lady, given by William Mackay, he is represented as guardian of the School.

When school opened in the fall of 1919, construction was started on the combination hockey rink / running track, which was completed in time for the hockey season that year. The rink— which was the gift of Mrs. Nicholas Brady —unfortunately was built on a rock ledge, causing water to seep out when it thawed. Dr. Hume took charge of many efforts to correct this defect, and would personally supervise the flooding and freezing of the rink after each thaw. The whole school would assemble to shovel the rink clear after each of the many New England snowstorms. "Armed with shovels, clad in gaudy, checkered shirts, smiling or scowling, everyone in the school at least makes an act of presence at this scene of many a historic hockey game. A white sheet of snow six inches thick presents a discouraging sight to this army of shovelers."[114]

Dr. Hume was an effective public speaker, taking every possible opportunity to speak to the boys. His rhetoric could move even the most hardened veteran at the school. He held class in public speaking from time to time, and the outgrowth of this was the "Canterbury Forum," which began in the fall of 1919. The Forum was a type of discussion group held once a week at which students would address the school and then field questions from the floor. It flourished for a number of years after its institution, faltered during the Depression, and was resumed for a time in the middle 1930s.

In his "sports for all" program, Dr. Hume organized a wide assortment of intramural sports, which filled in the gaps between seasons and provided opportunities for boys not active in either junior or varsity football. It was in this capacity that soccer was eventually introduced at the school. Although visiting luminaries—such as John McCormick, the tenor and soccer enthusiast—would visit the school and give informal exhibitions of the sport, it never really took hold until after Dr. Hume's death. The most illustrious of the intramural games, however, was the "Army-Navy" series, which usually followed the regular football season. The lower school was divided into teams that were coached by the Sixth Formers. They usually played three games, or until Thanksgiving. It was out of these teams that the eventual "midget" classification was derived.

Dances were a regular social function at the school. At the very least, a Thanksgiving dance and a graduation dance were held each year, and the boys were allowed to invite dates and friends to attend these affairs. The dances soon became reunion events for many of the alumni, and when the Homecoming tradition began in 1933, a dance was scheduled along with the football game. Card dancing began at 9:00 P.M., and there were usually sixteen to twenty dances on a card. A boy would pencil in his date for the first, last, and supper dance. The remaining dances on the card would be filled by swapping with dates of friends, and sisters or cousins who happened to be attending. According to Stephen Hume '43, any unfilled dances on the card would be "auctioned" off, so that no girl was ever left without a dance. Card dancing would continue until about 11:45, when supper was served. After supper, the dancing would continue, with cutting in allowed. The dances would end by 2:00 A.M.[115]

Other diversions at the school were generally of the outdoor variety. As has been noted, Dr. Hume sponsored extended hikes through the woods, tennis, golf on the school's developing course, skiing and sledding on Chapel Hill, and games in the woods. These games, unlike the modern variety, consisted mainly of "Hare and Hounds" chases and swimming. In fact, *The Quill*, and later, *The Tabard*, often published guides to the better swimming holes in the area, and also mapped out the best hiking routes and the time it took to hike them.

The first indoor activity sponsored by Dr. Hume was the fore-runner of the famous school tradition known as Saturday Night Movies. The first movies were played on a machine called the Pathescope, which was donated by Mrs. Havemeyer. By subscrib-ing to the Pathe service, the school received a newsreel and trave-logue each week, and often, a feature film. It was during one of the first showings of a travelogue, *Fishing in Portugal*, that the school's most successful stink bomb was loosed. The timing was perfect, and the bomb matured at precisely the moment in Dr. Hume's monologue when he was saying, "Boys, this is truly a wonderful film; why, you can almost smell those fish the men are catching." The next word was a thunderous, "LIGHTS!" The room was cleared. Although there was a minor inquisition, the culprit was never found.[116]

At Canterbury, Saturday Night Movies reached a peak in 1935, when one of the parents provided facilities for exhibiting 35mm feature films. For this purpose, a fireproof stone projection room was added to the old study hall (now the chaplain's resi-dence), which is still intact.[117] The feature shown at the school was the same one that played downtown. The reels were bicycled up the hill as soon as the New Milford Theater had finished with them.[118] The deliveries were often late, and the climax of the show had to be suspended while the messenger pedaled frantically up the hill with the next reel. By the mid-1950s, the size of the school demanded two showings, and the film (which had returned to the less-costly 16mm when the student body could no longer fit into the old study hall) was shuttled between South and Middle Houses in much the same way.

As soon as the corporate reorganization was completed, and it was made clear that any contributions to the School would remain *with* the School, Dr. Hume launched the Fifth Anniversary Fund and Development Drive. The plan was to expand the School to 160 boys, to put it in line with Groton, St. Mark, and Middlesex. To do this, the Main House was to be maintained as a lower school; Dr. Hume felt this was a unique service, which fed students into the upper school. The Bungalow was to be converted into an infirmary. On top of the hill, Dr. Hume proposed to build a gymnasium, a dormitory for 120 boys, a chapel, and a schoolhouse. These would be constructed out of granite in the Norman mode.[119] He also planned to have all the buildings joined by covered passageways.[120]

By graduation day in 1920, the plans for the new campus were on exhibition. Raphael Hume, Nelson's brother, then 32 years old, had drawn up the plans. Raphael was a highly qualified architect, whose work had appeared in such publications as *Architectural Record*.[121] Nelson was warming up for a drive that he hoped would raise $500,000. At the outset of the drive, he secured the blessing of Bishop Nilan of the Diocese of Hartford, and the good wishes of His Holiness Pope Benedict. Dr. Hume reminded Mr. Havemeyer of the importance of maintaining the good graces of Bishop Nilan:

> You may remember that when we first came into his diocese there was something of a misunderstanding about our attitude toward him, and I had to go very warily in dealing with him in securing his permission to have Mass at the school . . . I consulted Bishop Hickey, of Rochester . . . and he told me that the wisest thing would be to ask the Bishop . . . In fact, he pointed out that it was the only thing we could do now without giving him offense, and that it would be an uncomfortable state of affairs for us to be on the

wrong side of our own Bishop.[122]

The following fall the School opened with sixty-two boys. Morale was high, and the parents and patrons of the school were solidly behind expansion. Canterbury was becoming established as a preparatory school on equal footing with—and a charter member of—the interscholastic league that included The Gunnery, Westminster, Salisbury, and Berkshire.

In February 1921, Dr. Hume announced that the school had been promised a new chapel and a new gymnasium by two parents. William McPhee of Denver pledged $50,000 for the construction of a chapel in memory of his son, William Cranmer McPhee.[123] James and Nicholas Brady along with Clarence Mackay agreed to donate the gymnasium. James Cox Brady was a descendent of Anthony Brady of Albany, New York, a public utility and copper magnate. Along with his brother, Nicholas Brady, they contributed $150,000 toward the building of the new gym.[124] The original plan devised by the Bradys called for several indoor tennis courts, along with boxing and fencing rooms.[125] However, this was revised in favor of a basketball court and two squash courts. The first solicitation for additional funds was made in the form of a leaflet sent out to forty-five select parents and friends, along with a letter from one of the trustees. This was typical of Hume's tendency to rely on a relatively small number of people as the basis of the school's support.

The country slid into a recession in the spring of 1921, and because of this, Dr. Hume was forced to announce at an alumni meeting in June that there would be no building undertaken until the financial picture had brightened. The delay brought about a review and reconsideration of the basic plan. After considering several other alternatives, the trustees and Dr. Hume decided to place the new quadrangle on the hill. With that decision made, it became advisable to protect the site by purchasing the Elkington Farm property, which ran from the hill down to Highway 25, now known as Route 202.[126] Through the efforts of James A. Farrell, the property, along with a smaller annex (the Evitts farm), was purchased in March of 1922. Clarence Mackay, James Cox Brady, and John D. Ryan also contributed to the purchase price of those acres. In addition to securing complete control of the top of the hill, the purchase of the 62-acre Elkington Farm included a quarry,[127] although it is doubtful that Canterbury used this stone in any of its own buildings. The stone used in the construction of the gym came from a quarry in Roxbury, Connecticut.[128] While the fund drive had been temporarily halted, special gifts by the Bradys and Mr. Mackay made it possible to begin the gymnasium construction in the fall of 1922.

Building the gym was a slow process, and took more than a year. During that period, however, a new athletic field was put into readiness in the pasture adjoining the gym. The football games of the 1923 season were played there, but the locker rooms were not in use until midseason. The swimming pool and the basketball court of the new gym were in operation by January 1924. The first basketball games took place among intramural teams. The first official game was not played until after the close of the hockey season on February 28, 1924. Playing on their home court, the first varsity basketball team lost the game to Stanford by a score of 29–19. By the midwinter of 1924, the gym was in full use. It boasted a swimming pool, two squash courts, and a basketball court. Although the latter was of standard dimensions for the period, in later years it was sardonically labeled "the third squash court." The size of the basketball court did not disturb Dr. Hume. He always held basketball in lower regard as a salubrious indoor sport. He much preferred swimming, and was proud that so early in its development, Canterbury had one of the few 25-yard pools in New

England.

Dr. Hume's plans for the quadrangle on the hill involved closing off Aspetuck Avenue about 300 feet south of the site of the gymnasium, at the start of the Elkington Farm Road. It had not occurred to him that the town of New Milford would oppose the road closing, since Aspetuck Avenue to the north of the school had not been used for half a century or more, and, in fact, was a cow pasture. Not only did opposition arise, but it became quite intense. The town meeting held in early February 1923 drew close to seven hundred townsfolk, a record for the town.[129] The proposal to close the road was defeated by a wide margin (244–170) at a stormy town meeting.

A second proposal was made at a town meeting some months later, suggesting that the closing of Aspetuck Avenue be approved on the condition that Canterbury bear the cost of constructing a detour around the proposed hilltop buildings. That proposal was also defeated. As a result, rather than prolonging a contest with the town that had already developed unpleasant undercurrents, Dr. Hume and the trustees decided to abandon the plan for using the hill as the center of a new main quadrangle for the school.[130] Raphael Hume was asked to draw up new plans for the construction of North House, and to design the future campus of the school around the main building, leaving the new gymnasium in lonely eminence on the hilltop. However, as the fund drive continued to lag, further construction was postponed. Instead, the Wayside Inn[131] in town was leased for the lower school.

The School was visited by many dignitaries, both foreign and American. Two of the most famous were the French Benedictine abbots who stayed at the school for most of one year, entertaining the boys with ghost stories, and John McCormack, the famous tenor, whose son Cyril attended the school in the 1920s.[132] McCormack was a favorite visitor to the school, and Nelson

Hume's good friend. The headmaster and McCormack would spend long hours after lights-out, smoking cigars and drinking brandy in the common room of the Main House.[133]

In these early years, the Bungalow was often used as a school theater. Even as early as 1917,[134] it was the locale of such productions as *Katherine and Petruchio*. Canterbury's second venture into the world of theater took place in 1920, when John McCormack was in attendance at the School. McCormack received permission from Mr. George M. Cohan to present the latter's comedy, *Seven Keys to Baldpate*, then enjoying a successful run on Broadway. The Comedy Club Players, as they called themselves, were forced to postpone the opening night from February 20 to March 17 because of outbreaks of both flu and measles.[135] In the review, Joseph Campbell '21, John Hughes '20, Allan Ryan '20, Sidney Binns '20, and Theodore Ryan received plaudits. The play was presented in the Bungalow to an audience of approximately 175 people.[136] Just before the production, the power went out, and the play had to be acted by lamplight.[137]

In May 1921, the most extraordinary production of a play in the school's history took place. The play was *A Midsummer Night's Dream*, and included a prologue written by Cyril Hume, organ music by Jacques Pintell, and singing offstage by John McCormack. Nothing since has ever rivaled it. The distinguishing factor about the production was the lush appointments, including costumes. Also remarkable was the fact that the character of Bottom was played by none other than the headmaster himself. Joseph Campbell had been slated for the role but fell ill just before the performance. The only other person in the school who knew the lines was Nelson Hume; he could quote long passages of Shakespeare, and had been directing the production right from the start. Without any hesitation, he donned the donkey's head and gave a sterling performance, with no loss in prestige or discipline among his more fortunate players.[138]

In the spring of 1922 the golf course was expanded to seven full holes and two practice greens. It was laid out by Mr. Jerome Sullivan and Mr. Alexander Hume, of the faculty, and Harold Salembier '27. The greens were not much larger than a living-room rug and there were no traps, but noble and majestic trees furnished more than frustrating hazards,[139] with the hockey rink serving as the hardest trap of them all. The trap lay on the fourth hole, the green nestling in close to the wooden railing.[140]

On Sunday afternoons, the course was crowded. Alec Hume liked to play golf, and he ensured that the greens were kept mowed and the fairways playable. After his death, interest lagged. The course became too small for a new generation of long-ball hitters. Besides, the trees kept on growing until the course was no longer usable. By this time, the high point of the spring season had become the field day and school track meet that was held at the end of each school year. The obsolescence of the original little golf course on the school grounds caused an exodus to nearby links, where it was possible to arrange practice and play about once a week. Golf being the game that it is, skillful players would always be the exception. Skilled players that will remain in memory at Canterbury are Jack Routh '30, Bob Sweeny, ex '30,[141] and Charlie Sweeny '28, who later went on to achieve international acclaim as a golfer and as the golfing partner of the Duke of Windsor, when he was Prince of Wales.

Dr. Hume rewarded athletic prowess in the early days by block C's that were won not on the basis of varsity participation, but on terms of individual achievement. There were only three or four letters awarded in each sport. These letters each had a designated rank that corresponded to the order in which they were awarded. This kept the letter winners in a fairly tight community, and it was an honor to any student to receive even the

"Fourth Letter" in any sport.

Perhaps the most important event at Canterbury during the 1923–1924 academic year—even more important for the future of Canterbury than the opening of the new gym—was Dr. Hume's marriage. On December 15, 1923, he was married in Denver, Colorado, to May Desjardins, one of five daughters of Ella Purcell and Bernard Roi DesJardins. Dr. Hume had met May in Europe during the summer of 1923. A teacher and graduate student from Columbia's Teacher's College, she had gone to Europe to travel and study. After she went on a blind date with Nelson Hume, the two enjoyed a whirlwind courtship, resulting in a formal proposal before the European summer was over. He was forty-two; she was thirty-five.[142]

When Dr. Hume returned to the United States in the fall, he met May's sister Clotilde and her husband, William F. Russell, who was the dean of Teacher's College. They congratulated the couple, commending May's good fortune to her parents. Nelson and May were married four months later in Denver. In Denver Dr. Hume was the guest of Mr. and Mrs. McPhee, and McPhee, a member of the Board of Trustees and a personal friend of Hume's, acted as best man. A special dispensation for the wedding had to be obtained, because the wedding took place during the Advent season.[143] The Christmas holidays that year were extended to give the Humes a week's honeymoon at The Plaza in New York. While there, they met F. Scott Fitzgerald, an old student of Dr. Hume's from the Newman School.[144] When Nelson introduced his bride, Fitzgerald said, "I might have known, sir, I've never seen you look so high."[145]

The faculty, students, and friends from the village enthusiastically celebrated Dr. Hume's arrival at Canterbury with his new wife. The Humes took up residence on the top floor of the south wing of the Main House. Thus began Mrs. Hume's association with Canterbury, which would continue until her death sixty-five years later in 1988. She was an ideal headmaster's wife, managing to be everywhere she was needed while still remaining unobtrusive. Her many attributes included superlative tact and circumspection. She was a gifted wife and partner, and seemed to know when to oppose, when to guide, when to console, when to approve, when to comfort, and when to laugh at her ofttimes perplexed and harried husband. Her quick response to the humor in any situation, and her bright optimism and good nature, were valued at times when discouragement might have prevailed. The students and faculty thought the world of her, as reported in the *Pallium*: "Canterbury boys of the time testify that she brought a balance and amelioration to the schoolmasterly ferocity of her husband."[146]

Not only did she give help and inspiration to Canterbury's first headmaster, but she also gave three sons to Canterbury, each of whom became distinguished in his chosen profession. David Hume would go on to become the second headmaster of Saint David's School, a position he would hold for 37 years. Over the course of those years, he would serve as president of the New York State Association of Independent Schools as well as the NYC Guild of Independent Schools, The Elementary School Heads Association, and the Country Day School Headmasters Association.[147] Steve graduated from Columbia Law School and practiced law for the next forty-two years, the last thirty-five of which he was a partner in the firm of Cramer & Anderson in their New Milford office. Michael served twenty-five years as the Chief of Surgery at the New England Baptist Hospital in Boston.[148] If Canterbury had already been coeducational, their daughter, Rozanne, would also have been a Canterbury graduate. Rozanne, a graduate of Manhattanville College, raised five children of her own and served as the Director of Admissions at the Sacred Heart School at 91st Street in New York City. After Hume's death, May served continuously as a member of Canterbury's Board of Trustees until June 1980. According to the *Pallium*, hers was "an approving presence. She was strongly in favor of the change to coeducation, but spoke out vociferously and almost alone against plans to sell some of the school's land in the 1960s. Ten years later the school was buying land and the original plots thus conserved had grown in value by a factor of ten."[149]

The school year of 1924–1925 opened with sixty-seven students, the largest enrollment up to that time. Tuition had increased to $1,500. The school was at capacity, and Dr. Hume was anxious to get on with his plans to enlarge the school's enrollment to at least one hundred students. In sports, Canterbury was playing other schools on a regular basis. Those teams in the unofficial league were Berkshire, Salisbury, Pawling, Westminster, South Kent, and The Gunnery, with several other schools coming into the schedule from time to time.

Father Frederick H. Sill at Kent was especially interested in promoting relations with Canterbury. Dr. Hume promised the Pater, as he was known, that as soon as Canterbury's enrollment permitted, he would boat a crew to match the celebrated oarsmen from Kent. In fact, just before his death in 1948, Nelson Hume had invited Gerry Cassedy, the famous stroke of Harvard, to come to New Milford and to assess the nearby sections of the Housatonic River as suitable rowing places.

Kent, of course, was always bigger than Canterbury, and in football the Blue was no match for Kent. In its first game, Canterbury lost by a score of 97–0. In hockey, however, under Dr. Hume's own coaching, Canterbury was much more of a match for Kent. The contests were memorable and the rivalry hot, perhaps even more so between the two headmasters than between the players. Father Sill had begun it all when he had visited the school in its first fall, and told Dr. Hume that he was glad to see a school with a name so closely associated with Anglicanism. He welcomed Hume to the valley, saying that Kent was always glad to have another team they could beat so conveniently close. This, of course, drew a hot reply from Dr. Hume. The encounter, which began in front of the old Main House, was renewed with every game between the two schools. Exchanges grew louder as the years went by—not because the two men became less friendly, but because Father Sill became increasingly deaf.

> Once when we were playing hockey against Kent on our new outdoor rink, the referee ordered a Kent player off the ice—for what I do not remember. Father Sill was over the west side of the fence and *in medias res* before you could say Jack Robinson. And who, from our side of the fence was likewise—perhaps even beating Father Sill's time? Right! Then came the glorious denouement from any schoolboy's point of view—the referee ordered them both off the ice! Such laughter has not been heard since.[150]

Dr. Hume decided in 1924 to reactivate the drive for funds. He retained the plan for four new buildings, which would permit a division of facilities between the upper and lower schools, but he decided to limit the new campaign for funds to an amount sufficient to cover an enlargement of the Main House. For the School's tenth anniversary, Hume prepared a booklet called *Ten Years of Canterbury—And Its Future*. The booklet announced an appeal for $100,000 from parents and friends to match a similar gift from the trustees. With this sum, Canterbury hoped to enlarge the Main House to provide for forty more boys and at the same time, to pay off debts totaling $65,000, which had accumulated over the first decade of the School's existence. The report emphasized that the School was seeking wider support outside that provided by the twelve donors who had contributed the entire initial investment of $350,000.

The status of the School after the first decade was impressive.

It owned 135 acres and had just completed construction of a fully equipped gymnasium. In addition, the goal of the School to prepare Catholic men for higher studies in the best American colleges had been fulfilled. Scholastic standards at the School were high, and the *Quarterly*, bolstered by several essay and story contests, was becoming a learned journal known outside the Canterbury walls and quoted in national Catholic magazines such as *Commonweal*. Ninety-five percent of the graduates during the first ten years were admitted to college, the majority of them to Yale.

In 1925, Joseph F. Maloney, of Waterbury, Connecticut, joined the staff. Mr. Maloney had taught at Regis High School in Denver, Colorado, and was a graduate of St. Thomas Seminary in Bloomfield, Connecticut, and of Holy Cross College. He was assigned to remedial classes in Latin and mathematics, and he enlivened the spirit of the School for thirty-two years, until his death in 1955. He served in many capacities, particularly as coach of midget football and, for many years, of varsity baseball, following Mr. Brodie's retirement from that sport. With all the talents of a born detective, Mr. Maloney was especially adept at ferreting out young citizens guilty of devious attempts to beat the system. As a consequence, there were few, if any, unsolved mysteries in the gallery of boyish misdemeanors. He had a way with boys that made his services indispensable. It was useless to try anything on him; his humor was so sharp and his repartee so deadly that new boys soon learned not to try to match wits with him. He was widely known through his athletic contacts with the coaching staffs of other schools, was very fond of social life, and was a compendium of athletic knowledge and events in the world of sports.

What seemed at the outset to be a serene and fruitful year was suddenly turned into a crisis by two severe blows. The first was that the parent who had pledged money for the new chapel lost his business and was thus unable to meet his commitment. This deprived the fund drive of a great deal of momentum. It left a $50,000 hole in the plans for financing the school's expansion. In letters between Clarence Mackay, Henry Havemeyer, and Nelson Hume in early 1923, the men discussed postponing the building of the chapel and proceeding with the plans for the new dormitory. It was also clear at this point that the $50,000 pledged for the construction of the chapel would not be enough to construct the building according to the ideas of the Board of Directors.[151]

The second blow occurred on December 5, 1925. On the third floor of the Bungalow there was a hole in the wall that had become the boys' favorite depository of cigarette butts. Apparently some boy threw his after-breakfast cigarette down the hole before going to class. Around ten A.M., Mrs. Hume, on the third floor of the Main House, looked out the window and noticed smoke coming from the Bungalow. Nelson Hume was teaching on the second floor, but even the house burning down did not warrant interruption of one of his classes. Mrs. Hume, therefore, consulted Marie Hume in the infirmary, and they both confirmed that the Bungalow was, in fact, on fire. Marie went to phone in the alarm, but by that time some of the masters and boys were running toward the house. The first boys raced into the Bungalow to save some of their belongings. The story goes that the boys were throwing things like clocks, lamps, and typewriters out the windows while carefully bringing their blankets, shoes, and other unbreakables downstairs.[152]

"The tragedy of the fire was not unmixed with comedy . . . when a silver saxophone hurtled through the air to its owner's feet, a sigh arose and some people expressed the fear that the fire would accomplish no good at all."[153] However, the salvage operation did not last long, because as soon as the headmaster arrived on the scene, he stationed himself at the main door, armed with a golf club, and successfully repelled any further entrances. *The Tabard* of

December 8, 1925, included this account:

> At nine-twenty five the entire building was vacated. The whole roof was a sloping sheet of fire which crackled and spluttered as it sent curling tongues of flames into the rooms below. There was a bustle and commotion on the ground as the fellows ran about, collecting their clothes, commenting on the fierceness of the fire, and cheerfully remarking on the losses that they had sustained.
>
> A few minutes later, the whole second and third stories were a huge bonfire.[154]

The fire department could do little with the blaze, and by two P.M. in the afternoon, the Bungalow was a smoldering ruin. Plans were made immediately to house the boys in the gym. Beds were ordered from New Haven, and by four P.M. they had arrived. All of the neighboring schools offered to house some of the boys, but with Nelson Hume at the helm, this was unnecessary. The change of residence from the Bungalow to the gym was completed by lights out. The next day, wrecking crews tore down the chimneys and cleared the site. During the Christmas vacation the basketball court was divided into thirds for sleeping, study, and living rooms. The floor was carpeted, as were the squash courts. Masters' quarters were prepared in the balcony above the basketball court and in the rooms above the squash courts.

On January 15, a housewarming was held for the faculty and boys of both The Gunnery and Kent, who came over to inspect the ingenious way in which Dr. Hume had met the emergency. When school resumed in 1926, the upper-form boys were housed in the Main House and the lower forms were housed in the gymnasium. The biggest treat for the upper-form boys was the privilege of studying in their own rooms.[155] As reported in *The Quarterly*: "No more do these serious minded young gentlemen have to study together in one large room with only four arc lights to illuminate their way to knowledge, for they are allowed to study in their rooms, and each room is supplied with a writing desk and lamp."

The loss of the Bungalow changed the building plans for the school once more. There was lengthy discussion about whether to proceed with the North House, which had been planned along with improvements to the Main House, or whether to rebuild a bigger dormitory on the foundation of the Bungalow. The North House plan was favored at first, and plans were completed showing it, the Main House, and the store joined by passageways.[156] However, this proved to be too expensive for the funds at hand. To maintain the confidence of the present and future parents, Dr. Hume was anxious to begin building as soon as possible. It was therefore agreed to forgo the Main House addition in favor of building a dormitory on the Bungalow foundation, using the insurance money and funds from the fund drive. Thus it was that in the spring of 1926, construction of South House began (the present-day Carter House). The *Pallium* reported: "Desire to expand the new building's capacity accounts for the odd-shaped rooms and dormers in South House today."[157]

In the meantime, because the gym was being used in large part as a dormitory, swimming became a major sport at Canterbury. The first meet was held with Pawling on February 19, 1926, with Mr. Brodie as coach. The new team won all of its four meets that year and quickly became a power in the state. The other athletic highlight of that year was the golf team, which competed in the interscholastics and sent one boy to the semifinals.

Another change in the appearance of the campus that year came when the famous old stone wall that ran up the Chapel Hill was removed. Five thousand pine trees then were planted on the slope west of the soccer field that ran down to the river. A forest fire had burned off all the timber in 1915, shortly before school opened, and had blackened that entire hillside.

The bells that rang in an early Canterbury graduate's ears long after graduation were first sounded in January 1927. Corridor bells were used only to call attention to an oral announcement about to be made by the master in charge. It was soon evident that the bells themselves could be used to give commands, and at length the entire school schedule was controlled by bells. Even earlier, bells were used in the dorms. An "Impressions" column included in *The Tabard* at the time reported: "A relic was found among the ruins of the bungalow the other day, a much coveted relic which was borne proudly by its discoverer to his dormitory, there to be exhibited as the biggest electric bell ever seen at Canterbury. That bell had a short reign but an absolute one . . . This is the bell that killed the excuse, 'I overslept this morning, Sir.' "[158]

The South House, built in the stucco style of the Main House, was occupied on May 14, 1927. It had rooms for forty boys and apartments for two masters. The bathroom on the second floor was intended to service both floors. Years later, an abbreviated lavatory was added to the third-floor corridor. The first floor had a large common room and two magnificent porches, which were the pride of the upperclassmen who first occupied the dormitory. The half basement contained staff housing and a large laundry.

At graduation that year, Father Francis X. Byrne, SJ, a frequent visitor at the school, gave a sermon on the sorry condition of the school's chapel. The point of his talk was that the most important building on campus was, in fact, the smallest. He was deploring the contrast between the magnificent new gymnasium, with its commanding position on the hill of campus, and the little, insignificant chapel tucked away under the hill. A parent, John Thomas Smith—one of the nation's most distinguished lawyers, who at that time was general counsel of General Motors—was deeply moved by the sermon. Immediately after the Mass he pledged whatever financial support would be needed for a new chapel.[159]

The discarded plans for the chapel at the top of the hill were revised to adapt the structure to the site it currently occupies. Construction began in the fall of 1927.[160] The chapel was built out of the same granite used for the gym, taken from the Roxbury Quarry seven miles away.[161] Dr. Hume, working with his brother, Raphael, took great care in the design of the chapel. It bears Nelson's distinctive style, and shows his talent for aesthetic design. In fact, when it was completed the following June,[162] it was a masterpiece of liturgical art, incorporating the classic proportions of Norman Gothic with several innovations, such as having the main entrance not beneath the large west window, but on the side of the chapel.[163] By May, the chapel was nearly finished, but with no path to approach the chapel up the hill.

By the spring of 1929, two stained-glass windows had been given to the chapel.[164] The windows were made in Campden, Gloucestershire, England by Paul Woodroffe, an eminent artist in stained glass.[165] The two tall lancets in the north wall of the chancel were presented next.[166] Much later, through the generosity of Alec Hume, a new stained-glass window depicting the story of the Good Samaritan was erected.[167] The tower of the chapel, as planned by the headmaster, was to serve a most happy purpose: It was to house the new pipe organ donated by Mr. Michael Meehan in 1928, in memory of his mother, Sarah Ansbro Meehan.

The organ, a complicated instrument containing 967 pipes, was dedicated in a special ceremony on Sunday afternoon, May 26, 1929.[168] For its dedication, Pietro Yon, honorary organist of the Vatican, and the St. Patrick's quartet from New York City gave an organ and voice recital.[169] These pipes occupied two floors in the tower. The top floor of the tower, open to the weather with louvered windows, holds the mighty framework on which are hung the twenty-three bells of the carillon, donated in 1931 by Mrs. Irene O'Donohue Ferrer in memory of her husband, José Maria Ferrer, MD.[170] A carillon has at least twenty-three bells, which play half-tone notes, and can have a range of two octaves. The carillon can play accurately and without distortion any melody that can be sung. Dr. Hume spent months traveling through the East inspecting various carillons, and finally purchased the bells in Croydon, England.

Dr. Hume had been taking lessons from the eminent Mr. Kamiel Lefevere, carillonneur of the Riverside Carillon, and desired that Mr. Lefevere play at the dedication. Unfortunately, immigration laws prevented Mr. Lefevere from attending.[172] On May 10, 1931, Mr. Hailes of Albany dedicated the bells at Canterbury with a wonderful recital.[173] Before the dedication ceremony, Monsignor Michael J. Lavelle formally blessed the bells with oil, incense, and holy water. Bishop Nilan gave his permission for the full blessing ceremony to be performed.[174] Attending the dedication was Mr. William Gorham Rice of Albany, author of *Carillon Music and Singing Towers of the Old World and the New*, at the time the one complete book on carillons in any language.[175]

Mr. Rice's speech touched off an interesting exchange between Dr. Hume and Mr. Havemeyer. Mr. Rice referred to the tower as "a singing tower," which for some reason Havemeyer found inappropriate. The full text of Mr. Rice's dedication address can be found in the May 12, 1931, edition of *The Tabard*, but his opening was, "Today a new Singing Tower comes into full being and you are taking part in its creation."[176] Of course, the boys reporting for *The Tabard* picked up the phrase, and so did the local papers.[177] Dr. Hume had to hasten to assure Mr. Havemeyer that these references appeared in print before Havemeyer had voiced his objections, and that he would discourage further use of the phrase.

Mr. Edward Mack joined the Canterbury faculty in the fall of 1928, with two advanced degrees and teaching experience from his alma mater, Georgetown.[178] Before coming to Canterbury, he had taught history and Spanish at Gonzaga College, a Jesuit school located in Washington, D.C. He took over the history department at Canterbury, at the same time assuming the duties of organist and choirmaster. Mr. Mack also wrote a history of Canterbury School in celebration of the fiftieth anniversary of the School. This history was never published, but Canterbury's archives contains several copies of Mack's history.

Upon the installation of the José M. Ferrer Memorial Carillon, Mack became the official carillonneur of the School. Ed Mack, an accomplished musician, soon learned how to play the bells and eventually joined the exclusive Carillonneurs of America. He later gave recitals for both the town and the school. Carillonneurs Kamiel Lefevere, and Melvin Corbett also gave recitals over the years. Dr. Hume also occasionally played the carillon. Upon the passing of King Albert of Belgium, all carillonneurs were requested to play in his honor (Belgium being the place where carillons originated). Since Dr. Hume could not find anyone else to play on such short notice, he played Schubert's "Death Song."[179]

Before the carillon was in place, work began on the large west window of the chapel. This gift from John W. Mackay—Clarence Mackay's son, known as "Willie"—was to be the crowning adornment of the chapel. Work on it continued throughout the summer, and the school could not view the window until the following fall. Willie would present the window in early May 1931.[180] Mr. Mackay confided to Dr. Hume that "he wished Willie to give the window so that the Mackay name would be permanently identified with Canterbury School."[181]

The selection of a boy to be a sacristan was the most coveted honor in School life. The principal duty of the sacristan is to prepare the altar for every service in accordance with the liturgical calendar and to mark the Mass readings in the missal. Upon the installation of the José M. Ferrer Memorial Carillon, a duty was laid upon the sacristans to ring the Angelus at morning, noon, and night, and to toll the nine verses of the psalm "De Profundis" each night at nine o'clock in memory of Dr. Ferrer and of the Canterbury dead. These duties were performed for more than thirty-four years without a single lapse.

Ground was broken on April 11, 1928, for North House. The School had a new gymnasium and a beautiful new chapel commanding the campus. Enrollment now exceeded ninety, and the facilities fit the number of students. The additional dormitory had been in the original plans for the School before the Bungalow fire. Even after the larger South House was built, the School's facilities were hard-pressed to meet the increasing enrollment. North House would provide a dining room for the entire school and quarters for the headmaster and his family, thus freeing needed classroom space in the Main House. The cost of the South House and the incidental expenses of the chapel had exhausted the Capital Fund. In addition to about $20,000 in outright gifts, the trustees underwrote a $125,000 bond issue to raise enough money for the dormitory. Although the bonds were supposed to pay 5 percent interest, most of them were later returned to the School as gifts, and, through the efforts of Terence Carmody, the school's counsel, the School was eventually able to save most of the expense of this bond issue.

North House was occupied by October of 1928. Although it was the most economically constructed building on campus, the economies did not become necessary until after the first floor was completed. Thus, the dining hall and kitchen were far more elegant than were the upper stories. The light construction is saved by the molding and other tricks supplied by Raphael Hume. Dr. Hume laid out the basic dimensions of the dining room and designed it along the proportions of the "golden section" (in art and architecture, the most pleasing ratio, or 1 to 0.618). The living room in the headmaster's apartment was also designed using these principles. The center of the entire building was the dining room. The common room of North House was kept simple and small because Dr. Hume intended to keep the center of the school in the Main House. Unfortunately, he neglected to realize that the gathering place of any preparatory school is where the food is. Thus, with the completion of North House, the school split between the dining room and the two common rooms of Middle House and South House.

Mr. Mack was soon joined in teaching by Mr. Joseph Stanton, Mr. Rowland Hazard, and Mr. Edwin Lindman, a legendary teacher of mathematics. Mr. and Mrs. Lindman frequently entertained the boys, and according to an issue of *The Tabard* from the fall of 1932, a typical buffet dinner for the Sixth Form boys consisted of sandwiches, cake, and cocoa. After eating, they would work on jigsaw puzzles, play cards, and listen to the radio. Mrs. Lindman, a lovely lady, ran the school store for a while.[184] During this year, the policy of maintaining a general evening study hall was discontinued, and the experiment was begun of having all the boys, not just the upper-formers, meet the challenge of studying in their own rooms. That policy has been carried on ever since. When petitioning Mr. Havemeyer for faculty salaries in September 1931, Dr. Hume wrote:

> You will note that Mr. Mack is down for a raise of $500. Mr. Mack came to us on trial as a teacher of History, because he had never taught that subject before. He has turned out to be a good enough History teacher to qualify as a reader of the Board Examinations and has had good success with the boys. In addition to this, he plays the organ in the Chapel and conducts the Choral Club. I consider that he has always been somewhat underpaid . . . He is the finest sort of teacher, and he is the sort we wish to keep with us permanently.[185]

Further serving the School musically, Ed Mack founded the

Canterbury Choral Club in 1929.[186] Before Mack, the boys would sing only at Christmas. Hume thought that the boys should get away from the trite name of "Glee Club," so "Canterbury Choral Club" was adopted as a more distinctive title.[187] Dr. Hume set about to design a charm—a simple G-clef in gold with three letter C's surmounted. Tiffany made the die, and older Canterbury Choral Club alumni may still have their gold charms. The first Choral Club was exceptionally talented, and made its first appearance in 1929 during the intermission in Pietro Yon's Thanksgiving organ recital.

> The charter members were:
> FIRST TENORS: John P. Cohane '30, Charles Harding II '31, Gregory B. Smith '30
> FIRST BASSES: Henry F. Schenk '30, James H. McMahon Jr. '32, John D. Kernan Jr. '30, G. Paschall Swift '30
> SECOND TENORS: José M. Ferrer Jr. '30, Joseph P. Farrell '31, John W. Madden Jr. '31, Thomas K. Krug '31
> SECOND BASSES: H. Wisner Miller Jr. '30, Fred P. Hamilton Jr. '32, Anselme K. Mercier Jr. '30, Charles E. Fickinger '31

The annual concert of the Club took place the evening before graduation. The boys sang in the dining room at intermission during the graduation dance, with the student body, parents, and guests as audience. The programs adhered pretty closely to the classical tradition in choral singing, although Mr. Mack occasionally succumbed to some of the members' pleas for more "popular" music.

The old chapel now became the library and began its long series of metamorphoses until its current duty as the chaplain's residence. The next-oldest building, a barn that stood at the corner of the soccer field between North and Middle Houses, was moved behind the old tennis courts and eventually demolished. The infirmary at that time was in the suite that was formerly occupied by Nelson Hume and his family on the third floor of Middle House.

During the summer of 1929, Nelson Hume had to appear before the Town of New Milford to argue the case for property tax exemption for Canterbury School. The hearing took place over the course of three days: a day and a half of waiting to give testimony, and two half-days of testimony itself.[188] Near the end of July, a ruling came from Judge Foster of the Superior Court dismissing the appeal. The judge's ruling was based on the grounds that Canterbury was not operated chiefly for the public benefit. Terence Carmody, acting as legal counsel for the School, advised Nelson to appeal to the Supreme Court of Errors.[189] In the New Milford paper at the time, a reporter wrote: "There has been considerable interest in the case, for in the event the school corporation's claim was upheld, then the case could be used as a basis for similar claims by schools throughout the state, it is believed. Therefore, the case has been regarded as one of statewide importance."[190] In early April 1930, the Supreme Court of Errors handed down a decision against the School regarding Canterbury's tax-exempt status.[191]

Canterbury entered actively into relationships with other schools and became a charter member of the SSSIC (Secondary School Society for International Cooperation) in 1928. Mr. Brodie, along with Fortune Peter Ryan, traveled to the first meeting, beginning Canterbury's long and active participation in the organization. Canterbury's acceptance as a permanent member of the preparatory school group was also confirmed by the recognition given by Miss Mary Robbins Hillard, headmistress of Westover School for Girls. The faculties, as well as the student bodies, of the two schools often intermingled, and the Canterbury–Westover dances became notable social events.

In his year-end accounting to Henry Havemeyer, Dr. Hume summed up the end of the year:

I know you will be pleased to hear that the year that has

just closed has been by far the best year we have ever had. Standards of discipline, of scholarship, and of teaching have been unusually high. We have every reason to expect good results from the Board examinations that have just closed. The boys and their parents are all enthusiastic about the school, and there is no doubt that during the past year the school has come up several rungs in the ladder of accomplishment. It has improved not only in size and in equipment but has developed to a remarkable extent along the lines of efficient, smooth, harmonious administration. What you observed on your visit last Fall in regard to the development of its equipment is only an outward sign of something even more valuable and harder to attain in the actual life and accomplishment of the school.[192]

Canterbury School in the 1930s

As visible evidence of the School's success grew, interest in its activities also increased and benefactions multiplied. Enrollment increased slightly once again. Ninety-one boys enrolled for the 1929–1930 school year, of which thirty-two were new students.[193] Of the twenty-three graduates, twenty-one were admitted to college in the fall. Fourteen boys went to Yale or Princeton (seven each), and the remaining students went to Harvard, Amherst, Williams, Georgetown, Pennsylvania, Cornell, and Notre Dame. Hume wrote, "Of the two that did not go to college, one has given up the struggle, for he is not capable of getting there. The other might have gone to college this Fall, but, as he was only sixteen when he graduated from school, the Princeton authorities and his father thought he had better wait another year before entering."[194]

A Parents' Improvement Fund was organized in 1931, largely through the efforts of Terence Carmody. Hume had wished to begin the Parents' Fund a year earlier, but had recognized that this would have been an inopportune time.[196] Ever sensitive to the politics of a situation, Dr. Hume suggested waiting until the economy had stabilized a little and until parents had paid their tuition for the second half of the year. Dr. Hume recognized the psychological value of the gifts: "To the parents of the boys, such gifts are an evidence of the interest of people in the School and their confidence in its lasting future, which may in the long run have greater value than that much cash to spend on current needs."[197] Some gifts came in anyway. Mr. James T. Skelly of Wilmington donated $500 without being solicited. Mr. Carmody, along with the Appenzellar family, donated some new tennis courts in 1930. These courts, and two more built slightly to the north, expanded the facilities sufficiently to introduce a wider program of tennis. In the beginning, no coach was assigned, since the faculty was small in number, and the major sports demanded the services of most of the men. The captain of the team, who was generally a Sixth Former and number-one man, was looked to as an informal coach.

There was a brief period in the 1930s when field hockey was played at Canterbury. Mr. Leo Bellerose introduced the game, which aroused considerable interest and might have developed into a major sport had the School been large enough to support another fall sport. Mr. Bellerose, on one occasion, brought a picked team to Canterbury, many members of which had played on the previous Olympic Team. Canterbury gave a good account of itself, even against such quasi-professionals. So outstanding was the goalie work of Eddie Patera and Ben Halsey that both were invited to try out for the position on the next Olympic Team.

In the spring of 1931, one of the boys had an appendicitis attack and was taken out of school for the operation. This Second Former's name was John F. Kennedy. Canterbury was the only formal Catholic education that the future President would receive. The preceding fall Jack Kennedy arrived at school at the age of thirteen. Although constantly plagued with illness, he managed to star on the midget football team. He quickly gained a starting position on the team after registering the longest run of the afternoon in a game with the New Milford Sport Club. Later that fall he took part in the intramural "Army–Navy" games that were played as touch football at Canterbury. On April 29, 1931, he left Canterbury in an ambulance. After a rest in Europe, he entered Choate the next year. At Canterbury he had been moderately happy as a Second Form student, although homesick. In one letter home, he wrote, "We have chapel every morning and evening and I will be quite pius [sic] I guess when I get home."[198]

As the Great Depression tightened its hold on the country in the early 1930s, life at Canterbury hardly skipped a beat. This is not to say that the School itself was not yet feeling the weight of the crisis, but as before, Dr. Hume endeavored to maintain a protective fortress around his students. By 1931, declining enrollments were evident. Westminster School in Simsbury dropped from 135 to 100, The Gunnery dropped almost 25 percent, and Rosemary Hall in Greenwich dropped 35 percent.[199] In comparison to some other schools, Canterbury did not fare too badly. Ultimately, Canterbury's enrollment suffered a 32 percent drop, from a high of ninety-two in 1929 to sixty-three boys by 1933, but the only evidence that anything was amiss was the constant line of men who would make the journey up the hill from town for a handout at the school kitchen. The faculty were not as lucky as the students. In 1933 their salaries were reduced by 25 percent. Dr. Hume himself drew no salary whatsoever for two years. In a letter he wrote to Mr. Havemeyer, Dr. Hume expressed his concern in an understated fashion:

> One of the two boys I was counting on after the holidays may not come in. The other will come in on the first of February. The $750 to be paid by the second boy can, therefore, be counted on. It is likely that the warm weather we have been having up to the present may show some savings

in the coal account, though that will, of course, depend upon how severe a winter we will have.

I am continuing to watch everything as closely as possible.[200]

In the midst of this, Dr. Hume scheduled the School's first Homecoming Day, November 4, 1933. On what was described by *The Tabard* as a "crisp October afternoon," two hundred guests showed up to watch Coach David Adair's football team turn in an impressive victory over Kingswood with a score of 12–7.

In December of that year, the magnificent altar and canopy were dedicated in the chapel.[201] This was the gift of James A. Beha, father of James Beha '33. Bishop James A. Walsh, Superior General of Maryknoll, celebrated a High Mass at the chapel on Sunday, December 10. The Reverend John LaFarge, SJ, chaplain of the Liturgical Arts Society, gave the sermon at the impressive ceremony. Father LaFarge was also one of the editors of the Catholic weekly *America*. At the conclusion of the ceremony, Mr. Mack gave a short recital on the carillon.[202]

Mr. Joseph Campbell joined the faculty in 1932. He was the first alumnus of Canterbury to join the faculty. Mr. Campbell taught Fifth Form English, special work in German and French, and also taught history to the Third Form.[203] Sargent Shriver '34 called him an "inspiring teacher and an original thinker."[204] In a tribute written by Barney Brennan '33 for a *Pallium* article, Mr. Brennan says:

> He was a free spirit . . . He regaled us with stories of student life in Europe and about the expatriate writers in Paris . . . He talked about myths and their relation to religions and spoke quite a bit about the Grail legends, particularly as they related to the Knights Templar. He had read about their prosecution in the court documents of the time and seemed to have intensely explored the Bibliothèque Nationale [de France], learning to read Latin and early

French.[205]

Joseph Campbell went on to become the world's foremost authority on myth. He would achieve some popular recognition through his books and especially through his television interviews with Bill Moyers. Mr. Campbell's interest in mythology can be traced back at least as early as his Canterbury days. *The Quill* regularly published young Joseph's stories, one of which appeared in December 1919, called "Myths of the American Indians."[206] By Joe's graduation in 1921, he was editor of *The Quill* and business manager of *The Tabard.* He also was one of the founders of the Gun Club and was quite athletic.[207] For his scholastic and extracurricular achievements, Joseph Campbell earned his place as Head Boy of Canterbury.[208] Out of 342 students, Joseph would also receive the highest mark on the biology exam of the College Entrance Examination Board in 1921. He received a 92 percent, and was the first at Canterbury School to earn the honor of this high mark.[209] In the years immediately preceding his return to Canterbury, Campbell had been awarded a fellowship to study at Cambridge and at the Sorbonne,[210] and after returning stateside, was invited to Canterbury as a guest lecturer to speak about short story writing.[211]

Between 1929 and 1934, *The Tabard* made great strides. In 1929 Andrew Haire was responsible for enlarging the booklet-size publication to a format more befitting a newspaper. Dr. Hume permitted Andrew, as chairman of the editorial staff, to expand the paper to six pages instead of the customary four. The vigorous administration of Andrew Haire was followed by an equally energetic one under the editorship of his brother, Thomas B. Haire '30, who was later to serve most effectively on the Board of Trustees of the School, and as the head and moving spirit of the fiftieth anniversary celebration committee.

Under the Swift brothers and the Krug brothers,[212] who alternately ran the paper for four years, the internal format was further sharpened. Sargent Shriver's *Tabard* was the culmination of these efforts to modernize the school paper. Shriver would go on after his graduation from Yale to become an assistant editor of *Newsweek* magazine. He would participate in John F. Kennedy's successful presidential campaign, and in 1961 would be appointed the first director of the U.S. Peace Corps. In the fall of 1933, he stream-lined the type of *The Tabard*, cleaned up the front page, increased the use of pictures, and returned to the high grade of paper with which Paul Krug had experimented. The result was one of the most readable *Tabards* in the School's history. "Gleams and Glooms," the most enduring of *Tabard* features, had been founded by Parton Swift in the fall of 1931 to replace "Impressions," which had been the toast of the early *Tabards*. Swift was the editor-in-chief of *The Tabard* in 1930, but stepped down the following year to devote his time to "Gleams and Glooms" and the *Quarterly*, which he later edited.

Other notable achievements in *The Tabard* during the first half of the 1930s were the expanded *Alumni Notes*, complete with pic-tures and the institution of a sports column called "Sport Shots," initiated by John P. McMahon in the fall of 1932. *The Tabard* also updated the timing of new staff appointments. Traditionally, new editorial staff had taken over the reins in April. This was changed to the fall, so that experienced staff would still be in charge of the graduation issue.[213] Within a couple of years, when the School went back to a graduation issue of *The Tabard* instead of a year-book, this was changed back to the spring so that the graduating Sixth Formers could prepare better for their College Boards (then administered in June).[214]

In addition to adding professionalism to *The Tabard*, which earned it a rank of second in the Princetonian Newspaper Association Contest, Sargent Shriver brought out the first yearbook in the history of Canterbury, even though the first plea for a yearbook had been published as a *Tabard* editorial several years earlier.[215] Dr. Hume had always been opposed to a yearbook—possibly because he felt *The Tabard* served quite well as the official record of the school year's news, and that it should continue to function as such. Nevertheless, Shriver—along with John Purcell, who co-edited the book—persuaded the headmaster to allow them to publish a yearbook of limited scope. The clinching argument seems to have been the fact that the boys had managed to acquire sufficient amounts of pledged advertising to cover the publication costs.

Thus, the class of 1934 produced a creditable yearbook that included summaries of all the sports and news events of the year, as well as pictures of the teams and the graduating class. In short, it was a formal presentation of the expanded final issue of *The Tabard*, which had previously covered the subject. They dedicated the volume to the then Bishop of Hartford, Right Reverend Maurice F. McAuliffe, DD. The following year a slightly larger and more ambitious yearbook was published. This one was dedicated to Mr. Brodie, and gave more lengthy accounts of the school year. It also included an "In Memoriam" to Mr. Alexander Hume, who had died earlier that year of a heart attack. They called this book *The Canterbury Pilgrim*. This custom lasted only two years and then returned to the old *Tabard* supplement until 1946, when the yearbook once more appeared. It has been continued ever since.

Assistant Headmaster Alexander Hume's death, which occurred on February 24, 1935,[216] was a significant event at the school. Alec Hume had been Nelson's alter ego at Canterbury for twenty years, and as such, had always been content to remain in Nelson's shadow. In addition to his general duties as his brother's assistant, he had been in charge of the boys in the lower school. He was a quiet man, and not the dynamic leader that his brother was.

The students realized this and often tried to take advantage of him when Nelson would leave the school in Alec's charge, but they soon found out that any infraction against Alec was a direct affront to the headmaster himself. On one occasion, the Sixth Formers conducted chapel services with the response "Pray for Al" after the incantations.[217] Upon hearing of it, the headmaster threatened to expel the entire class unless a public apology to the assembled school was made by each of the boys.

Alec's funeral was the first to be held in the Canterbury chapel. Pietro Yon played the organ for the services and directed the quartet from St. Patrick's. Because of the relationship between the two Hume brothers, and the subsequent effect on the school, the loss of Alec was far greater than merely the departure of a beloved master. It meant that Nelson, who was not wont to delegate authority except to his brother, now had to cope with all the details of business management. This new dynamic was dramatically evident even at Alec's funeral. During the High Mass, the groundsmen were shoveling the walk outside the chapel, and the grating sound of the shovel against the cement was loud and distracting. Nelson Hume got up from his seat in the back of the chapel and started down the aisle toward Alec's customary pew, presumably to send the assistant headmaster outside to quiet the shoveling. After a few steps, Nelson realized what he was doing and returned to his seat again. For Dr. Hume and Canterbury, the pattern of twenty years had been broken.

The School would see another calamitous event just one year later. At 6:00 A.M. on St. Patrick's Day 1936, the night watchman discovered a fire on the second floor of Middle House. Fortunately, it was during the spring vacation. Apparently, rags and cleaning materials that were being used to refinish the floors had been stored in a closet on the second floor. These rags ignited, and by the time the watchman discovered it, the fire was raging throughout the second floor. Ultimately, the entire building was destroyed.

Oddly, unlike the Bungalow fire in 1925, the Middle House fire didn't even make front-page news in *The Tabard*, although it did make the first page of the *New Milford Times*.[218] As before, Dr. Hume moved swiftly to maintain the normal routine and, if at all possible, to capitalize on the situation, but the loss of the old Middle House was in many ways irreparable. All 3,500 volumes in the library went up in smoke, including recent donations by Gregory Smith '30 and many others.[219] The books had only recently been transferred to Middle House from South House. Just that January, the headmaster had accepted applications to the library club, which extended library privileges to those who signed a pledge promising to help with library upkeep. Second Former Michael Hume '41 and First Former Steve Hume '43, Nelson's sons, were among those who had signed this pledge.[220] In addition, all of the pictures and memorabilia that lined the corridor walls were lost. Where the Bungalow fire had deprived the school of pleasant sleeping and recreational quarters, the Middle House fire deprived the school of office space, classrooms, the infirmary, and staff housing. Dr. Hume, however, was able to reorganize the school without missing a beat.

Upper-form students were housed in the gymnasium as before. With the destruction of the old Middle House, the gymnasium had to be used for classrooms as well as sleeping quarters. There were shifts in masters' duties, with Mr. Brodie, Mr. Mack, and Mr. Lindman reassigned to the gym.[221] Ed Mack writes in his history:

> As a lesson in pedagogy, and as a personal experience, it was found that Modern European history could be as effectively taught in the locker room of a gymnasium as in more elegantly appointed surroundings. And matter rather than form, substance rather than environment was demonstrated to be the essence of education. Yet, even with the pressing into use of the squash courts, there was not room enough in

the gymnasium.[222]

A Hodgson portable house was erected next to the gym to provide classrooms for the upperclassmen. Thus, when the students
returned for the spring term, the campus was in fact divided
according to Dr. Hume's original design. The school office traveled
first to Dr. Hume's apartment in North House. That summer the
office moved to the North House common room but, by the time
school opened in the fall, the office had been established in the
adaptable old chapel. The School rented a private house down
near the village and fitted it as an infirmary, with Miss Marie
Hume in charge. A squad of boys not actively engaged in a sport
was formed to clear up the rubble outside the ruins. Their task was
to clear an area for a larger parking space for faculty and visitors,
and also to stack all the usable bricks they could find from the
demolished Middle House.[223]

Construction was immediately started on a new Middle
House. For once in Dr. Hume's career at Canterbury, funds to
meet the emergency were on hand. Unfortunately, the low bid by
the contractor sent the contractor into bankruptcy halfway
through construction, so there was an added delay in the building's
completion. Again Raphael Hume supplied the plans, but with this
project, there was time and money enough for Nelson Hume to
attach his own trademark to one of the buildings: floor-length windows in the common room, permitting an inspiring view of the
valley.

The headmaster planned for the new Middle House to be the
keystone of the campus—the showplace and center of school life.
In this, he had one of his few lapses in his ability to foresee the
future. The new Middle House could not replace the old one—
which had already eroded with the construction of North
House—in either its physical or symbolic role. The old Main
House was a multifaceted building that had been able to

accommodate the many diverse activities that went on inside it. Until 1925, there was no question that it was indeed the center of the school. Not only did it hold every facility necessary to school life, but it also held the headmaster himself. The erection of South House did not alter this fact much. The two common rooms were about the same size, and the small number of students in the School felt more comfortable holding their meetings in the Main House.

North House, however, definitely altered the pattern of school life. The kitchen had been taken away from Middle House and so had the headmaster, who took up residence in the apartment there. Thus, the two most important forces in Canterbury had been removed from the Main House. Through architecture, Dr. Hume hoped to reinstate the symmetry of influence on the campus. He moved the site for the new building 100 feet to the west so that it would take a more related and thus commanding position between the two other buildings, and provide a view of the Housatonic Valley.[224]

The upperclassmen occupied the new dormitory, but Middle House never again became the Main House, and with the later construction of a separate classroom and an infirmary at the north end of the campus, it became less distinctive. Dr. Hume's original plan was to use the room in the south end of Middle House as his study and office.[225] However, he moved the public administrative offices to the other end of the building. He liked the bay window on the north side, from which he could survey the campus.

During the construction period, the School rented the neighboring Hickory Hearth to provide temporary classroom and library space. The new Middle House was ready for occupancy in December 1936. It may be noted here that Hickory Hearth also eventually burned down. The little stone gatehouse is the only surviving building of Mrs. Black's original compound at the top of the hill, except the old chapel, which she had moved to that location in 1901.

The 1936 school year began with an enrollment of eighty-seven boys. Dr. Hume dedicated the new dormitory on Homecoming Day. At those ceremonies, Dr. Hume ended his speech with the words *Cantuaria floreat*. He had used this same expression at the groundbreaking for Middle House. He used it again in a telegram to Sargent Shriver, congratulating the former student on his election as editor of the *Yale Daily News*. Legend has it that Shriver wrote back and recommended that the phrase be adopted as the school motto, but perhaps the suggestion came from E. Barry Ryan '37, the editor of *The Tabard* who wrote,

> As the telegram implied, Canterbury flourishes and flowers through the deeds and victories of her sons. Should not *Floreat Cantuaria!*, as a school slogan, be taken to heart by all those fellows who have entered the portals of the school to graduate finished and molded men?[226] Four years later, Mr. Mack wrote the school hymn under the same name.[227]

Cantuaria floreat did indeed signal a new era for Canterbury School. The final ten years of Dr. Hume's life would be spent watching his school flourish as a full-grown institution. Everything at Canterbury was a tangible product of the Canterbury idea. The fruits of this remarkable twenty-year achievement included five imposing structures surrounded by 135 acres of the Housatonic River Valley.

The years preceding World War II were relatively quiet ones. In 1937, the school focused on finishing the new Middle House and restoring the gym. When the school office was completed at the north end of Middle House, the school's first mailboxes, obtained from the old post office in New Milford, were installed. In February of 1937, artist F. Luis Mora's painting of George Washington with his horse arrived at the school through Mr.

Mora's generosity, and was hung in the dining room.

Born in 1874, Mr. Mora was a close friend of Dr. Hume's and a frequent visitor to the campus. He often spoke to the boys about art and how it is created.[228] A legend, not true, soon developed around the school that Mr. Brodie had served as the model for the figure standing beside George Washington's horse. Of all the paintings donated to the school, the George Washington has best weathered the storm, despite a hole in George's knee caused by an airborne fork. In 1963, Mr. Sheehan would have the painting completely cleaned and restored, including George's damaged knee. The painting still hangs at the entryway of Sheehan House.

In 1943, three years after the death of her husband, Mrs. May Mora donated his bronze statue of St. Francis of Assisi. Mr. Mora's interpretation of St. Francis of Assisi differed from the usual artistic interpretations of the saint. Mr. Mora depicted St. Francis as a man conscious of the fleeting nature of time, his robes flowing as he strides forward to accomplish God's work.[229] Along with the statue of St. Jude, crafted by Reed Armstrong '55, the statue of St. Francis was cleaned and the finish restored in 2002.[230]

By the fall of 1937, Canterbury had recouped the losses suffered by the Depression and enrolled ninety-two boys. Hickory Hearth was no longer rented, as Dr. Hume had found there was enough room in the bottom floor of Middle House to accommodate the students. The library, which had already been restored to about four hundred volumes at Hickory Hearth, was moved to its old quarters in the small room adjacent to the study hall in Middle House,[231] and then in December distributed to three house libraries established initially in the three masters' rooms. The new plan was put into effect to make the books more accessible to the boys and to increase library circulation.[232]

There was one interesting addition to the faculty during this time. Mr. James Herlihy arrived from Maine with his tweeds and bridge cards to take up residence on the second floor of Middle House. Mr. Herlihy had spent the last five years traveling and studying in Europe, and was also an accomplished pianist. Mr. Herlihy taught all sections of French and revived the study of Spanish at Canterbury.[233] He remained on the faculty throughout the war, and during all that time was an urbane influence at the school. Mr. Herlihy supervised a group of boys on trail-riding trips at the Timber Trails Riding Academy in nearby Sherman, Connecticut. With the close of football season, Mr. Herlihy took the boys riding two or three times each week until the weather became unsuitable.[234]

The winter of 1938 saw the addition of ski races and a squash tournament to the athletic schedule. Twenty-five boys turned out for tryouts for the ski team, which were held on the Chapel Hill. The chosen team of four practiced for the Salisbury tourney all winter at the Timber Trails Inn, on Route 37 in Sherman, Connecticut, but an early thaw that year forced the cancellation of the Salisbury meet. The squash tourney, however, proved to be a great success. George Mergenthaler, a Fifth Former, emerged as the champion of a schoolwide round robin that occupied the winter athletes shortly before spring vacation. In later years he met a hero's death in the Battle of the Bulge.

Also in 1938, the swimming team won the third leg of the Connecticut Preparatory School Swim Association (CPSSA) cup at Trinity. Through the efforts of Ed Haag, who held the state record in the breaststroke at 1:07.4, the Blue maintained its supremacy in the medley relay.

The Quarterly came to an end in 1938. *The Quarterly* had become a source of envy for the staff of *The Tabard*, since the latter felt pressure to meet the demands of expansion and the rising costs of publication. In reality, both business staffs had merged as early as 1932, and the publications shared many staff members. Even if

The Quarterly had a superior cash position, student tastes were leaning to the news format of *The Tabard*. Whatever the reason, the Graduation Number of the 1941 *Tabard* contained an extra section, captioned "*The Canterbury Quarterly.*" This, it would seem, was the obituary notice of *The Quarterly*. Without competition from *The Quarterly*, *The Tabard* would be able to increase its cash through ad sales. Ads in *The Tabard* cost $40 for a full page and were especially popular for the graduation issue, since this was the one most likely to be kept for a long period of time.[235]

Graduation in 1938 that year provided the occasion for two important announcements. The first was that Pius XI had conferred upon Dr. Hume the Order of St. Gregory the Great "in recognition of conspicuous services in the field of education." Of the honor, Dr. Hume said, "I consider the honor as really having been bestowed on Canterbury School as such, and that I have been selected as the person upon whom to pin the medal . . . for Canterbury has been built up by the good work and good will of everybody that has been connected with the school."[236]

The second announcement concerned plans to erect a schoolhouse. For sixteen years, Dr. Hume had been voicing the need for such a building. The two fires and the Depression had kept it low on the priority list. However, Mr. Hubert McDonnell, upon his election to the Board of Trustees in 1936, undertook the task of raising the necessary funds. Mr. McDonnell had attended Loyola School from 1901 to 1905, during Nelson Hume's first years of teaching; the friendship that began during these years would last until Dr. Hume's death in 1948.[237] As evidenced in his correspondence with Mr. Havemeyer and Dr. Hume, Mr. McDonnell was a take-charge man. Within two years of his appointment to the Board of Trustees, McDonnell had set several objectives for the School, most of them concerned with devising a concrete plan to end the School's indebtedness, preferably by the twenty-fifth anniversary. McDonnell also felt the board should be expanded "by adding one or two graduates and one or two older individuals, who have sympathy with the type of work done, and who have substantial financial resources."[238] He suggested that Dr. Hume invite "John Burke to join the Board, also Mr. F. Peter Ryan, a wealthy young graduate, and also Mr. Gerard Smith,[239] son of Mr. John Thomas Smith, one of the school's principal benefactors."[240] At a meeting of the Board of Trustees held at Clarence Mackay's New York office on June 10, 1938,

> Plans and specifications prepared by Edward B. Caldwell, an architect of Hartford, Conn., for a classroom building were submitted and explained by Dr. Hume; and
> Upon motion duly seconded, it was unanimously
> Voted: That said plans and specifications, subject to such modifications as Dr. Hume may deem advisable, be and they are hereby accepted and approved.[241]

Present at this board meeting were Messrs. Mackay, McDonnell, Hume, and Carmody. By graduation in 1938, three-quarters of the amount needed for the construction of the main corridor of the proposed two-winged structure was on hand. Toward the end of July, construction began on the main section of the building.[242]

On November 12, 1938, Clarence Mackay died. As one of the founding trustees, Mackay had played a decisive role in the school's struggle to survive. His faith in Dr. Hume had been unshakable, and he had shared Dr. Hume's passion for excellence. Dr. Hume could always turn to Mr. Mackay in times of crisis, knowing he could rely on his unwavering support.[243] To fill Mackay's place on the executive committee (one of three), the trustees selected Hubert McDonnell of New York at the June 1939 board meeting. McDonnell represented a new generation in the life of Canterbury, and was the first new member of the Board in more than ten years.

Soon after McDonnell's election to the executive committee, John S. Burke, president of B. Altman and Co., and Carlton J. H. Hayes,[245] professor of history at Columbia, were elected to the Board. This new blood came to the organization just as the school faced the difficult period of World War II. Writes Dr. Hume, "Mr. Burke, a short time ago, was appointed a Papal Chamberlain by the Pope for his activities in helping the Cardinal in his Catholic charities. Mr. Burke has two sons in the school and another one coming up. He is deeply interested in our work."[246] Nelson Hume, John Burke, Carlton J. H. Hayes, T. F. Carmody, James Cox Brady, Hubert McDonnell, and Henry O. Havemeyer constituted the Board of Trustees in 1941.[247]

Part of the new schoolhouse was finished and dedicated on December 8, 1938, the feast day of the Immaculate Conception. It was large enough to provide a study hall for thirty-five students, a laboratory, classrooms, and rooms for the faculty and *The Tabard*. At the dedication ceremonies, Dr. Hume announced that construction on the north wing would begin that summer. Dr. Hume reported on the new schoolhouse in a letter to Henry Havemeyer:

> The addition of the new schoolhouse is one of the most important benefits that has come to the school in a long time. It is like a real school now during class hours. The boys and masters are all delighted with the new building, and the parents who have seen it are loud in its praises. It gives the impression of the actual fact that we are making first-class provision for the boys during their working hours. The fine laboratory is particularly impressive. It is really a thing to be proud of.[248]

The enrollment for the 1939–1940 academic season topped out at ninety-eight, a new record for the school, including thirteen sets of brothers. Although impressive, it fell short of Dr. Hume's goal of one hundred students. Dr. Hume wrote, "It would be especially satisfactory to begin our twenty-fifth year in September 1939 with 100 boys on the roster."[249]

The new schoolhouse had released space in Middle House to accommodate the large Fifth Form and the reopened First Form,[250] which, for a number of years, had not been enrolled. In the same letter, Dr. Hume appealed to Mr. Havemeyer to help recruit boys of good Catholic families to increase enrollment. Dr. Hume outlined how he believed Mr. Havemeyer should go about this:

> A casual approach to the parents is best at first; a suggestion that a fine boy like that ought to have the advantage of being educated in a fine school,—in Canterbury, in fact; an offer to write to the Headmaster to get him interested in that particular boy, and to send booklets to the parents; and then an occasional question or comment by way of "follow-up."[251]

The second (north) wing of the school building opened for use on January 9, 1940. Mr. Havemeyer was reluctant to proceed until all the funds were raised, but Dr. Hume pressed for the go-ahead, as the increased enrollment had already caused overcrowding. At times, there were not enough chairs to accommodate all the boys in the study hall. These boys sat in the corridor, while at the other end a blackboard screen was erected to create additional classroom space.[252] The plans included the large study hall on the second floor, which could seat 112 students, and the shop on the first floor for arts and crafts. This number—112—seemed to be approximately the school size that Dr. Hume had envisioned, since the number of cleat lockers that fit exactly into the gymnasium hallway was also 112.

During this time, Mr. Havemeyer chastised Dr. Hume for embarking on new construction before more funds were raised: "You do not see nor appreciate the other side of the picture, when I am put on the mat by the Examiners, with respect to Canterbury School's liability to the Chase National Bank. . . . It is, to say the least, most embarrassing." Nelson replied, "I wish to assure you that I never get my mind off the ultimate objective, that is, to get the school altogether out of debt, but there is a long way to go and sometimes it is necessary to pause on the way to improve our earning capacity as we have done by all the capital expenditures we have made in the last three years."[254]

Just before Christmas vacation in 1939, the death of the Reverend Joseph King—the pastor of St. Francis Xavier and the school's chaplain since 1921—saddened the school. Father King had been close to the boys and the school, and had been a special companion of Dr. Hume. Dr. Hume had appreciated Reverend King's tact and tolerance, qualities the official priest of the school needed in his relationship with the lay head of the school, who considered himself a qualified liturgist.

Canterbury, in 1922, had become the only congregation outside Vatican City to celebrate the *missa recitata*.[255] The student body could say in unison the "Kyrie," "Gloria," "Credo," and later, the "Sanctus" and the "Agnus Dei" of the Mass. Father King had also encouraged Dr. Hume to lead many of the religious ceremonies in the chapel. Father King allowed Dr. Hume to design the chapel with such laity-inspired innovations as the absence of an altar rail, because Dr. Hume considered the boys as the choir. This rare partnership gave to Canterbury more than eighty years ago the kind of enlightened lay participation in liturgy that has become widespread since the Second Vatican Council. Thus, religion and religious activity were integrated into the daily life of the Canterbury boy through morning prayers, the reminder of the "Angelus," evening prayers, and the solemn tolling of the "De Profundis" each night.[256]

Mention should also be made of the early cultivation of art at Canterbury. Not only were exhibits of individual artists encouraged at the school, but Canterbury joined in sponsorship of traveling art shows from larger museums. Connecticut Valley Schools Art Exhibit Groups, begun by the art departments of various area schools, instituted a traveling circuit, limited to twelve schools. Six museums and galleries loaned works, including the Wadsworth Atheneum of Hartford and the Museum of Modern Art in New York City.

The Wadsworth Atheneum loaned several pieces to the School for an exhibit on surrealism. Canterbury was fortunate to display works by Salvador Dali, Joan Miro, and Paul Klee. The fourth exhibit in the series featured a drawing called *The Bather* by Cezanne, Two Dancers by Picasso, and another piece by Dali.[258] The success of this program prompted Mr. P. Penn Prince of the *New Milford Times* to arrange an exhibit of the oils and watercolors of Charles Liedl, a naturalist painter.[259] Mr. Liedl painted landscapes of scenes in and around the town of New Milford, where Mr. Liedl spent his summers.[260] Forensics (the art or study of formal debate) and writing also flourished during this period. Dr. Hume's English class broadened to provide presentations before the entire school body. *The Tabard* reached a high degree of competence, and in 1940 received third place in the annual contest among secondary school publications sponsored by the Princetonian. The competition included such prep schools as Exeter, Choate, Taft, and Andover.[261]

Dr. Hume had the honor of being elected to the Headmasters' Association in 1939. Membership in the Association was limited to just one hundred educators, and was composed of all the outstanding, long-established schools. In his typically modest fashion, Dr. Hume saw the honor more as a reflection upon the School than on his own personality.[262]

The graduates of the class of 1939 had the distinction of receiving the first issue of the Canterbury Alumni Medals. Through the suggestion and efforts of Mr. Hubert McDonnell, the medals were cast in sterling silver by Tiffany & Co. The medal became the symbol of the spiritual heritage that a Canterbury student takes with him when he leaves. It depicts Our Lady Queen of all Saints on one side and the chapel on the other.

It is interesting that the twenty-fifth anniversary year unwittingly captured the flavor of Canterbury's first year. In 1940 there was that distinct feeling of *Camelot*, where life was lush and leisurely, a time and place set aside from the rest of the world. Buoyed by a remarkable 92.6 record on the College Boards with twenty papers receiving honor grades, the school began its anniversary year. Dr. and Mrs. Hume hosted the school at a turkey dinner commemorating the first meal eaten at the School.[263] Dr. Hume telegraphed Mr. Havemeyer on September 27, 1940, inviting him to celebrate the twenty-fifth anniversary of the opening: "[W]hile I am not planning to mark our anniversary in any special way until early December, I do think it would be most appropriate for you and me to spend a few hours together here at school on that day as we did 25 years ago."[264] Dr. Hume further reminisces:

> I can remember Mr. Mackay saying so often in his earnest way during those early years, "Let us keep up our standards in all phases of school life." If Mr. Mackay were here now, I think I could tell him honestly that we have done so, and I could assure him, as I assure you, that there is no school in the country in which the standards are any higher in any department . . . We seem finally to have matured into a full-grown institution with the benefit of a good deal of tradition behind us.[265]

Dr. Hume credited the success of the school with God's favor. In one of his school-year-opening letters to Mr. Havemeyer, he expounds on this idea. "When we consider the hard days through which the school, and everybody else, in fact, has had to live, it is quite obvious that the work of Canterbury in its growth and improvement has certainly been favored by God. There is no other explanation. This thought, which recurs to me so often in these days, makes me look upon it all with sincere reverence and a sense of my obligation of greater and greater personal dedication to the work."[266]

Mr. Claremont Koenig arrived at Canterbury at this time, and proved to be an important addition to the faculty.[267] Mr. Koenig came with firsthand experience in the operation of a preparatory school and with advanced degrees in chemistry at Yale. Mr. Koenig was one of Canterbury's few non-Catholic faculty at this time, so his fellow faculty members gave him the sobriquet of "Black Mike." He reorganized the science department and added dynamism and a certain sense of mischief to the school. He was a man of positive statements, and left no doubt in anyone's mind as to the indisputable nature of his judgments. Canterbury never had a more loyal rooter for its athletic teams, and he was indiscriminate in his support of them, whether it was football, baseball, hockey, basketball, swimming, soccer, or chess. He was seldom known to agree with any decision or ruling of an official that was against Canterbury. He also took charge of the Camera Club and with serious effort, turned it into a constructive extracurricular activity. In sleepy New Milford at the time, Bruce Nearing, the town constable, had "Black Mike" Koenig pegged as one of Canterbury's troublemakers for his numerous traffic violations and speedy driving. One time after a big snowstorm, "Black Mike" got a running start up Canterbury's hill by driving up the wrong side of the green.[268]

The Choral Club was also greatly improved that year under the direction of Mr. Mack, and for the first time gave concerts at school dances and sang at High Mass. At the Graduation Mass that year, the Choral Club introduced the school hymn, *Cantuaria Floreat*, which Mr. Mack had written that spring.

The social life at Canterbury was never brighter. In addition to the traditional Homecoming and graduation dances, there were also tea dances with the girls from Westover and from St. Margaret's in Waterbury.

It is probably no coincidence that Canterbury adopted a regulation school blazer in 1941. Dr. Hume announced the design, created by Brooks Brothers, in February. The jacket was a deep blue color with silver buttons at cuff and breast. The left breast pocket displayed the school seal, and on a guidon beneath the seal, the school motto. Members of the Sixth Form were allowed to wear the embroidered numerals of their graduating class above the seal.[269]

The twenty-fifth anniversary also officially marked the passing of one of the older fixtures of the school. "Old Geyser," the school truck that had served the school for almost a decade, finally collapsed. The various uses of the "Geyser" covered a wide range of services, from removing snowdrifts bit by bit, to taking hockey teams to practice, to light farm work.[270] Dr. Hume purchased a sawed-off two-ton truck as its replacement. It took its place in the hearts of the Canterbury boys, and during the war years, when gas rationing curtailed vehicle use on campus, it became *the* status symbol of privilege on campus.

The only formal celebration marking the school's twenty-fifth anniversary was a dinner at the Yale Club in December 1940. Ninety-two alumni, headed by John Hughes '21, the president of the association, attended. Mr. Terence Carmody, Mr. James A. Farrell, Mr. John S. Burke, and Mr. Hubert McDonnell represented the Board of Trustees on the dais. The main address was a speech by Mr. R. Dana Skinner, reviewer for *Commonweal* and publisher of *America*. Francis Carmody '20 presented Dr. Hume with a silver cigarette case.[271] Mr. Havemeyer wrote to Dr. Hume, expressing his regrets that he was unable to attend.[272] Havemeyer does note, "I suppose you have seen the article concerning the

School and your good self in *Time* for the week ending December 30th. The free advertising we got should be very beneficial to the School, as *Time* is read over the length and breadth of the country."[273]

Perhaps what added most to the air of luxury at Canterbury in 1940–1941 were the Filipino staff members. The number had grown along with the enrollment so that the boys were always well attended. There was one Filipino worker for each table in the dining hall, and a head waiter, named Ernesto, who stayed close to Dr. Hume's table. Ernesto was a stately and unusually tall man who directed his corps with the dignity of a field marshal.

The Filipino staff also took care of the students' rooms. Once, out of curiosity, a Filipino worker asked several students what they were studying. "Geometry," they answered, and prepared to give an explanation. "Geometry?" he replied. "I thought you would be at least up to trigonometry. I was studying calculus at your age."[274] By the spring of 1942, however, a great many of the Filipinos were being drafted into the U.S. Merchant Marine, marking the end of an era.[275]

One day in early May of 1941, Dr. Hume was talking to his Third Form religion class and asked them what they thought the Blessed Virgin Mary looked like. A description was compiled that also included her vestments. Dr. Hume then took the entire class to where workmen were uncrating a large wooden statue, which had recently arrived as the gift of J. Banigan Sullivan. Mr. Sullivan '25 wished to make this gift of the Blessed Virgin in memory of his own mother.[276] Irving and Casson of Boston[277] did the work on the new shrine, which consisted of a carved-oak pedestal and a spired canopy supporting the statue.[278] The shrine arrived on campus unassembled and with only the gold-leaf base painted; the artist completed the painting in a studio behind North House.[279] The dedication occurred on May 11, during the month traditionally devoted to Mary; a congregation of 150 parents, alumni, students, and guests were in attendance.

At the graduation ceremonies held on June 6, 1942, two memorial gifts were dedicated. The first was the Window of the Assumption, given by Mrs. Carl W. Badenhausen. The second was the Panel of Saint Michael, gift of Mr. and Mrs. John S. Burke.[280]

As the school began its twenty-sixth year and a new age, the first son of an alumnus entered Canterbury. He was John King, son of Gilbert King of the class of 1919.[281] That same year Miss Hume retired, leaving Nelson the last survivor of the school's original staff. To fill her place as infirmarian, the school hired its first nurse, Miss Mary Walsh.[282]

Frank Fisher also joined the faculty in 1941. He had taught for three years at the Carteret School after his graduation from Fordham University, and would teach math and science to the lower forms. Mr. Fisher proved very versatile. He reorganized the Gun Club that year into a formal school activity, complete with its fully equipped range behind North House. In addition to the Gun Club activities, Mr. Fisher found time outside the regular curriculum to conduct classes in Morse Code, mechanical drawing, first aid, and model-airplane building. Before he left Canterbury after sixteen years of service, he had helped construct the new wing on the schoolhouse, built his own home on top of Canterbury Hill, and coached one of the finest swimming teams in Canterbury's history.

The World War II Years

Even in the fall of 1941, the impending war was casting its shadow over Canterbury life. In order to meet restrictions mandated by national defense, new cloth book bags replaced the older canvas bags. Canvas and woolen goods used in football pants and jersey became difficult to come by. Other materials, such as casters for beds and certain lab materials, became cost-prohibitive. *The Tabard* carried weekly reports of alumni who had signed up both with the U.S. Armed Forces and the Royal Air Force. By 1942, Dr. Hume was worried about getting along with a reduced number of faculty. He writes,

> The reason for the reduced faculty, of course, is the enlisting or drafting of schoolmasters. I need two more men than I have at present, and I am likely to lose one of those that I am counting on,—the football coach, who, even though he is a married man with a child, is likely to be inducted into the Army within the next month. Of course, I am being very busy about finding other men to fill these vacancies, but the kind of men I want are the very kind of men Uncle Sam needs, and he is likely to win out in this competition.[283]

In December 1941, for the second time in its history, the School began to operate on a wartime basis. Dr. Hume was a leader among the Independent Schools in mapping programs for Moral Preparation for the call to arms, and for increasing emphasis in the war years on physical education.[284] This latter part of the program was directed by Mr. Brodie, who had been a regimental athletic director in World War I. Mr. Mack and Mr. Koenig had charge of the lectures on Moral Preparation.

Every boy was required to enroll in at least one extra activity that would develop his skills and prepare him intellectually for the war. These extra courses were Morse Code and rifle practice, given by Mr. Fisher; military mathematics, given by Mr. Lindman; radio maintenance, given by Mr. Koenig; automobile maintenance, supervised by Mr. Maloney; first aid and map making, conducted by Mr. Fisher; and finally, an expansion of the Camera Club to study war photography, under Mr. Koenig.

Even with the School on a wartime footing, Dr. Hume tried to maintain tradition and keep the spirit of the School alive.

Although gasoline rationing was already in effect, Dr. Hume sent a letter to parents encouraging them to attend Homecoming Day in 1942. Dr. Hume suggested that Homecoming guests arise early enough to catch the 8:05 A.M. train from Grand Central, arriving in New Milford at 10:28. He exhorted, "We can get along without the cars; but we surely would miss the folks and the chance to entertain them here at school."[285] Even the trustees were not exempt from the impact of the war, as James Brady was called into service in the Navy.[286]

It was natural to compare Canterbury in 1942 with the School during the First World War. In most respects, conditions at the School were comparable. During both wars, Canterbury, like all other institutions, had to cope with rationing. In both periods the School engaged in emergency vegetable growing, with emphasis on potatoes. May Hume's response, according to an issue of *Pallium*, was to "raise chickens in back of North House and take over the housekeeping management of the three dormitories, as well as to step in as dietician and director of the kitchen staff. She worked with head, hands, and heart, and was so much a part of the short-handed housekeeping team that one new worker once warned her to 'Look busy, the boss is coming!' when the headmaster made a surprise appearance in South House in search of his wife."

The school had begun to feel the pinch during the autumn prior to Pearl Harbor Day, when shipments of supplies had been seriously delayed or items substituted. As soon as war broke out, the food rationing matched that of the First World War, with added restrictions placed on gasoline and paper. Squads of boys organized to collect paper from the dormitories for government use.[287] The school schedule remained the same except for the addition of daily calisthenics and the previously mentioned special war courses. At the War Department's request, Dr. Hume placed emphasis on basic instruction and obedience over military training.[288]

Graduation was moved up a few days to allow the boys some vacation time before they entered the college summer semesters. There was also a midyear graduation in 1944. Father Walter F. Kenny, pastor of St. Francis Xavier Church in New Milford, celebrated High Mass in the forenoon, and Father Edward J. Sullivan, SJ, Prefect of Discipline at Boston College, preached the graduation sermon. The actual graduation ceremony took place in the study hall, when Dr. Hume, after a fitting address to the graduates and entire School, presented diplomas to Dominick Dunne,[289] Clifford McCormick, Joseph Mora, and John Rumely. Dominick Dunne would receive a Bronze Star for his actions in rescuing two wounded men in Felsberg, Germany, at the age of eighteen. This midyear graduation was strange, new, and touching in its simplicity and in its implications.[290]

The first wartime blackout experienced by the School occurred on the evening of March 1, 1942. The School was dark within four minutes and fifty-five seconds, while Dr. Hume commanded his staff from his position just outside his front door.[291] The clap of his hands could call a boy to attention from anywhere within the quad, whether at night or in broad daylight. During the blackout, one boy underestimated the headmaster's ability to control the quad, and while the boys were waiting for the all-clear signal, he began threatening Dr. Hume in his best Japanese/American accent. The threat was short-lived. Dr. Hume summoned the impersonator to his office by name and warned any other would-be offenders by a single clap of his hands.

Canterbury was no longer exempt from war's tragedies, as had been the case in 1917–1918, when the school had fewer students. *The Tabard* printed news of alumni missing in action or taken prisoner. Eleven boys gave their lives during World War II, and this came home poignantly to Mr. Brodie, Mr. Maloney, Mr. Lindman, and Mr. Mack, who kept seeing the boys' "shining morning faces" before them as each name was uttered and prayed for in the chapel. On Thursday, April 22, 1943, a service flag for all graduates of Canterbury in the services was hung in the chapel, as a gift from the class of 1943. The flag arrived on campus with 140 blue stars, and one gold star. By placing additional stars between the rows, the flag could accommodate another 100 stars. The first gold star was for Captain Jack Miller '31, killed in action. Captain of the winning 1930 football team, Jack went on to graduate from Princeton, had a successful career, married, and fathered two children. He served with the Marines in the Solomon Islands and was in the first landing boat when attacked. Dr. Hume told the assembled Canterbury boys, "Among our alumni there is none worthier than Jack to achieve the honor of being the first to die for his country."[292] The service flag was originally placed to the left of the shrine to the Blessed Virgin.[293] It now resides in the Copley Library along with a list of each member of the Canterbury community who served in the armed forces.[294]

Other changes that year were in the College Board examinations. The old essay tests were dropped in favor of scholastic aptitude and achievement tests. This change came almost simultaneously with the revision of college entrance requirements. The mounting number of applications would present the schools and colleges with new pressures after the war.

The Tabard, with new editor Stephen Hume, ceased its twenty-five years of weekly publication in 1942 and became a biweekly[295]. This move was made for economic reasons, and to conserve paper for the war effort. Weekly publication was expected to resume after the war, but by then, college entrance pressures were such that the boys found they could not afford to spend as much time on the paper as their counterparts had during the 1930s. Furthermore,

Dr. Hume was growing older and was finding it difficult to meet the many demands on his time. Shortly after *The Tabard* schedule was cut in half, he reduced his teaching load and thereafter concerned himself with only the older boys in religion and English.

An era at Canterbury had, quite definitely, come to an end. The luxury of the early days had disappeared by degrees. Having one's bed turned down by a Filipino worker in the early evening went the way of finger bowls and other manifestations of *la dolce vita*. Once, a boy had only to hang up his pajamas every morning to merit an extra day's vacation. The boys were now required to clean their own rooms and make their beds. They soon found, however, that this provided a certain autonomy in their rooms that they had not enjoyed before, when very little contraband, such as radios, phonograph records, or inappropriate magazines and comic books, escaped attention.

With the staff of the school cut down to a bare minimum because of the draft, the students took up the slack in various other areas of school life, as well. Students waited on tables for the first time. The tables themselves were denuded, and the fresh linen replaced with more prosaic linoleum. Each of these new tasks had unexpected compensations, however. One by-product of the emergency was the increased popularity of the work squad, made up of boys not involved in a regular sport. The gas ration for the school truck was the largest dole on campus. The head of the work squad had the only keys to the truck, and thus was courted by students and teachers alike for his services. The Fifth and Sixth Formers were responsible for keeping the coal-fired furnaces stoked during the evening.[296] This provided a certain basement camaraderie, a break from the study hall routine, and a most welcomed cigarette. In some schools, scholarships had been available to needier boys as waiters. This practice was never introduced at Canterbury. When the time came for room-care and dining-room duties, each boy had to take his turn, and no social stigma became attached to these tasks.

Two of Canterbury's great athletic personalities, one a student and the other a coach, came on the scene in 1943. Student Tony Cudahy would achieve fourteen varsity letters over a four-year period at Canterbury. He played varsity football for three seasons, played the full four periods of every game, was never taken out, nor ever injured. In addition, he played hockey and baseball, and he swam. In his Sixth Form year, Tony was elected captain of the football, baseball, and hockey teams. He was elected captain of the hockey team in his Fifth Form year but nevertheless continued his position in the sprints with the swimming team. On a day when both the swimming and hockey squads were playing at home, Tony was ferried between the pool and the farm pond. It was not uncommon for him to absent himself from the ice twice during a game, depending on how the swim meet was going.

During this same year, George Stirnweiss was looking for something to do when he wasn't playing second base with the New York Yankees.[297] Coincidentally, Canterbury's football coach was drafted in the middle of the 1943 season. George Stirnweiss became his successor and continued as basketball coach at Canterbury, leading the team to its first successful season in many years. The following year the record was topped when the team won nine games in an eleven-game schedule despite the absence of the team captain, Charlie Kip, who had been called into the service. The presence of Stirnweiss on the athletic field seemed to galvanize the rest of the sports program, which had definitely been in the doldrums before his arrival. He had a magic talent for getting the most out of his boys.

The painting of the Canterbury Pilgrims that would hang in Middle House for years to come was given to the School in 1943 by Mr. James B. McCahey of Chicago as a gift on behalf of his son, Fred M. McCahey '43. He had purchased it especially for Dr. Hume after the headmaster had publicly announced his desire for such a painting. The mural originally came from England, where it had been owned by friends of Alfred, Lord Tennyson.[298] Unfortunately, the painting has not survived the years.

By the fall of 1943, the School's 108 students were fully accustomed to the wartime routine. *The Tabard* was published once a month except for an extra issue in the fall. In 1944, the Second Form succumbed under the pressure of the war. With the war at its peak in 1944 and the draft age diminishing, the headmaster was forced to make room for the older boys at the sacrifice of his lower school. Also, since the death of Alec Hume in 1935, there had been no one to whom Nelson Hume could hand over that part of the School. Consequently, the First Form had been dropped after Alec's death, and only the Second Form continued, with some interruption, as a remnant of the old school.

It was the size of the study hall that limited the School's capacity in 1944. The addition of forty-one new boys swelled the enrollment to a record 111—too many boys to fit comfortably in the small study hall. Before the year was out, however, eight had left to serve in the armed forces.

After fourteen years of not being used because of the ice's poor quality, the old rink behind South House was recommissioned and used throughout the winter season. The rink was fitted with new boards that avoided the chronic bad spots in the ice, and the season was further blessed by a cold winter. The result was that the hockey team turned in one of the best seasons in fifteen years by winning three and tying one to remain undefeated.

Canterbury emerged from the war a distinctly different school. There was no rush to take up where school life had left off, as there had been after the First World War. Even though the summer months intervened between the end of the war and the beginning of a new school year, the sobering effect of the war years lingered on. Because the School and its headmaster were so intimately connected with each other, the lingering melancholy that stayed with Canterbury through that year was an extension of Nelson Hume's own sorrow for the loss of his students—for the war had taken its toll of Canterbury boys. The service flag in the chapel bore twelve gold stars for the Canterbury fallen. Dr. Hume's close relationship with every Canterbury boy made each of these losses a personal one for him. He turned toward his second postwar era with a heavy heart.

His first undertaking was to raise funds for a new school infirmary, which he proposed to dedicate as a memorial to the alumni who had died in the war. He also had in mind the enlargements of the chapel and the gymnasium. The chapel had to undergo some minor repairs, as a lightning strike had damaged the tower during a severe thunderstorm in the spring of 1946, knocking off a cornerstone and loosening others.[299] During this time, Dr. Hume was devoting energy to reassembling his faculty, and intensifying the preparation of Canterbury boys for the stepped-up requirements for college entrance. Signs of the vigor and enthusiasm of the prewar Canterbury began to reappear in 1947. *The Tabard* and the yearbook produced creditable editions, and the athletic teams began winning. Led by captain Bernard "Boo" Berry, along with Ed Duffy and Tom Landry, the hockey team boasted an outstanding 6-2 record, and many compared it to the earlier great team of 1918.

Both his wife and his physician had warned Dr. Hume to slow down. Even as early as 1941, Dr. Hume wrote, "[E]very boy and every set of parents require a great deal of my personal attention . . . besides that, I still have a fair-sized schedule of teaching periods and the general administration of the whole place, indoors and out."[300] But he was determined by his own personal leadership to reestablish the school on a firm peacetime basis. Throughout the spring of 1948, he pressed forward in all departments of the School, in addition to handling administrative matters and giving his personal attention to each of the college admission officers, who were now embarked on their new policy of school visitation.

In perhaps one of his last official acts, Dr. Hume engaged Mr. Jean Hebert, of Holyoke, Massachusetts, and a graduate of Middlebury College, who was fluent in both French and Spanish. Mr. Hebert spoke glowingly of Dr. Hume, noting, "He was per-haps the most dynamic individual I had ever met. He made this great impression on people . . . very forceful, very dynamic. A man of tremendous energy."[301] Dr. Hume invited Jean to Canterbury, gave him a tour, and took him into the chapel, where the doctor played the organ for him. Jean said that in terms of volume, Dr. Hume knew only loud, louder, and loudest.[302]

A few days before the end of school in May 1948, Dr. Hume left his English class and went to his house, saying to Mrs. Hume: "A man who feels as sick as I do should be in bed!" He was, unknowingly, suffering from a heart attack, from which he would never recover. He sent word to Mr. Mack to take over the prepa-ration of the Graduation Mass, but insisted that he was not ill; sim-ply, that his doctor had said he must rest. As the day of graduation approached, there was no apparent improvement in his condition. On graduation morning, the Sixth Form gathered gloomily in his living room at the foot of the stairs, and he sent down, with Mrs. Hume, what was to be his last message, wishing them all the suc-cess and happiness he was wont to express to and for them when he officiated at graduation exercises.

Mr. John S. Burke, president of the Board of Trustees, gra-ciously presided in Dr. Hume's place while the traditional exercis-es were carried out. At this time, there was no general feeling of depression or foreboding. It was true that Dr. Hume had never before had a serious illness, save for an appendectomy many years earlier. The graduating class was sent on its way, reunions took place as they always did at this point of the school year, luncheon was served, and Canterbury settled down to its summer somnolence.

Dr. Nelson Hume died on June 14, 1948, having contended earnestly for the faith once delivered to the saints. Unquestionably, the most important work of his thirty-three years at Canterbury was the weaving of his Catholic faith into the warp and woof of the fabric of the School. He felt that the traditional Jesuit schools established and maintained themselves in a milieu of ultra-parochialism, and that they tended both to insulate and to isolate the student from a realistic awareness of his religious position in a pluralistic society. Dr. Hume's philosophy of preparing his charges to succeed in a diverse society is still evident in the last line of Canterbury's mission statement today: "The hallmark of a Canterbury education is the School's willingness to accept students as they are, support them where necessary, stretch them where appropriate, and inspire them to become moral leaders in a secular world." It must be noted that this was fifty years before the Vatican Council opened up new fields for proper religious activity by the laity.

And so, by 1948, there were seven buildings, whereas in 1915 there had been but two of any size—and these two had been destroyed by fire. The School could boast of some unusual and distinctive features: few schools of Canterbury's size possessed a swimming pool and there were even fewer institutions of learning that had a carillon. Few people could sense the significance of the School's chapel as the boys of Canterbury could. Time and vision, added to executive ability, would add lustrous substance to this aggregation of scholastic facilities and graces. By 1948, Canterbury was well established, flourishing, of unassailable posi-

tion in the scholastic world, respected, and, best of all, loved by
nearly four hundred grateful alumni.

**Nelson Hume, one of the founders of Canterbury School, and Canterbury's
first headmaster.**

Mr. Henry O. Havemeyer
Mr. Clarence H. Mackay
Mr. Nelson Hume
Mr. Condé B. Pallen
Mr. Allan A. Ryan
and Mr. George Cabot Ward
have the honour of announcing the opening of

Canterbury School
at New Milford, Connecticut
on Thursday, the twenty-third of September
One thousand, nine hundred and fifteen
as a college preparatory school for boys
under the patronage of

His Eminence John Cardinal Farley
Archbishop of New York

Applications for admission and requests for information
may be addressed to
Nelson Hume, Ph. D. Headmaster
at Eighteen East Forty-first Street, New York, until the twentieth of August
and thereafter at New Milford, Connecticut

The engraved announcement of the opening of Canterbury School. 1915.

Nelson Hume with two unidentified students. 1917.

Alec Hume with two Lower Form boys.

Cyril Hume, Headmaster Nelson Hume's youngest brother, skiing in back of the Main House.

Henry Havemeyer Jr. in goalie position on the old rink.

Charlie Martin, a nephew of founder Henry O. Havemeyer, and one of Canterbury's first students. Charlie enrolled at midterm and so missed the distinction of being one of Canterbury's charter students.

The mile marker on the road by Canterbury's chapel. A familiar sight to legions of Canterbury students.

Early postcard showing the Main House from Aspetuck Avenue.

LIVING ROOM IN "THE BUNGALOW"

The living room in the Bungalow, from an early prospectus advertising the School.

The front of the Bungalow, on the site of present-day Carter House. The Bungalow was destroyed by fire in

A glimpse inside the Bungalow ca. 1921. This picture was included in an early prospectus advertising the School.

The dining
room, 1921,
from an
early School
brochure.

Inside
Canterbury's
original
chapel, now
part of the
chaplain's
house. This is
the oldest
building on
campus.
1921.

In the early years, golf was a favorite
pastime of both students and masters.
For a time, the School had a par-3 nine-
hole course. Main House, Chapel, and
barn in the background, ca. 1917.

Faculty, ca. 1920. Headmaster Nelson Hume
third from left, followed by James McCarthy,
Philip Brodie, Alec Hume, and Maximillian
von der Porten.

The Canterbury Corps of Cadets drilling on the lawn in back of the Main House. 1917.

The School truck decked out as a victory wagon to celebrate the end of World War I. 1918.

Students smoothing out the ground to prepare the hockey rink for icing, ca. 1917.

Students were responsible for shoveling snow off the hockey rink. Main House in the background, ca. 1917.

The first hockey rink, built 1919. The Bungalow is in back; the Main House in the far background.

Football on the athletic fields in back of the Main House. 1919.

Off for a joyride with "Duke." Tom Denehy '19 at the reins; Gilbert King '19, Joe Lilly '20, Ralph Sturgis '21, and Dick Salembier '21 on board. From the photo archive of John Hughes '21. Denehy, King, Lilly, and Hughes were instrumental in the founding of *The Tabard,* the School newspaper.

Nelson Hume during one of the early outings to a Yale football game. Taking all the boys to a Yale game was one of the School's earliest and most welcome traditions. Trips discontinued when the enrollment grew so large as to make transportation unwieldy.

Hockey on what is now called Conn's Pond, or sometimes Canterbury Pond. Route 202 runs between the pond and the house. In the earliest years of the School, this may have also been referred to as Pell Pond.

Trapshooting in the fields north of the School, just beyond where Duffy House now stands. 1919.

Flames shooting through the roof during the Bungalow fire in 1925. This picture was taken from the Main House.

South House, now called Carter House, built in 1926 on the Bungalow foundation. Late 1940s.

Dedication of the Chapel of Our Lady, Graduation Weekend, June 10, 1928.

Chapel of Our Lady prior to the addition. Although plans to build a chapel were on file as early as 1920, construction did not begin on the Chapel of Our Lady until the fall of 1927.

A close-up of the carillons, donated in 1931, and dedicated by Monsignor Michael J. Lavelle in May 1931.

Headmaster Nelson Hume believed in a "hands-on" approach to running the School.

Ground was broken for North House on April 19, 1928. Now called Duffy House, North House provided a dining room, headmaster's quarters, and dormitories for the expanding enrollment. Late 1940s.

An aerial view of the campus in the 1930s. The gym and chapel are in the upper left. The Main House is on the site of the present-day Sheehan House parking lot, flanked by North House on the left and South House on the right.

**1939
Faculty.
Seated L-R:
Kimball,
Lindman,
Mack,
Bellerose,
Doyle.
Standing
L-R: Collier,
Maloney,
Halsey,
Elms,
Adair.**

Only the chimneys remained standing after the Main or Middle House fire in 1936.

**1948 photo
of Sheehan
House built
in 1936 to
replace the
Middle
House.**

George Stirnweiss, second baseman for the Yankees, took over when Canterbury's football coach was drafted into the service in the middle of the 1943 season. He continued as basketball coach at Canterbury, leading the team to its first successful season in many years.

CANTUARIA FLOREAT

Ut Cantuaria floreat,
  Quae Sanctam Fidem tenuit,
Et gloria famaque sua
  Sic apparuit.
Quae lumen ostendit
  Virtute triumphantium,
Et animas incendit
  Quo magis venerari.
O Cantuaria Floreas
  Ad multos annos felices!
Per Sanctum Spiritum nos Deum
  Semper induces.

CANTERBURY FOOTBALL SONG

All hail to the Canterbury Pilgrims!
  All hail to the boys who wear the blue!
As down the field we'll make them yield,
  We'll fight for the score that's overdue.
We'll cheer for the backs who make the touchdowns,
  We'll shout for the line that's like a wall.
We'll sing for the sturdy sons of Canterbury,
  Hail to them one and all!

Cantuaria Floreat, Canterbury's school song, written by Ed Mack. Mack also wrote the now obscure football song, which makes reference to the Canterbury Pilgrims. The "Pilgrim" name was later replaced by "Saints." From an undated Canterbury songbook.

Seated (L-R): Edwin Lindman, Philip Brodie, Nelson Hume, Joseph Maloney, and Edward Mack; Standing (L-R): Frank Fisher, James Herlihy, William Hanrahan, Claremont Koenig, John Dolan, and Vincent McCrossen.

Nelson Hume in his later years.

116

2

THE SHEEHAN YEARS

Walter Sheehan, Second Headmaster

The selection of a successor to the headmaster became the urgent and compelling task of the Board of Trustees. A committee of Canterbury's Board, consisting of Francis Carmody, John Burke, and Hubert McDonnell, formed to consider candidates and make a selection. Although some members felt that the School would surely fold without Nelson Hume at the helm, Mr. Carmody's steadfast belief in the school's future was persuasive.[303]

In choosing a new headmaster, it seemed likely that the trustees would be guided by certain factors. Age was a primary consideration—choosing a young man would ensure, as much as possible, a reasonably long tenure. The candidate would, of course, have to be a practicing Catholic. Other factors would include teaching and administrative experience in a preparatory school and, if possible, acquaintance with the problems of college admission. They soon determined that the ideal candidate was Walter Sheehan.

Mr. Sheehan often told the interesting story of his coming to Canterbury. It seemed that at the annual meeting of the

Headmasters' Association in Rye, New York, in February of 1948, Dr. Hume was chatting with Mr. Wickenden, the headmaster of Tabor Academy in Marion, Massachusetts, and asked him if he knew any Catholic men in secondary schools who might make good headmasters. Mr. Wickenden told Dr. Hume of his friend and former colleague, Walter Sheehan, who, at that time, was the first Dean of Freshmen and Director of Athletics at Williams College, and who had taught with him at Deerfield. At that moment, Mr. Frank Boyden, the well-known headmaster of Deerfield, came by and told Dr. Hume that Sheehan would make a fine headmaster. Dr. Hume made a mental note of this recommendation, and in early May invited Mr. and Mrs. Sheehan to Canterbury for a visit and to talk to the Sixth Form about some of the problems and situations that lay ahead of them when they went to college in the fall. Dr. Hume was impressed "by Sheehan's tall, athletic frame (he was a college basketball star), his straightforward manner, and his common sense."[304] Some time after the visit, Dr. Hume recommended that Sheehan be contacted in case the matter of a successor ever were to arise.

After Dr. Hume's death, the trustees contacted Mr. Sheehan's pastor in Williamstown, Massachusetts, and were satisfied with what they learned about Sheehan's religious background. They suggested that Mr. and Mrs. Sheehan visit Professor and Mrs. Carlton J. H. Hayes at Afton, New York, Dr. Hayes being the only educator on the Board of Trustees. This visit completed, and with Dr. Hayes's recommendation, the committee offered the headmastership to Mr. Sheehan, who accepted.

At that time, Mr. Sheehan was thirty-eight years old and fulfilled the requirements for headmaster in every respect. He had graduated from Deerfield after transferring from the Sacred Heart High School in Holyoke. He had had twelve years of teaching experience under Mr. Boyden at Deerfield, and was attuned to the secular school. He was also an alumnus of Williams College. While serving as dean of freshmen and director of athletics at Williams, he was on the admissions committee and thus had gained valuable experience in the field of college entrance policies and requirements. He had the distinction of having captained the Williams varsity basketball team, and had pitched on the baseball team while an undergraduate.

Walter Sheehan was married to the former Lillian Fontaine, of Belmont, Massachusetts, and they had two sons: Peter, a graduate of Deerfield and Williams, and Kevin, a Canterbury and Williams graduate. Their daughter, Monica, also was a Canterbury and Williams graduate. Following his appointment to succeed Dr. Hume, Williams College granted Mr. Sheehan the Honorary Degree of Doctor of Humane Letters. In 1964, he would be awarded the Degree of Doctor of Laws by Portland (Oregon) University when he delivered the commencement address there. Years later, Jules Viau, by then a senior master, recollected,

> Mr. Sheehan was a complex man, not easily identified with any stereotypical head of school, and although very kind and tolerant of adolescent nonsense, he was no Mr. Chips, but a figure who commanded respect and could effectively reduce the most recalcitrant student to respectful silence.[305]

There was never any halfway with Walter Sheehan. Mr. Sheehan decided on sweeping changes at Canterbury. The system of discipline—the carrot-or-the-stick approach of extra days' vacation for exemplary behavior—was abolished. No special system of discipline was substituted; boys were simply expected to behave. A general persistence in rebellion or nonconformity could result in loss of privileges, such as curtailment or deprivation of a weekend or vacation days. The custom of permitting the boys to go downtown for an hour on specified days of the week was done away with, as was afternoon tea. Instead of tea, the school store opened after athletic practices for students to purchase candy or cigarettes. After evening study hall ended at 9:30, students could purchase milk and cookies, and the funds that were raised were used to purchase athletic uniforms[306]. Some athletic teas and tea dances still occurred, so losing the custom of daily tea did not elicit a reaction from the students.

One unchanging practice was that boys still had to walk downtown to have their yearbook photographs taken at Simpson's Studio (then located at Bridge and Main). Early on during Mr. Sheehan's tenure, one of the boys was returning from his photo session when a boy from town made a remark. The Canterbury boy backed the offender into the ash cans in front of Sloan's Pharmacy and dropped him with one blow. The boy wasn't even back to the top of the hill before Mr. Sheehan knew of the incident and suspended all further permission for boys to go downtown.[307]

Despite his relatively strict approach to discipline, Walter Sheehan was tolerant and uncannily intuitive when it came to understanding his young charges, according to James Moore, his assistant headmaster for five years: "The incident never hid the person for Mr. Sheehan."[308] Many a student was exhorted to "stay in and pitch," or was complimented for "turning the corner." Students delighted in imitating or mimicking many of these speech patterns or gestures, sometimes quite accurately.[309]

Mr. Sheehan had already begun to emulate his former mentor, Mr. Frank Boyden of Deerfield, as a maker of headmasters. Mr. James Moore came to Canterbury in Mr. Sheehan's first year, taught English, acquired a master's degree at Columbia, and coached basketball. He was named assistant headmaster in 1958, the first one named since Alec Hume's death, In 1963 he moved on to the headship of a new Catholic lay school, LaLumiere,[310] a counterpart of Canterbury located in Indiana. Mr. Moore headed

LaLumiere from 1963 through 1979, and again from 1988 through 1993.[311] As an expression of his admiration for Mr. Moore, Mr. Sheehan magnanimously served on the board of LaLumiere for a number of years.[312] Mr. Moore passed away on December 4, 2004.

Walter Sheehan had the same impact on his faculty that he had on his students. For Mr. Sheehan, "loyalty [was] everything, disloyalty must be terminated."[313] Walter could silence a complaining faculty member—usually Jean Hebert, according to Jules Viau—by using the "zip-it" gesture later made famous by Mike Myers as the character Dr. Evil in *Austin Powers*. When Walter considered the faculty meeting over, he would signal JP Mandler to switch off the lights. At another faculty meeting, Walter suggested that if a certain complaining faculty member was so unhappy, he could certainly deliver his resignation to the headmaster's desk by the following morning. The faculty member backed down and remained cautious in his speech at faculty meetings thereafter. "Walter didn't brook any complaints."[314] Ed Mack once remarked, "If you want to be happy and keep your job, stay out of the office."

Walter Sheehan was very formal with his faculty. Phil Brodie and Ed Mack always referred to Mr. Sheehan as "Sir." However, Walter Sheehan was known as "Twit" to his Holyoke cronies or administrative equals.[315] No faculty member would have dared call Walter Sheehan "Twit" to his face. Walter believed in running a tight ship, and such informality would have been highly inappropriate. Even when Mr. Sheehan appointed James Moore as the assistant headmaster, Moore could not bring himself to call Mr. Sheehan "Walter."[316] At one point, Mr. Sheehan felt that the faculty were too lax in their behavior in Middle House. To rectify the problem, Walter moved John Martiska to a faculty apartment on the first floor and Jules Viau to a faculty apartment on the third floor. When the presence of these two faculty members still did not restore enough order for Sheehan's satisfaction, he moved one of the offending faculty members right off campus.

Walter Sheehan could also be cagey when presenting new tasks to his faculty members. It was not unusual for him to notify a faculty member of a new responsibility by congratulating him on it.[317]

Lillian (Lynn) Sheehan was an excellent counterpart to her husband. Described as a formidable woman, Mrs. Sheehan was always very much a lady, very much in possession of herself. Mrs. Sheehan always wanted to make sure that everything was "just so." Unofficially, she was in charge of campus beautification.[318] Lynn Sheehan was great with the single faculty members, and did what she could to make their lives comfortable by inviting them in for meals and bridge. Jean Hebert thought she was one of the loveliest ladies he had ever met. On Sunday mornings, she would have all the faculty in for brunch, instead of dining "with the troops." The Sheehans entertained frequently (although Lynn expected faculty spouses to help serve). Teas, especially near the beginning of the school year, took place at the headmaster's house. Bridge nights were also popular events. Jules Viau recalls that Mrs. Sheehan was a very sharp bridge player and it was quite a feather in your cap to play as her partner.[319] The Sheehans were clearly devoted to each other, and Lynn took care of Walter in his declining years, even though Walter outlived Lynn.

The English department had always been in the hands of Dr. Hume, with some assistance in running the lower forms. In 1957, Mr. William D'Alton assumed direction and guided the department. Bill D'Alton and Mr. Roderick Clarke were two faculty members who were also alumni of Canterbury; Mr. D'Alton graduated in 1942 and Mr. Clarke in 1946. Mr. Clarke carried on the traditions of Canterbury in his teaching of history, in addition to his duties as director of studies and college counseling. In 1978 he would become the School's fourth headmaster.

Mr. Sheehan felt the need for a resident chaplain, and the first was Father Thomas Quinn, who came in September of 1948, freshly ordained. The headmaster and the trustees felt that a resident chaplain would be a constructive force in the school and would carry on the spiritual ideals of the founders. In addition to Father Quinn's ecclesiastical duties, he also taught religion classes to each form twice per week; taught two Latin courses; served as housemaster in North House; and assisted in coaching the athletic teams in the fall.[320] Father Quinn remained at Canterbury for ten years.

Father Quinn also brought the world of the theater to Canterbury. Each year he would direct a stage production, beginning with a play called *Room Service*. For the next few years, the students had to use the St. Francis school auditorium when they successively staged *Ten Little Indians*, *Arsenic and Old Lace*, and *Stalag 17*, among other plays. Father Quinn once experimented with using the old New Milford Town Hall, which had a stage and equipment dating back to the 1870s. In these fusty surroundings, the Mimers, as the dramatic organization was named, excelled in *The Ghost Train*. Father Quinn received assistance from various students, faculty, and faculty wives.

Mr. Hugh Campbell, husband of Lorli von Trapp of the Trapp Family singers, and Howard Junker '57[321] helped with production and stage decoration. Isabelle Reilly, wife of faculty member Gene Reilly, designed sets, and Frances Hebert, wife of Jean Hebert, assisted with makeup.[322] These later productions were presented in the school gymnasium (now known as the old wrestling room).

Father Quinn demonstrated a special aptitude for and a genuine interest in education. Because of this, Archbishop Henry J. O'Brien of Hartford felt that he needed Father Quinn, who left Canterbury in 1958 and later became principal of Saint Thomas

Aquinas High School in New Britain, Connecticut.

Upon Father Quinn's departure, the burden of directing the annual dramatic production fell upon the shoulders of Mr. Moore and Mr. D'Alton, and after Mr. Moore left, on those of Mr. D'Alton alone. Limited seating in the gym necessitated that the play run for three nights. The final performance was reserved for upper-formers, faculty, parents, and friends. After the final performance, all were invited to the headmaster's residence for an informal tea.[323]

Bill D'Alton could be called the original Canterbury diehard. After graduating from Canterbury in 1942, Bill started the fall term at Yale, but then enlisted in the army and saw combat in Europe. After a brief stint as head of the English department at the Cate School, near Santa Barbara, California, Bill returned to Canterbury in 1957, where he stayed until his retirement in 1989.

In the interim that transpired in the search for another chaplain, Father Fox and Father McCabe, of the Maryknoll Fathers, gave brief service to the school. The following year, in 1959, Father Regis Ryan, of the Dominican Order, became Canterbury's second long-term chaplain. Father Ryan was assisted in his religious teaching by Mr. James Breene and Mr. Jules Viau.[324] After seven years of devotion to the spiritual needs of the community, Father Ryan was needed by his superiors as a teacher. Father Clement Greenan, also a Dominican, came over from Ireland at Mr. Sheehan's invitation to succeed Father Ryan as Canterbury's next chaplain. In a comparatively short time, he endeared himself to all.

Perhaps the most conspicuous difference between Dr. Hume's technique of administration and that of Mr. Sheehan was that Dr. Hume's was strictly personal, and Mr. Sheehan was a staff man. The small school, with its intimate, personal supervision of every phase of school life, was the essence of preparatory school management in earlier days. The constantly expanding school, with its proliferation in numbers of students and faculty, made such pilotage out of the question, and recourse was made to distributive administration.

The Canterbury of Mr. Sheehan's day was an organization of divisions and subdivisions. Most of the details of school management were in the hands of the staff. During the summer, this allowed the Sheehans time for travel, frequently to Ireland; this was in contrast to the Humes, who in 1939 finally took a two-week vacation, the longest they had had in more than ten years.[325] This travel time also allowed Walter the chance to indulge in one of his favorite pastimes—golf. In times of expansion, this system of management gave proper opportunity for travel, contact with alumni and, especially, for all-important fund-raising efforts. A typical fall circuit might consist of travel to Cincinnati, Detroit, Chicago, and Florida.[326]

Walter Sheehan worked with his board to identify and woo benefactors. In one letter, Walter suggested that the time was ripe to pin down a potential donor, and "push the ball across the goal line."[327] However, in the area of student contact, Sheehan remained very much hands-on. For many years, Walter Sheehan wrote a progress report to every boy's parents each marking period. A sample paragraph might read as follows: "He is to be commended for his fine gain in class standing, and I am certain he has turned his corner in this regard, and from now on will always be in the first quarter of his class."[328] Sheehan ably demonstrated his take-charge style in 1954, when polio struck the school and four boys were afflicted. He decided to close the school and send all the boys home, potentially saving the school from more serious consequences. Staff had to get the boys home on extremely short notice, but they carried out the operation efficiently and smoothly.[329]

In 1951, Mr. Sheehan revived the idea of the Student Council.

The new Student Council began as a senior group, composed of the four sacristans and three elected Sixth Formers. Representatives of the Fifth and Fourth Forms were included later. With the rapid expansion of the student body—156 by 1951—and the difficulties of providing for sufficient supervision, Mr. Sheehan found it necessary to extend authority to the student body. First, he introduced the proctorial system to assist the faculty masters; in turn, the proctorial idea was further enlarged to include four committees of proctors that would have charge of the dining room, the gymnasium, the chapel, and the schoolhouse. When the practice of having boys live off-campus was introduced, Mr. Sheehan appointed an additional proctor to supervise such boys. So that the entire control of discipline should not be in the hands of the students, a discipline committee consisting of the assistant headmaster and two other faculty appointees acted as a supreme court in exercising jurisdiction over all disciplinary questions.

Many schools considered the problem of honesty versus cheating in the classroom as a disciplinary rather than a moral issue. This feeling led to the adoption, in 1956, of an honor system, first for the Sixth Form on a trial basis, and eventually extended to all forms. Policing of classroom integrity became the direct concern of the students themselves. The members of the Student Council were the first recipients of complaints or accusations. They worked to resolve the matter and then presented it to the faculty for a final decision.

Scholastically, under Mr. Sheehan, the School kept pace with what was new in the educational world. As a matter of course, the math department introduced the "new" mathematics shortly after its general introduction into the public schools, about 1955. Since the trend in all schools then was toward "honors" courses, Mr. Sheehan introduced them in English, history, foreign languages, and science. The modernization of the curriculum was generally free of the extremes being explored by some of the public schools at the time. There were sporadic attempts to reintroduce Greek into the curriculum, with limited success. In fact, there were some who predicted that within a short time the new liturgy would cause Latin to die out altogether in any secular school, along with the classics. (As a matter of fact, as early as 1931, Yale *had* made the decision to omit the Latin requirement for the BA degree. At the time, Dr. Hume replied, "Our plan at Canterbury is to require Latin of all the boys up to and including the Fourth Form . . . [a]fter all, Latin is a fine subject for instruction and does a boy a great deal of good in many other respects, particularly in English and in French.")[330]

Art as a hands-on activity was introduced at this time by Mrs. Isabelle Reilly. The program was offered as an extracurricular club activity at this time, and students were allowed to meet once a week in the basement of the infirmary during evening study hall. Art did not become part of the curriculum until the 1970s.[331]

In physical appearance, *The Tabard* edition of October 5, 1950, presented a new format of five columns instead of four, an increased abundance of photographs and illustrations, and bolder treatment of the news in headlines. A larger Canterbury School could provide more news of diversified activities, so the editors kept athletics off the front page. These physical changes were less important than what was happening between the lines of type. One noticed more freedom in the presentation of various facets of School life, less accuracy in factual content, less circumspection in presentation, and less orthodoxy in classical journalism. *The Tabard* crackled with life and vibrancy, and editorialized with some maturity, though still with a certain amount of self-important profundity. During this time, the publication evolved into more of an expression of a way of life than a limited journal of record.

After a publication hiatus of a few years, a new literary magazine called the *Carillon* started appearing three times a year by the early 1950s. The *Carillon* differed from *The Quarterly* in appearance, format, and other physical features. While the binding was modest and there was no formal table of contents on the cover, it effectively served as a creative outlet for Canterbury's youth.

Following the departure of Mr. Edward G. Roddy, Mr. Sheehan appointed Williams graduate Mr. James Shea of Holyoke, Massachusetts, as head of the history department. Mr. Shea had already served two years on the faculty, and was also one of the first faculty members to live in the new Carmody House dormitory. Additionally, Jim Shea served as the housemaster in North House until 1958[332] and was the faculty advisor to *The Tabard*. An avid baseball fan, Jim managed to coach all three levels of baseball while at Canterbury. Beginning in 1984, Jim taught the very popular "America in the 1960s" history course,[333] which he continued teaching until his retirement in 1997.

Jim Shea was also involved with the school library, which, after a long struggle, was finally coming into its own. The library had grown from the days when the books were kept and checked out in the little annex to the old chapel, and from the time in 1935 when the fine library in the old Middle House had been lost to fire. It had also evolved since the period when the study hall had been converted into a handsomely appointed research and study center. Under the guidance of Jim Shea in the 1960s, the library became more and more the scholastic power center of the school. Helen Lataif became the school's first full-time librarian in 1968,[334] and the library expanded to encompass the two classrooms at the northwest end of the Schoolhouse. Those two classrooms were used as an office and a periodical reading room.[335] The library would remain here until January 1984, when Robert Markey Steele Hall opened, with the David Casey Copley Library situated upstairs and the new dining hall downstairs.

One of the most valuable legacies Dr. Hume left to Mr. Sheehan was Miss Madeline Powers, who completed forty years of service as secretary to the headmaster in the mid-1960s. In earlier days, Miss Powers had been largely responsible for recording and averaging grades, overseeing applications for college, transferring credits, and several other tasks connected with keeping abreast of scholastic records. As the School continued to grow, it was no longer possible to follow this procedure. Mr. Roderick Clarke '46, who had been a member of the faculty for several years and was later to became the school's fourth headmaster, was installed as director of studies, and he coordinated those activities under the auspices of a separate department.

Mr. Sheehan took a sympathetic attitude toward his faculty. The trustees had stipulated that he not dismiss or replace any of the existing faculty before the lapse of a year's time. However, it quickly became apparent that the new headmaster was more than content with the faculty he had inherited. Nonetheless, Mr. Sheehan had several concerns related to the faculty: He immediately raised the salaries of the older men, while at the same time relieving them of the long hours of dormitory supervision. The faculty, which numbered approximately ten, rotated dorm duty about every third weekend, plus a couple of nights during the week. Roughly four of the faculty actually lived in and ran the dormitories.[336] Later, in 1955, Walter persuaded the trustees to inaugurate a pension system, whereby faculty members who had served twenty-five or more years would receive a regular annuity after retirement.[337] The twenty-five years began in 1955, so the men who had already served for many years could not be included. Instead, a lump-sum payment was made to provide small annuities for these men.

The question of faculty housing had always been a difficult one at Canterbury. With the exception of Mr. Brodie, all masters had to find what living quarters they could on their own. Due to the shortage of housing in town, this became nearly impossible at times, and valuable men were lost, or nearly lost, because of their inability to find decent housing. Mr. Sheehan began to address this issue, and beginning in 1957, he had three houses constructed on school grounds, in addition to purchasing and renting other houses in the village.[338] Thus was recognized the importance of a stable and comfortably housed faculty, and the maintenance of normal family life.

Many of the masters so well known to scores of Canterbury students throughout the next forty years began teaching at Canterbury around this time. Upon the retirement of Mr. Brodie in 1956,[339] Mr. Sheehan requested Mr. Mack to lay aside his Sixth Form English and history classes and step into the classical shoes of Mr. Brodie. Mr. Mack was finally forced out of action in 1957 by a heart attack. He retired and lived next to the campus until his death in 1977. His two sons are Canterbury alumni, Edward R., of the class of 1951, and Michael A., of the class of 1954. With Mr. Mack's retirement in 1957, Mr. James Breene, who had been a member of the faculty since 1955, assumed the direction of that department. Mr. Breene came to Canterbury after two years of teaching, bringing with him from Georgetown the classical Jesuit training and an unusual predilection for Greek, which he introduced into the curriculum with some success.

Mr. Jules Viau ultimately followed Mr. Breene. Mr. Viau originally came to Canterbury in 1954 to teach sections in French and in Spanish, but was also pressed into service over the years to teach theology and Latin. Through his many years of coaching, it is hard to think of Jules Viau in conjunction with any sport other than tennis, but he also coached baseball for some years.[340] Reluctant Canterbury scholars will remember Mr. Viau's taps to the back of the head to call their wandering minds back to the task at hand. As a young faculty member, Jules admitted he didn't always know the appropriate dress code, and he relied on his proctors to keep him out of hot water with Phil Brodie and Walter Sheehan, especially in the dining hall. Particularly astute students would alert Jules to proper dress code by commenting, "Tonight is a special night; you shouldn't wear a sport coat." Or, "Perhaps you should wear a different pair of socks." Dress shoes for dinner had to be black or cordovan, and socks had to be black or navy blue.

A few years later, two more Canterbury alumni were added to the history department: Peter Cashman '55 from Yale, and James Briggs '56 from Williams. Mr. Cashman functioned with great success as director of development of the fiftieth anniversary drive. Mr. Briggs, currently a Canterbury trustee, was the first son of an alumnus (Walter O. Briggs Jr. '30) to become a member of the school faculty.

Each year, Mr. Hebert, Mr. Viau, Mr. Shea, Mr. D'Alton, Mr. Breene, and Mr. Clarke added experience to their capability and diligence. The mathematics department was strengthened by the addition of able instructors such as Mr. John F. Graney Jr., who had arrived around 1960 and headed the department, and Mr. Weldon Knox in 1959.[341] Mr. Weldon Knox came to Canterbury not only as an experienced and very able teacher, but also as a former superintendent of schools in New Milford (1943–1959).[342] Mr. Graney was assisted in his department by Mr. John Coffin and Mr. Walter Burke.

John Martiska, from Providence College, rendered service to the English department and assisted in the business management of the School previous to the appointment, on a full-time basis, of Mr. Arthur Betz, to assume the duties of the first official business manager since the death of Alexander Hume in 1935.[343] Probably no one in the history of Canterbury filled as many roles within the School as John Martiska. He taught Third Form English for seventeen years, Fourth Form theology for fifteen years, and served two separate times as the School's business manager (1958–1964, and 1970–1979). He also served for fifteen years as a dormitory master in Havemeyer House and nine years in South House.[344] John, or "Rock" as he was called, was director of School services for many years, and his domain included the school store, snack bar, Canterbury's small farm (a barn with some chickens and a horse), Saturday Night Movies, and the mail.

When interviewed for *The Tabard* on at least two separate occasions, John claimed not to understand why he had earned the nickname "Rock." It will forever remain a Canterbury mystery. Rock was also responsible for coordinating the driver's education program. Starting a tradition that would endure for many years, Mr. Martiska helped acclimate new students during orientation by outlining the laundry, bookstore, and mail routines. To fill in his remaining free time, John was honored to serve as a Eucharistic minister, and was an active force in the Mission Society. Even when school was not in session, Rock coordinated the soccer and music camps that regularly rented Canterbury's grounds.[345] He was known and feared for his bark, which seldom gave way to a bite, and scores of new students were terrified by Rock's annual "tampering with the U.S. mail is a 'Class A' felony" speech. Master of the dining hall, Mr. Martiska, bedecked in his Michael Jackson glove and Budweiser-print pants, would signal the start of sit-down dinner by ringing his set of bells. At faculty meetings, Rock would deliver pithy announcements (in Russian) along these lines: "When the turkey flies overhead, and the mice begin to play the balalaika, it's time for the bear to watch out."[346]

Besides chapel and religious instruction, one additional religious experience was afforded to the boys during the school year, in the form of the annual retreat. This observance dates from the first days of the School. Nelson Hume felt so strongly about the retreat that when petitioned by Mr. Havemeyer to excuse his son Henry from the retreat, Dr. Hume wrote in exasperation: "What is of most importance in this connection, however, is that Henry will miss the most important religious training of the entire year, and I fear that his being taken away from it might give him a wrong impression of the relative importance of religious matters, because a retreat under a competent priest is always an 'event' in a school."[347] As the enrollment expanded greatly, Mr. Sheehan felt that a more personal experience would result from smaller groups, and so the two upper forms began the experiment of journeying to one of the many religious retreat houses in New England—the Sixth Form to one, the Fifth Form to another. The two lower forms followed through the routine of the retreat on school grounds.

The new headmaster was an on-the-spot observer of the rapid growth of Deerfield and was a firm believer in the big school. At Canterbury, the motives for a big school were somewhat blurred by a conflict between desire and necessity. A big school meant greatly enlarged facilities, and greatly enlarged facilities meant building projects—and lots of them. In addition to accommodation in space, the headmaster was faced with the fact that the plant was getting old and was in vital need of repair and rebuilding. The only way in which money for these things could be obtained on a short-term basis was through tuitions. Because additional students were needed for revenue, the demand for housing increased. Double rooms were made out of single ones, and every available space was converted into sleeping quarters for boys. Students were housed with faculty and in off-campus homes. A policy of accepting day students was inaugurated. Postwar prosperity was on the upswing, and demand for admission to educational institutions was at an all-time high, so that there was no dearth of applicants. Mr. Sheehan proved himself to be a builder by temperament. He began, within two years of his appointment, to construct the much-needed infirmary, and by 1951 a well-built and functional building was dedicated, blessed by Father Quinn, and ready for use, generously equipped and furnished by B. Altman and Company.

If needs for dormitory accommodations were pressing, Mr. Sheehan was also faced with still more necessary but less enjoyable projects. The roof of the swimming pool was in a dangerous condition as a result of nearly twenty-five years of moisture condensation. The heating plants of all the buildings were obsolete, and it was becoming more and more difficult to find reliable men to care for the furnaces. Oil burners had to be installed throughout the entire plant. These major replacements and rehabilitative undertakings required a great deal of money, which the School did not have in reserve; as a result, it had to borrow the funds for these projects. The answer to these and other expenditures, for the time being, had to be cash income from tuitions. Hence, the annual increase in enrollment. In time, the old plant was rejuvenated and attention could be focused on new expansion projects.

Although the gymnasium was outdated, both in size and efficiency, the question of the chapel took precedence. Designed for a school of one hundred boys, it could not accommodate the burgeoning population. Boys were crowded into the aisles and into every corner of space. In 1960, the building was enlarged. It was a happy circumstance that the atmosphere on the hill was free from any smoke or pollution, and the original granite had retained its freshness, so that the matching stones of the addition blended well. One viewing the building for the first time would not be aware that the two sections were built thirty-five years apart. The moving of the great west window to its new location in a wall sixty feet farther west engendered speculation as to the delicacy of the operation, and even whether it could be accomplished at all. Ingenuity triumphed, as each minuscule portion of stained glass was first photographed in color, so that when the window was to be reassembled, a perfectly completed jigsaw puzzle provided the guide. Thus, the glass was easily and accurately set back in place.

The new chapel had some novel features. Always called the Chapel of Our Lady, the gradient of the terrain allowed for a large basement room to be used as a theology classroom with facilities for hanging wearing apparel and made possible a staircase leading to the auditorium. A regulation confessional, lacking in the former smaller chapel, was placed in the rear. The chapel presented an inspiring vista down its new length to the west window, and had seating for 250 people.

As later reported in the *Pallium*, "Over the years, devotion to St. Jude developed in the school, but it was Philip Brodie . . . who truly fostered it . . . [He] persuaded Walter Sheehan, Hume's successor, that the chapel should have a statue of St. Jude."[348] Reed Armstrong '55 was commissioned to create the statue. Although Reed sculpted the statue in his Princeton, New Jersey, studio, the statue was sent to a foundry in Italy to be cast in bronze.

The Chapel of Our Lady was the one of the first churches in Connecticut, along with the Chapel of St. Thomas More at Yale, to place an altar so that it allowed the celebrant to face the congregation and to employ the temporary new English translation at Mass.[349] Vatican II in 1963 published statements in favor of three important understandings held by Canterbury's founders: "the regional diversity of the Catholic experience, the importance of a participating laity, and the obligation of ecumenical outreach."[350] Canterbury incorporated all three into the fabric of the School, still highlighted today in Canterbury's mission statement. Canterbury's philosophy is best summed up by Conn Nugent '64.[351] When asked about how his Canterbury experiences led him to his path in life, Nugent responded:

> I can seriously say that I got a crackerjack classical education at Canterbury. Men like Clarke and Shea and Breene

and Moore, and D'Alton, and I would have to include Regis
Ryan, the chaplain at the time, really had a wonderful sort
of blend of traditional education with a progressive cosmo-
politan world view. Their point of view was not isolationist
or protective at all. I hate to sound cliché, but they honestly
imparted a great thirst for knowledge in me.

The other thing was the spiritual aspect: that being a
Christian meant that you had to live one's ethics through
interactions with other human beings. I took it to heart, and
I still do. That to me is the Canterbury legacy.[352]

The headmaster was always in favor of all the boys in the
School taking part in the High Mass on the occasions when it was
sung. In later years, the custom was revamped, and a smaller
group, under more intensive training, functioned as the choir and
became known as The Schola Cantorum.[353] Mrs. Hugh Campbell,
whose husband was a faculty member, first directed this group. She
was well trained in the technique of Gregorian chant, since, before
her marriage, she had been Lorli von Trapp, a member of the
widely known Trapp Family Singers.[354] When the Campbells left
Canterbury, Walter Sheehan informed Jean Hebert that Jean was
going to be the new choral director. Walter gave as his reason the
fact that he never had any worries about Jean "controlling the
troops." Jean always felt that he was chosen because Walter knew
he slipped down to Brookfield now and again to play in a jazz
band.[355] The Schola later became the Chapel Choir under the able
direction of Mr. Gerald Vanasse.

Gerry Vanasse arrived at Canterbury in the fall of 1960. A
native of New Bedford, Massachusetts, Gerry taught in the New
Bedford high school before coming to Canterbury. Although hired
to teach French and German, Gerry was immediately tapped for
his musical abilities. In his first year at Canterbury, Gerry replaced
Mr. Mack at the chapel organ. He also was pressed into assisting
Mr. Jean Hebert with the Choral Club.[356] With his jaunty beret

and a twinkle in his eye, Gerry served Canterbury for thirty years. Marc Vanasse '73, Gerry's son, reminisces:

> The history of faculty-chaperoned trips dates back to the early 1960s, when Walter Sheehan asked my dad to lead a group of Canterbury boys on a summer tour of Europe. They went in grand style in those days—an ocean liner to and fro, deluxe accommodations, and an itinerary that would make any traveler envious. He led many groups, and what I remember most is that he always brought back great presents. One in particular, a portable Telefunken tape recorder, provided my siblings and me many hours of pleasure.

By 1962, a need for new headmaster's quarters was apparent, and so a new residence for Mr. Sheehan was constructed across the road from the chapel, commanding an exquisite view of the valley[357]. The old residence, an appendage to North House, was converted to good use. Mr. Sheehan had the former sun porch rebuilt for his office. The dining room became the sanctuary of Miss Powers, his secretary. The kitchen was transformed into an office for Roderick Clarke, the director of studies and college counselor. Dr. Hume's living room, the site of so many pleasant occasions in former days, became a reception room for those waiting to see the headmaster. The second and third floors were easily converted into students' rooms, and furnished additional revenue.

By 1962, most of the Fourth Form was living off-campus in masters' or former masters' houses, in residences assigned to faculty members, and in private homes. Mr. Sheehan and the trustees became increasingly unhappy about this condition, feeling it was not conducive to an integrated school life. Something had to be done immediately. Fortunately for Canterbury and for Mr. Sheehan, Francis Carmody '25 was president of the Board of Trustees at this time. A man of faith and determination, believing deeply in the Canterbury ideal, he worked tirelessly for the good of the School. As the headmaster was to say, nobody had a greater part in the growth and development of the School than Carmody through his foresight, leadership, and character. Years later, Roderick Clarke, fourth headmaster, would reflect, "Francis Carmody was the best example of a perfect gentleman." Francis could make anybody feel at ease in his presence. He remembered all the faculty names, what they taught, what they coached, and all the small details that make conversation comfortable.[358] It was Francis Carmody who sparked the decision to go ahead with a drive to meet the School's needs, and his faith in the eventual outcome was infectious.

Canterbury had never had a large capital gifts campaign. In 1952, the school started on the road to endowment, and raised enough to support a pension plan and introduce other fringe benefits for the faculty. Through annual appeals, Mr. Sheehan had raised money on a yearly basis for maintenance and additions, but it was evident to all that the time had come for bigger projects, including plant expansion, and facilities that would simultaneously meet existing needs and enable the faculty to do a better job in several areas. To this end, and in anticipation of the coming fiftieth anniversary of the founding of the school in 1962, an organized drive for a goal of $1,800,000 was set in motion in the capable hands of Marts and Lundy, a professional fund-raising firm. The following program was recommended and agreed upon according to priority:

- new dormitory (Havemeyer)
- a new gymnasium
- a new residence for the headmaster
- a combination classroom and auditorium (Hume)
- a second dormitory (Carmody)

The trustees had wanted to set aside some of the drive money for endowment after the building costs had been met, but yearly and marked increases in these costs ultimately would not allow this position.

The success of the drive was evident in the new Havemeyer House, a dormitory housing forty boys and containing apartments for two masters and families. On the graduation day on which Havemeyer House was dedicated, ground was broken for the new gymnasium. Mr. Brodie had the honor of turning over the first spadeful of dirt, because of his many years of service in coaching athletic teams. Construction progressed apace, and the following February, Canterbury played its first basketball game on its new floor. One feature of this new building was the donation by the Briggs family—Walter O. Briggs Jr. '30 and his three sons, Walter O. III '52, Basil M. '54, and James R. '56—of a large lounge for after-game teas, small dances, and social gatherings. It was named the Brodie Room, and Mr. Brodie's portrait, painted at the time of his retirement as a gift of the trustees, hangs on the south wall.

The completion of the gymnasium brought to within two buildings the fulfillment of the expansion program. The second-to-the-last building, the lack of which the School had felt keenly through the years, was begun in the summer of 1966. It was a new classroom building, named in honor of Dr. Nelson Hume. Perhaps most gratifying was the fact that it contained a 400-seat theater for dramatics, school meetings, and general gatherings. The Hume Building also contained the School's first room dedicated to art, Room 207.[359] During the Homecoming ceremonies on September 30, 1967,[360] Father Quinn, Canterbury's first resident chaplain, came back to officially dedicate Nelson Hume Hall.[361]

Not quite a month later, ground was broken for a new dorm, to be called the Francis T. Carmody dormitory. When Francis was enrolled at Yale, he shared living quarters with James Cox Brady, Peter Folger, and Paul Mellon. Later, when Carmody was president of the Board, he approached Mr. Mellon to help establish a

retirement fund for faculty. Mr. Mellon was happy to do so, provided the source remained anonymous. As an alumnus of Choate,
Mr. Mellon did not want any conflict of interest. Later, when it was
time to solicit funds for the new dormitory, Canterbury
approached Mr. Mellon again. In an astounding act of generosity
and as a testament to his old friend, Paul Mellon made the largest
single donation received at Canterbury up to that point.[362] "On
Saturday, October 5, 1968, at 11:15 A.M., the formal blessing and
dedication of Carmody House took place. Edward T. Carmody
'22 was at Canterbury to make the address to the assembled parents and alumni. Father Greenan performed the blessing of the
new building."[363]

The construction of Carmody completed the building program of the previous five years. "The new gymnasium, Mr.
Sheehan's present residence, Nelson Hume Hall, with its fine laboratory and auditorium facilities, and Havemeyer Hall are the
other four buildings that have been erected under this program."[364]
This would be the last major construction until 1983, when ground
was broken to build Steele Hall. Because the Hume Building
became the new classroom building, the Schoolhouse gradually
became known as the Old Schoolhouse.

Beyond this construction, the headmaster had another project
that came to the forefront at this time. There was increasing need
for more playing space and better grounds to accommodate the
rising interest in soccer and a need for a permanent home for the
track and field team,. Mr. Sheehan had a visionary plan for the
apple orchard, which, over the years, had grown old and neglected. During Nelson Hume's tenure, the fruits of the apple orchard
had contributed to the dining hall and to afternoon tea, as reported in a 1926 issue of *The Tabard*: "A call was sent for all the boys
who were not on the football team to help in the picking of apples.
With the aid of these boys, twenty barrels were filled. Two of these

barrels have been pressed into cider and are being enjoyed by the boys each afternoon after football practice is over."[365]

Walter Sheehan had the apple orchard bulldozed out of existence, and had the land graded to form playing fields. Within the track was the new football field, and to the west was the baseball diamond, laid out by the engineers for the Detroit Tigers, through the cooperation of Mr. Walter O. Briggs Jr. '30, the former owner of the Detroit Tigers. West of the baseball diamond was the new soccer field. Since it was developed in a depression between the old football field and the road, the surrounding grassy banks were vantage points from which to watch baseball on one side and football on the other. Still more playing and practice space was located to the east of the old field, and new tennis courts were built close to those donated by Donald Appenzellar '30.

The Fiftieth Anniversary and Beyond

Throughout the 1960s and into the 1970s, *The Tabard* regularly featured reports of the war in Vietnam and contained editorials reflecting both sides of the United States' involvement. Generally, as the war progressed, the feeling of protest grew stronger among the student body. With Paul Salembier as editor-in-chief, William Randolph Hearst III '67, scion of the famous publishing family, started as a staff reporter for *The Tabard*, rising to associate editor by 1967. For the first time, Form reporters were also appointed to *The Tabard* staff. The first issue of the 1965 school year headlined the fiftieth anniversary of Canterbury, which was kicked off with Homecoming festivities on October 16. More than two hundred alumni, parents, and friends returned for the ceremonies.

Three hundred attendees came to Canterbury's campus for a fiftieth anniversary three-day symposium on "The Christian Humanist in an Age of Technology," while the students were on their spring break in 1966. Bishop John J. Wright of Pittsburgh delivered the keynote address, with eight speakers representing theologians, philosophers, historians, businessmen, and clerics.[366]

The culmination of the fiftieth celebration year occurred on May 2, as eight hundred members of the Canterbury family gathered at the Waldorf-Astoria Hotel in NYC for dinner. Cardinal Spellman gave the invocation, and the president of the Board of Trustees, Mr. Donal McDonnell '39,[367] extended the welcome. Deerfield's Headmaster Frank Boyden, a longtime friend and associate of Mr. Sheehan, was guest speaker.[368] *The Tabard* relates a story regarding the chalice sent to Rome in the weeks preceding the dinner:

> Shortly before noon on May 2, Monsignor Ahern called Mr. Haire and told him that the Papal Secretary of State had cabled special Papal blessings, which the Cardinal would read at the dinner. While Mr. Haire was waiting to escort the Cardinal to the Waldorf the evening of the dinner, he heard the doorbell ring. The housekeeper answered it and Mr. Haire heard her call to Monsignor Ahern: "There is a man down here with a box for His Eminence." The Monsignor came down immediately, opened the letter that came with the box, and turning to Mr. Haire said, "Here is the Canterbury chalice. It left Rome this morning and came in from the airport by special messenger." The Monsignor himself was startled to read in the letter that His Holiness Pope Paul VI had used the chalice that very morning in saying a private Mass.[369]

At graduation that year, Mr. Sheehan inaugurated the Carmody awards. The Carmody graduation prizes recognized achievement in the arts and other creative pursuits at Canterbury. In 1966, the headmaster awarded two first prizes: one in poetry and one for the short story.

> Mr. Carmody, a graduate of Canterbury, class of 1925, and of Yale, was very interested in literature. He was the

head of The DeVere Association, an organization which attempts to prove that DeVere, Earl of Oxford, wrote the works attributed to William Shakespeare. His friends, knowing how devoted Mr. Carmody was to literature, felt that these awards would preserve the memory of his interest while stimulating the creative ability of Canterbury students.[370]

One day during the summer of 1966, Mrs. Gilda Martin, then a teacher in the New Milford public school system, received a telephone call from Walter Sheehan. Although Walter Sheehan and his wife, Lynn, knew Gilda's in-laws and socialized with them, Gilda was surprised that Walter would be calling her.

"How do you feel about teaching boys?" he asked. Jean Hebert had highly recommended Gilda's skills as a teacher and Walter was confident of Gilda's character.

Thus began another long and fruitful Canterbury partnership. Although there had been one or two part-time female faculty members at Canterbury, Mrs. Gilda Martin was the first full-time female faculty member hired. Among the many peculiarities associated with having a woman on the faculty was Mr. Sheehan's admonishment, "Gilda, you *will* stay out of the boys' locker room."

Señora Martin ran a tight ship. At 8:00 A.M. on the dot, Señora locked the door to her classroom. Anyone arriving after she locked the door had to produce a note and an apology. A garish necktie and equally garish jacket hung in the closet in the back of the classroom for any boy foolish enough to come to class out of dress code. The boys adjusted quickly to having a female teacher, but were unsure of how to address her. Frequently, they would address Gilda as "Sir," because that was what they were used to. Even the headmaster had difficulty addressing the faculty with its new female member. As she sat in her favorite spot in the back row, Gilda remembers Walter Sheehan addressing the faculty as

"Gentlemen." It was a long time before he addressed the faculty as "Gentlemen and Gilda."[371]

September 1966 brought the acquisition of a General Electric computer terminal directly coupled to a mainframe located in Valley Forge, Pennsylvania. "By telephone to Bridgeport, Connecticut, one could hook up to this large computer for an hourly rate of $30, not including the monthly fee for the terminal itself."[372] After renting a computer at the cost of $3,000 per year, the School made the jump to enter the technological age by purchasing a new computer system, the digital PDP8, for the cost of approximately $11,000.[373] This was the first real introduction to computing at Canterbury. To help promote use of the computer, Mr. Paul Cauchon inaugurated a Saturday morning class in the study of the FORTRAN programming language. Nine brave students enrolled in the five-week course. Mr. Cauchon had started teaching at Canterbury in 1962. After graduation from Providence College with a degree in chemistry, Mr. Cauchon had joined the Marines and saw active duty in Europe during the Korean War. While in the Marines, Paul helped develop and design the computer-training center in Norfolk, Virginia.[374]

There were many educational and entertaining programs offered at Canterbury during this era. Several students traveled with Mr. Cauchon to MIT for a seminar on laser technology. Jimmy Breslin spoke at the fall sports banquet, and baritone Gilbert Price performed musical selections for the Canterbury community. In late spring, through the auspices of Paul Hanly '69 and his grandfather, Mr. Kenny, Canterbury hosted a performance of the vocal group The Four Seasons. This performance and the Gilbert Price concert were both benefits to raise money for the African Project, led by Father Michael Duffy '51, a Maryknoll priest then stationed in Tanzania. Father Duffy had requested funds for the purchase of a tractor, and the proceeds from the two fund-raising events netted close to $2,100. The students of Canterbury were able to meet Father Duffy's need and purchase the tractor.

During the mid-1960s, faculty member Jim Shea started a lecture series on world affairs for the edification of the student body, and clubs remained active on campus as well. The Art and Architecture Club, in its second year under Mrs. Briggs, helped design sets for the theater as well as completing various other projects. The Choral Club continued to grow, and listed as its accomplishments the making of two records and a local broadcast of a recital by Danbury radio station, WLAD.[375] Continuing the work of reporting sports scores to local newspapers was Mike Meserole '68 as the newly appointed head of the Press Club. While it was a quiet year overall for Canterbury's sports teams, the varsity swimmers did garner their third consecutive Connecticut Independent School Swim Association award (formerly known as the Connecticut Preparatory School Swim Association).

In the spring of 1965, the Canterbury Mission Society came into being. Its primary goal was to promote the spirit of Christian living by urging Canterbury students to give of their time and money to help others who are less fortunate. To raise money for the needy, the Mission Society sponsored a bake sale in the late spring. Baked goods and other food items were auctioned off to the students. Mrs. Weldon Knox's Vintage Vanilla Cake raised the most money for a single item, with the winner paying $26. A full lasagna dinner in the home of Mr. Roberts sold to six juniors for $100. Faculty children also contributed. Mary Kate Shea baked oatmeal cookies, and the Martiska children offered Rice Krispy Squares for sale.[376]

That spring, William F. Buckley, editor of *The National Review*, spoke on campus through the generosity of the Hearst family. Mr. Frank Conniff, father of Mike '72 and a Pulitzer Prize–winning news correspondent, also gave a lecture for the upper-form students that year on Vietnam and the communist threat. Paul Salembier '66 published an interview with then Governor Nelson A. Rockefeller, which appeared in the issue of *The Tabard* published on March 11, 1966.

Every so often an event comes along that is so rare and special, it is remembered and talked about long afterward. Such was the graduation-night performance of *A Man for All Seasons*. Directed by William D'Alton, *Man* will surely hold a place with the 1921 production of *A Midsummer Night's Dream*. The play was the first one performed in the brand-new Maguire Auditorium of Nelson Hume Hall, and it was the first Canterbury production in which girls filled the women's roles. Female students from New Milford High School had been invited to audition for these parts. The cast of *A Man for All Seasons* featured some of the best and brightest in Canterbury's history. Paul Tucker '68, a Fifth Former, received one of the drama awards, usually reserved for Sixth Form students, for his portrayal of The Common Man. William Hearst played the part of Sir Thomas More, while Patrick Tokarz '67, Christopher Doyle '67, and others rounded out the cast. The three girls selected from New Milford High School were Shelley Lang, Mary Douglas, and Chris Coffin, daughter of Mr. and Mrs. John Coffin.

Paul Tucker returned to the stage in the Christmastime production of *The Man Who Came to Dinner*. Later in the winter, both Paul Tucker and Mike Burgess were invited to participate in Kent School's First Annual Drama Festival. Both boys won citations for their performances, although the play, *Bound East for Cardiff*, did not win a prize. Paul earned the Hume Award at his graduation for his many achievements.[377]

On September 9, 1967, The Equestrian Order of the Holy Sepulchre invested Mr. and Mrs. Sheehan into their order. The ceremony took place at Saint Patrick's Cathedral in New York City, officiated by His Eminence, Francis Cardinal Spellman. This Papal Order dates back to the Crusades, when men were rewarded for their defense of the faith.[378]

Peter Bordonaro and Don Roberts joined the faculty in 1967, while Jim Breene became the new development director. Ed Mack, retired from teaching since 1957, debuted his musical *Rip Van Winkle* at the New Milford High School in October. A contingent of Choral Club and other interested students attended the premiere.

Varsity football enjoyed its best season in eleven years with a finishing record of 6-1. The only loss came in the final game of the season, against rival Trinity-Pawling. Although Paul Hanly '69 and Peter O'Donnell '70 played good defense, they were unable to come up with a win for an undefeated season. *A Tabard* editorial noted, however, that the sportsmanship displayed by the Canterbury boys was exemplary. Despite a promising outlook for the spring season, varsity tennis ended with a 6-4 record. The team was headed by Captain Alex Fanjul '69. Fourth Former Bob Steers '71 managed to garner a top spot on the team. The spring teams of golf and track had one of their best seasons. Finishing with a record of 11-2, a highlight of the season occurred on May 24, when Third Former Bobby Steele '72 played a 71-stroke round against The Gunnery, with two eagles and a birdie. Although they didn't end with a winning season, varsity track set new records in the mile, half-mile, and discus, and placed third in the Quads.[379]

The spring of 1969 brought two Canterbury alumni back to speak to the student body. Bob Giegengack '56, then assistant professor of geology at the University of Pennsylvania, returned to speak to the student body on the study of geology. Sargent Shriver '34 spoke to the students about his newly appointed position as U.S. Ambassador to France, a post he would hold until 1970. Ambassador Shriver was appointed director of the Peace Corps in early 1961. "An effective head of this organization, he was named in 1964 director of the Office of Economic Opportunity (OEO) by President Lyndon B. Johnson and held both posts until 1966, when he resigned from the Peace Corps to devote himself to OEO . . . [H]e became George McGovern's vice-presidential running mate in 1972, after Thomas Eagleton withdrew from the Democratic ticket. McGovern and Shriver were defeated."[380]

Editors announced the new heads of school publications in the spring. The new editors and staff were responsible for finishing the year's publications. A record six students left campus to complete senior projects in 1969, mainly from *The Tabard* and *Cantuarian* staffs. Rory Nugent received a promotion to editor-in-chief of *The Tabard*.[381]

Following the general mood in the country, several changes were made to both the Canterbury curriculum and the School's privilege system for the 1969–1970 school year. More electives were offered, including half-year courses in theology, such as "Introduction to Philosophy," "Existentialism," and "Love, Sex, and Morals." The Student Council elected to open their meetings to all students. Mr. Sheehan loosened restrictions on downtown visits, and, in one of the most welcome changes, breakfast became cafeteria-style instead of a sit-down meal. Instead of waiting in the common room for everyone to arrive before sitting down to breakfast, students were free to come and go during the allotted breakfast time.[382]

Other minor changes were taking place on campus as well. The director of studies made several scheduling modifications to the curriculum. In place of a mandatory Saturday-morning study hall, students had the option of participating in various activities. Janet Huntington offered a class in typing, Gerry Vanasse offered music appreciation, and members of the history department joined to offered a current events class.[383] Other changes included altering the daily schedule to give the students a greater block of free time in the afternoon. Breakfast began ten minutes earlier, and lunch was shortened to allow for an extended mid-morning break. This change in the daily schedule also allowed students a forty-five-minute break between classes, and sports in the afternoon.[384]

The dining hall and kitchen had been experiencing growing pains due to the increased enrollment throughout the 1960s. A student-led walkout during the 1968–1969 school year was designed to call attention to the need for modernization in the kitchen. The walkout brought the situation to a head, and significant renovations were soon made to both the kitchen and to the library in the Old Schoolhouse. A new dishwasher, steam tables, and new refrigeration facilities were added. Displeasure with the meal offerings continued, however, so a food committee consisting of several students and faculty members was formed to address these concerns. Although acceptable by institutional food standards, the quality of the food in no way matched the early days, when Dr. Hume had insisted on top quality in the dining hall. The dining service agreed to replace cornflakes with a more palatable breakfast cereal, and to offer French fries or hash browns as a supplement to meals of "dubious edibility" (such as corned beef and cabbage).[385] An International Week created more variety in the food offerings for the students. The dining hall offered theme dinners such as "Soul Food Night" or "Italian Night" twice a month.

In an unusual move, Mr. Sheehan appointed two head proctors in 1969–1970: Rory Nugent and Steve Van Schoyck. Nugent and Van Schoyck alternated their responsibilities, with Nugent acting as head proctor for the first half of the year, and Van Schoyck the latter. They also switched their responsibilities as representatives on the Student Council. In another unusual move, six boys in the class of 1970—Bruce Dominick Angiolillo, Edward James Calhoun Jr., Roger Pierre Kavanagh III, James Peter O'Donnell,

Rory Nugent, and Steve Van Schoyck—received Hume Awards upon graduating.

Charlie Huntington from Williams College joined the faculty, and in the spring, he introduced lacrosse as a sport at Canterbury. Although varsity soccer had a fairly mediocre season, the JV team under Coach Huntington was undefeated with a record of 5-0-1. Athletics in general fared well, if not in overall team records, than with strong individuals. Varsity wrestling had its best season in Canterbury history and earned third place in the state competitions. James Peter O'Donnell, captain of both the football and the wrestling teams, scored impressive victories. In track, Greg Coleman '72 took first place in the pole vault, clearing 9'6".[386] Chappy LeBlond had a great season on both the football and wrestling teams as well, and earned a reputation as a very versatile player.[387]

During the athletic banquet held the night before graduation, Chappy LeBlond won an award for "most remarkable achievement," as he went on to become the National Prep School Champion in wrestling, while Peter O'Donnell won a leadership award.[388] In the spring, the baseball, track, and tennis teams had winning seasons. Three-year varsity tennis player Bob Steers became captain of the 1971 team. Baseball finished second in the league, which was its best finish in eight years. Under the leadership of Coach Walter Burke, the track team won the Quads by one point. Throughout the early 1970s, the school enjoyed continued good sports records, especially in the winter sports. Opponents knew Bob Steele for his backcourt speed and agility in basketball; wrestling enjoyed its second undefeated season in a row; and hockey celebrated its best season in six years. Soccer also enjoyed one of its finest seasons, and, in the spring of 1972, Greg Coleman cleared 12'2" in pole-vaulting for track.[389]

Possibly the biggest change to come to Canterbury in the

1970s was the decision to go coeducational. "America was experiencing the first strong wave of modern feminism . . . [t]he coeducation movement of the early '70s had a financial impetus, but it probably would not have occurred without the spadework done by Freidan and her cohorts."[390] Mr. Sheehan had announced in early October 1968 that he had invited eight girls from the Sacred Heart School in Noroton to spend a week at Canterbury in a reciprocal program. He hastened to explain that this would not be a first step in becoming coed, although many felt this would be inevitable.[391]

On Friday, October 30, 1970, Mr. Sheehan announced at lunch that Canterbury would become a coed school.[392] Thus, in the fall of 1971, Canterbury admitted nine girls as day students. The first nine girls to attend Canterbury were Terry D'Alton '73, Gail Erwin, Valerie Gumpper '74, Sarah Huntington '75, Sarah Krieger, Lizette Michelman '74, Judy Sullivan '74, Anne Wagenbrenner '73, and Vicky Weill '74. Surprisingly little appears in *The Tabards* issued during the 1971–1972 school year regarding this major move, perhaps because having the girls from the Sacred Heart School in the previous two years had already somewhat accustomed the boys to the presence of girls on campus. Once this step was taken, however, there was no going back. Appearing in *The Tabard* of February 12, 1972, was the announcement that boarding girls would be accepted in the fall of 1972, and would live in the Havemeyer dormitory.

Valerie Gumpper '74 pointed out some of the difficulties the administration faced with this development: "We fit easily into the academic program; that is no problem. Aside from that, what are they to do with us? There is no sports program for girls . . . [a]s day students, we are sometimes unable to join in evening activities."[393] An article in *The Pallium* discussed further changes made to the school during the transition phase:

> When girls became boarders in 1972, washers and dryers
> were installed in their dorm, Havemeyer, whereas boys had

to wait until 1981 before they could do their own laundry on campus. Also in 1972, Kim Smith was hired as a boarding female faculty member. She was housed in two dorm rooms in Havemeyer, and she shared the bathroom with girls on the hall. Girls' soccer, basketball, and lacrosse were added to the athletic program. Little in the curriculum changed in those first years, although when Betsy Conley was hired in 1973, she taught a course in women's literature.[394]

Sarah Huntington '75 said, "Looking back I think the male students adapted to us more easily than did the faculty. Our presence upset the chemistry of the school; we kept having to be accommodated."[395]

Mrs. Sheehan had her own thoughts about what the girls would wear and how they should behave, which she communicated to Mrs. Martin through Mr. Sheehan. Administration and faculty had to grapple with defining new rules for dress code, dormitory visitation, and appropriate language. The school prepared a small lounge area in the Old Schoolhouse to serve as the girls' separate common room. Ever conscious of the comfort and tastes of the girls, Mrs. Sheehan decreed the room should be painted a salmon color. Years later it came out that the girls never really liked the color, which they came to associate with their confinement and sense of not really fitting in with the life of the School.

Of equal import to the Canterbury community during this time was the announcement in the fall of 1972 that headmaster Walter Sheehan planned to retire after twenty-five years of service.[396] Earlier, in the spring of 1971, before entering the hospital for hip replacement surgery, Mr. Sheehan had appointed Mr. James Breene as assistant and acting headmaster.[397] Stories told by longtime faculty members related that Walter Sheehan had strongly espoused the traditional concept of the single-sex preparatory school, vowing he would retire when Canterbury became coeducational. Despite these feelings, Sheehan realized that financially, the Board felt the School could only survive by going coeducational, especially since many schools with profiles similar to Canterbury's were going coed. In an interview in *The Tabard* of October 21, 1972, Sheehan ". . . reported that he has long held the belief that the final years of his service to the school should be devoted to the task of solidifying Canterbury's positions financially . . . [a]s a result of his decision . . . the Board of Trustees on October 11 elected him President of the Corporation, to be in charge of fund-raising and development."[398]

The new headmaster, Canterbury's third, would be Mr. John Reydel. His appointment was announced to the student body in the early spring of 1973.[399] Later that same spring, Mr. James Breene announced his acceptance as headmaster of the Country Day School of the Sacred Heart at Overbrook, Pennsylvania.[400] Jean Hebert, the last faculty member hired by Dr. Nelson Hume, celebrated his twenty-fifth anniversary at Canterbury.[401] Although not leaving, Mr. Weldon Knox announced his intention to teach only one section of mathematics instead of his typical four.[402] Philip Brodie celebrated fifty years of service to Canterbury in December 1969, as some two hundred alumni, parents, and faculty gathered in New York to view the performance of *Goodbye, Mr. Chips*, and pay tribute to the seventy-seven-year-old Mr. Chips of Canterbury.[403]

As reported in the *Pallium*, "During his 25-year career as Canterbury's second headmaster, Walter F. Sheehan oversaw the school's greatest period of expansion and left an indelible imprint on the school he loved." The *Pallium* would report this bittersweet news: "Ironically, the day of Mr. Sheehan's death, October 23, [1993], coincided with the annual battle for the Sheehan Cup. Canterbury prevailed on the day and retained the trophy it had captured the year before."[405]

No longer will we hear Mr. Sheehan's hearty "How goes the battles!", his conclusive "Carry on!", or his favorite valediction, "Peace!" He strove mightily indeed for the faith handed down to the saints, just as he devoted himself to his "boys" and "girls," for the "saints" of Canterbury School.[406]

Canterbury's second headmaster, Walter Sheehan, and his wife, Lynn.

Walter Sheehan exhorting the student body to turn the corner.

Jean Hebert, known by faculty and students alike as The Bear, relaxing after teaching "the troops."

Bill D'Alton illustrating a point in English literature.

After a fruitful career as superintendent of the New Milford Schools, Weldon Knox "retired" to teach and tutor math for another thirty years at Canterbury.

Former Assistant Headmaster Jim Breene speaking at the Canterbury medal dinner honoring Jim Shea. Fall 1999

John Martiska, fondly and mysteriously called Rock, held more positions on the faculty than did anyone else.

Dinner in the North House dining hall. John Martiska is visible in the lower left corner. The picture of George Washington, given to the school in 1937 by F. Luis Mora, hangs in the background.

A late 1950s view of students going to chapel; the chapel addition was built shortly thereafter, in 1960.

Interior view of the Chapel of Our Lady, c. 1959.

A 1949 picture of the gym; the facility was expanded in the mid-1960s.

Gerry Vanasse, a member of the Foreign Language Department for thirty-eight years, in the Steele Hall Business Office.

Students busily working in the Old Schoolhouse library, c. 1959.

Groundbreaking for Havemeyer House, May 11, 1963. The headmaster's house is in the background.

Named in honor of Dr. Nelson Hume, the new classroom building contained a 400-seat theater for dramatics, school meetings, and general gatherings. The Hume building also contained the School's first room dedicated to art, Room 207.

Portrait of Nelson Hume, which hangs in the entrance to the Hume Building. May Hume was present for the dedication of the building.

1967 photograph of Maguire Auditorium in the newly opened Hume Building. The main-stage curtain was finally replaced in the fall of 2005.

Carmody House, and its twin, Havemeyer House, were built in the mid-1960s. The first boarding girls were housed in Carmody.

Even after his retirement, Phil Brodie remained a fixture on campus.

Fiftieth anniversary celebration. Frank Boyden, former Deerfield headmaster and friend of Walter Sheehan, at the podium. Walter Sheehan is to his left.

Walter Sheehan receiving a chalice from Cardinal Spellman on the occasion of Canterbury's fiftieth anniversary. The chalice was flown in that morning from Rome, where the Pope Paul VI had blessed and used the chalice that very morning in a private mass.

Señora Gilda Martin, first full-time female faculty member. Gilda joined the faculty in the fall of 1966.

Sargent Shriver '34, center, flanked by two of his former teachers, Phil Brodie and Ed Mack.

A 1970 aerial view of the campus looking northeast.

The first girls to attend
Canterbury: Vicky Weill '74, seat-
ed left; Sarah Krieger, standing
center; Anne Wagenbrenner '73,
seated right. Up in tree: Sarah
Huntington '75 and Valerie
Gumpper '74. Not pictured:
Lizette Michelman '74, Judy
Sullivan '74, Terry D'Alton '73,
and Gail Erwin.

3

THE LONG LOOK BACKWARDS[407]

> . . . *as I cast my eyes,*
> *I see what was, and is, and will abide;*
> *Still glides the Stream, and shall forever glide;*
> *The Form remains, the Function never dies.*
> *—Wordsworth*

Walter Sheehan's retirement and the beginning of coeducation at Canterbury make a fitting divide between the old and the new. It seems appropriate at this point to include, verbatim, Edward Mack's closing pages from his Canterbury history, part of the School's archives:

> The vista of Canterbury, looking backward, is suggestive of a medieval painting, where, in the foreground, loom the subject personalities, and the background brings into perspective the charming minutiae and previous trivia, the distant detail, in exquisite miniature, of the dramatic scenery through which the principals have found their ways to the foreground of the canvas.
>
> One brings into view personalities—innocently important in the greenness of salad days at school, later to be famed, even historic figures. One remembers little Jack Kennedy, seated at one's table, a shock of auburn hair, a Boston accent, highly reserved and somewhat on the defen-

sive, not quite certain of himself, a future President of the United States, who spent a fleeting eight months within the atmosphere of Canterbury.

One is in Chapel, and the virtuoso quartet from St. Patrick's Cathedral is singing the Requiem Mass for Alec Hume, and one hears, before the Mass begins, the sotto voce warning of Maestro Pietro Yon to his artists: "You will watch even the lift of my eyebrow!" And minutes later, Dr. Hume, shading his eyes against the blizzard blowing through the open door of the Sacristy, as he tolls the "De Profundis" bell for his brother's last departure from Canterbury.

And one remembers the graceful old Middle House—old Weantinaug Hall—hidden in a massive shroud of black smoke, then suddenly bursting into cataclysmic flame, and one hour later one sees rubble, ruin, and the stark skeleton bones of chimneys.

One is again in Chapel, and the Choral Club, with sorrowed and anxious faces, singing the Requiem for Dr. Hume as he lies beneath a great pall in the midst of all that was his life and his dream.

Now we are in School, and there is a pot-bellied stove for warmth and a portable blackboard in a temporary Schoolhouse, with boys taking a novelty for what it was and getting on with the daily job at Canterbury.

Or we can see the boys gathering for morning prayers in the main hall of Mrs. Black's "Hickory Hearth," when that staid old residence served as a schoolhouse following the last fire.

Or a faculty skating party on a brisk winter night, with Dr. and Mrs. Hume gathering the flock afterwards for something warm to eat and drink.

Or the annual intramural track meet on Memorial Day and in the midst of events, Dr. Hume racing up the drive in his Buick, with Mrs. Hume en route to the hospital and to the reception into the world of Rozanne.

Or Big Tony, muffled out of sight, pushing mountains of snow with his plow.

Or dozens of pretty girls and happy boys in summer formals jewelling the hillside near the Chapel in the soft evening light, while Kamiel Lefevere evokes magic from the beautiful bells of the carillon.

Or in a great scene on the old athletic field, with vast tents and thousands of Canterbury people eating lunch at the great Homecoming in October 1965; in reunion, in reminiscence, in happy abandon as Canterbury begins to celebrate her Fiftieth Year.

Or in March 1965, in the shining new gymnasium, a symposium of Catholic and Christian thought striving, in a distraught world, to maintain the integrity and the significance of Christian intellectualism, probing the profundities of "The Christian Humanist in an Age of Technology."

Or a final remembrance of the Fiftieth Anniversary Celebration: the ballroom of The Waldorf-Astoria on the evening of May 2, 1966, when over eight hundred Cantuarians gathered at dinner to bring to a close the Anniversary Celebration; Mr. Frank Boyden, as a guest speaker, commenting humorously on preparatory school life; Father Campbell, the new President of Georgetown, speaking on the challenges in education today; Cardinal Spellman presenting to Mr. Sheehan, for the School, the Chalice consecrated and used by Pope Paul that morning and flown that day from Rome; the choice decorations by Mrs. Thomas B. Haire and her Committee; the *élan* of the occasion.

And back at School, one remembers the pageantry of Archbishop O'Brien's rededication of the Chapel;

The Thanksgiving Dances of long ago, the Tea Dances with girls' schools—dances for the awkward and the agile; Club Night in the cozy Common Room of the old Middle House, with a bright fire burning and the boys gathered around the grand piano;

Ernesto, the tall Filipino, who presided over the Dining Room for so many years with the gravity of a Prime Minister and the deportment of an English butler;

A procession of buses going down the hill in the golden autumn en route to a football game, with snatches of song and the smell of burning leaves;

One remembers—one remembers . . .

Fifty years of Canterbury have been fifty years of interest and profit. An educational institution is a collective effort, and one applies obvious and simple criteria for evaluation. It is successful, in the primary sense, if it accomplishes its mission. Canterbury's mission has been the historic, twofold one of the Christian school based upon the principle that education is inseparable from religion. Canterbury, in its constant adherence, scholastically, to the academic college preparatory program, has never lost sight of the overall belief that the primary end of all education— using the latter term in its absolute sense—is to mold the human being into the intellectual and spiritual likeness of God. In this concept, it is one with all Catholic schools. To the extent to which faltering humans can succeed in any quest, Canterbury hopes that it has succeeded. It has given to some twelve hundred alumni an orthodox notion of the relationship of education to religion. It has fulfilled its mission in meeting the academic standards established by the prestige colleges of the United States. It has demonstrated to nearly three generations the dignified balance that should be maintained in all the various activities of school life as a guide for such balance of activities in more mature life.

4

THE REYDEL YEARS

John Reydel, Third Headmaster

On February 1, 1973, Mr. Sheehan announced to students and faculty that John Reydel would be his replacement, and would serve as the third headmaster at Canterbury. John Reydel came to Canterbury from the Lawrenceville School in New Jersey, where he had served since 1956 in various capacities, including housemaster, varsity football coach, and chairman of the history department. A native of New Jersey, John Reydel graduated from Princeton University in 1951. In a letter to the Connecticut State Department of Education, Walter Sheehan wrote, "As you can see, he is a very impressive individual, and since we felt that we ought to go outside, I cannot think of a better man on the basis of his combination of scholarship, athletic ability, and administrative skill."[408]

Partly as a result of the times and partly because of personality differences in the two men, the Reydel administration was less formal than Walter Sheehan's. Jack Reydel was headmaster during an era when faculty were more apt to criticize and question.[409] One

of his first acts as headmaster was to grant amnesty to any student
currently on disciplinary probation, which raised eyebrows among
the older faculty.[410] While Walter Sheehan believed in firm deci-
sion-making at the top, Jack Reydel was more of a consensus
builder. Jack Reydel's opening remarks to the faculty conveyed a
sense of cautiousness not evident under Walter Sheehan. Mr.
Reydel's vision of education was somewhat based on the Outward
Bound philosophy, in that he believed students should find qualities in themselves that they didn't know they had. One important
trait he hoped to foster in the students was pride in themselves and
in their school. In the opening month of school, he wrote:

> We open our football schedule this Saturday with a
> young but untested coaching staff and with a squad of play-
> ers who have seen Canterbury win only three games in
> three years, so we really have no place to go but up. What
> we need is some kind of a psychological breakthrough to get
> our kids to believe in themselves.[411]

Jack Reydel stated that he would be more than happy—
indeed, he would love—for the students to wear their Canterbury
shirts at all times.[412] Within a month, Canterbury students would
receive their psychological boost by beating undefeated Cranwell
on Parents' Day, followed by another win over Westminster during
their Parents' Weekend. Enthusiasm and school spirit was high,
and Jack made sure to mention the wins in fund-raising letters, and
in his first report to the Board of Trustees.[413]

Jack came to Canterbury with his wife, Bradley, and their two
children, Amy and JJ. Along with her daughter, Amy, Bradley
Reydel helped coach the girls' soccer team. The Reydels also
organized a Pee Wee Soccer Program for the community, in which
Canterbury soccer players coached the community participants on
School fields.

Mr. Reydel expanded the faculty's retirement fund from a
small private endowment to TIAA-CREF. Walter Sheehan had

always liked to do things his own way, choosing to avoid involvement with larger organizations. Jack Reydel recognized the benefits of an outside-managed retirement program and brought TIAA to Canterbury, which continues as the School's retirement plan today.[414]

John J. Reydel's appointment as headmaster coincided with the second major fund drive of the School's history, the purpose of which was to increase the School's endowment. The drive kicked off on Friday, October 26, 1973, with a dinner for one hundred alumni, parents, and friends. Long-standing Board member, Mr. Guerin Carmody '28, son of Terence F. Carmody, served as toast-master for the dinner.[415] Although retired from his administrative duties, Walter Sheehan still remained very much a part of the School as director of the fund-raising effort.

As early as December 1973, Mr. Reydel and his wife planned some travel with Mr. and Mrs. Sheehan to assist in the campaign drive. The travel was mostly local, with trips to the New York and Boston areas.[416] Mr. Sheehan, as director of the drive, had two able assistants in Gerard C. Smith '31, national campaign chairman, and John Whelon, Archbishop of Hartford, as honorary chair-man. The School was most fortunate in that Peter Cashman '55, lieutenant governor of Connecticut, was willing to handle the leadership solicitation for the fund drive. Mr. Cashman had a long association with Canterbury. A graduate of the School and of Yale University, Mr. Cashman taught from 1959 to 1963 before taking the position as director of development for the school year 1963–1964. Politics eventually drew Mr. Cashman away, and in 1970, he won a state senate seat. Peter would remain involved with the School, however, and ultimately returned to serve on the Board of Trustees.[417]

In addition to increasing the School's endowment, Mr. Reydel announced plans to build an addition to the gym for the girls, to construct a new hockey rink, and to renovate the older dormitories. Because the dormitories were built when boys all showered in the gym, showering facilities were inadequate. Even in the new girls' dormitory, the girls shared four showers among thirty-eight girls.[418] The fund drive progressed slowly throughout 1974 and 1975. Economic uncertainty, particularly in the stock market, was to blame.[419]

In the fall of 1975, Canterbury's girls finally got their own locker room.[420] In a drive led by hockey coach Charlie Huntington, funds were raised for a new ice rink. Mr. Thomas F. Gilbane of Providence, Rhode Island, offered to build the rink at cost. In his letter to Mr. Gilbane, Mr. Reydel wrote, "Pride doesn't just happen—the kids have to learn it; but they must be well coached and have the support of the administration. From my point of view, that is what we hope to continue at Canterbury."[421]

At this point, pledges and gifts totaling more than $250,000 had accumulated.[422] The new ice rink opened on November 13, 1976, with the first varsity hockey game held on December 1. In the years preceding the opening of the rink, practices had been sporadic, dependent on ice availability[423]. Three times a week, coaches held practice at The Gunnery, if ice was available. Jean Hebert reminisces: "I've seen four rinks come and go: the rink behind South House, Conn's Pond, the Bleachery rink, and the gym rink."[424] Right from the beginning, Canterbury made the ice arena available to the community. Groups such as New Milford Youth Hockey used the rink, and the town of New Milford also used it for town-sponsored figure- and free-skating times.[425] This spirit of openness continues to this day, with many groups making use of ice time throughout the winter season. The new rink must have brought good luck to the hockey team. In the 1976–1977 season, varsity hockey finished with a 22-3 record. The Canterbury team shared the Connatonic League title with the The Gunnery.[426]

During the spring of 1977, Mr. Sheehan completed his retirement from Canterbury. After a twenty-nine-year affiliation with the school, Walter Sheehan stepped down from his position as fund drive director.[427] The school completed another piece of its fundraising objectives by sprucing up both North and South Houses. New carpeting was installed, as well as new plumbing and new boilers. Workers renovated the Brodie Room as a snack bar and lounge for the students.[428]

One of the biggest changes that Mr. Reydel brought to Canterbury School was the institution of Saturday classes. The new schedule began with the 1974–1975 school year, with classes held six days a week. Students had a full schedule on Monday, Tuesday, Thursday, and Friday; five classes were held on Wednesdays; and four classes on Saturdays. Despite initial grumblings expressed through *The Tabard*, by the end of the year, students had accepted, if not embraced, the concept of Saturday classes. In his final editorial in *The Tabard*, Sixth Former Gregory Kiernan '75 endorsed Saturday classes based on improved academic involvement, quicker intervention for those needing help, increased opportunities for extracurricular activities, and the greater participation of day students in activities. The drawbacks, then, as now, are that some sporting events, weekends for students, and special programs (such as the SATs) interfere with Saturday classes.[430]

The early to mid-1970s were a time of long lines at gas pumps and worry about decreasing supplies of oil. Concern about the energy situation led to a number of steps toward conservation at Canterbury. The dormitory heads lowered thermostats during the academic day, and the headmaster limited school trips. For the 1973–1974 school year, Mr. Reydel announced a revised school schedule. He extended the winter break an extra week, and the March break began a week earlier. School that year ended on June

8 instead of June 3, although graduation still took place on Wednesday, May 29.[431]

In keeping with the tenor of the '70s, a wide variety of courses and clubs sprang into being. In one of his first letters home to parents, Jack Reydel introduced new programs in wilderness, driver education, and a coeducational choral group.[432] A jug band, featuring Mr. Jean Paul Mandler on guitar and banjo, was popular, as well as a Sound Effects Club, sponsored by Mr. Bill D'Alton. The club's purpose was to create commercials.[433] Several students proposed a chemistry project involving turning grapes into wine.

> The idea was met with immediate enthusiasm . . . Jay Kuenzle and Walter Briggs were assigned the research aspect of the experiment, and Greg Kiernan was appointed the task of supplying the grapes . . . Jay gave a lengthy and somewhat involved report of the procedure with side help from Walter. Greg then brought up the desponding fact that wine grapes were out of season.[434]

Academic departments offered new courses covering subjects such as Sports Literature, Science Fiction, America Revolts, and The Virtuous Person.[435] They were later joined, or replaced by, Ecology (which included a five-day camping trip), The Study of Fantasy, and, in the theology department, Psychic Phenomena.[436] In 1975, John Martiska taught a half-year theology course, Examination of Moral Conduct.[437] Along more traditional academic lines, Jack Reydel established an honors-level American history course. He hoped that it would stretch the students, and lead to greater advanced placement testing scores.[438] A rival student newspaper, *The Spectrum*, appeared, while *The Tabard* carried a comic strip called "The Canterbury Kid," drawn by Walter von Egidy '77. Through the generosity of retired CBS sound engineer Hamilton O'Hara, Canterbury students produced and staged several radio broadcasts. On Halloween night, 1974, WINE, a Danbury radio station, broadcast the students' production of *Sorry, Wrong Number*, featuring Nicole Vanasse '75 and Stephanie D'Alton '76.[440]

Both the day student and the female populations continued to grow during this time. The 1974–1975 school year brought the largest enrollment to date in the School's history. On opening day the enrollment totaled 283 students: 205 boarding students and 78 day students.[441] Since 1967, day students had grown from representing less than 10 percent of the student body to almost 33 percent of the school's population.[442] Steve Reynolds '78 wrote an article in the November 20, 1976, issue of *The Tabard*, titled "Day Students Find a Home," describing the newest attempt to provide day students with a place to unwind—a common room located off the lobby of Hume, in what is now the dean of students' offices.

In a testament to the value of a Canterbury education, thirty-one members of the Sixth Form class in 1977 had relatives who were alumni of the school.[443] At the same time, students voiced dissatisfaction with a general lack of diversity on campus. A letter to the editor in *The Tabard* dated April 29, 1977, stated that there were no black females on campus, and recommended closer affiliation with A Better Chance (commonly referred to as ABC)[444] , a program administered out of New York City and dedicated to "recruiting, identifying and developing leaders among young people of color"[445] Enrollment in 1976 topped all records, with an opening student body numbering 323. This number would not be reached again for almost twenty years.[446]

The 1970s were a time for experimenting with Canterbury's rules and regulations. In a four-year period, from 1971 to 1975, "the dress code went from jackets and ties to a less rigid code and then back again."[447] Reydel tried a brief program of using Sixth Formers to proctor daytime study hall on a volunteer basis.[448] In addition, the Mission Society acted as a security force to watch over the pinball machines installed in the school store.[449] The

School's work program was once again resuscitated, under the supervision of Mr. Paul Cauchon. Work crews toiled forty-five minutes every day performing such jobs as kitchen and dining-hall cleanup, library duty, or vacuuming and cleaning the common rooms and dorms.[450]

Students also served on the welcome committee, which was responsible for four areas in the school: admissions, concert ushering, receptions at athletic teas, and office work.[451] Changes continued to be made to the school's disciplinary committee. The most long-awaited change was a shortening of the length of the meetings. When replying to the question of how long he had served as the head of [the] committee, Walter Burke wryly said, "Too long, but it's my only stepping-stone to the Supreme Court."[452]

There was a resurgence in sports during the Reydel years. Many teams during this time enjoyed winning or record-setting seasons. Wrestling and cross-country, in particular, enjoyed strong winning seasons. In 1973, a young Third Former by the name of Chris Adams finished first in seven out of eleven cross-country meets.[453] This same Third Former would come back eight years later as a teacher of Spanish and the cross-country coach. The following year, the cross-country team finished the season with a 15-0-1 dual meet record.[454]

That same winter, Canterbury held its first wrestling invitational, against Trinity-Pawling, The Gunnery, and Salisbury. Canterbury finished with three trophies, awarded to Bill O'Connor '75, Craig Neff '75, and Harmon Moats '75, presented by Mr. Gordon Lawson, father of Francis Gordon Lawson '68 and, in 1966, the founder of wrestling at Canterbury. Bill O'Connor would go on to win the state championship on February 22, in the 152-pound weight class at the Taft School. Canterbury would finish ninth out of seventeen.[456]

The fall season of the 1975–1976 school year was probably the athletic highlight of this time. Boys' varsity soccer finished 9-1-3, and was deemed one of the best in New England. The girls' team did equally well, and, in a notable match against Wilbraham-Monson, Stephanie D'Alton '76 set an overall record for scoring. Mary Kate Shea '77 and sisters Debbie O'Connor '79 and Sheila O'Connor Kuhn '76 assisted Stephanie. The cross-country team, with Chris Adams '77 and Gerry Vanasse '78, won the New Englands for the second consecutive year.[457] Chris Adams set a course record at Hopkins and broke the meet record at the Williston Invitational. Gerry set course records at Avon and The Gunnery. He became the first Saints' runner to break 14:00, with a time of 13:56.[458] Both young men traveled to Portland, Maine, to run in the Northeast Regional Junior Olympics, the qualifying race for the National Junior Olympic Championship, held in St. Louis, Missouri. Gerry Vanasse finished second in the fourteen-to-fifteen-year-old division, while Chris Adams finished seventh in the sixteen-to-seventeen-year-old division. In St. Louis, Gerry placed twenty-seven out of eighty-eight.[459] The following year, 1977, Canterbury again took the Cross-Country Invitational. In a field of eighty runners, four of the top five were Canterbury students, with Gerry leading the way.

On Sunday, April 28, 1974, four new tennis courts were dedicated, a gift of Mr. James A. Farrell Jr. of Darien in memory of his father, a member of the founding corporation in 1915. Mr. Farrell, president of Farrell Steamship Lines, was a trustee of Canterbury School and a member of the second class to graduate from Canterbury. Following the dedication, John F. Lowman (summer circuit, USLTA) and William Lofgren (teaching pro) played an exhibition match, umpired by Mr. Hugh Magoun of New Milford High School. Credit belonged to Jules Viau for arranging the day.[460]

Varsity basketball, led by Captain Bob O'Connor '76, finished with a record of 17-3. They were edged from the league championship with a loss to Avon by four points. Paul Daley was selected to All New England from the team.[461]

Although relatively new to Canterbury, lacrosse quickly became a strong Canterbury sport. The boys' lacrosse team won its first league title in 1975 with an 11-1 record, led by Larry "Turk" Turkheimer and Captain John Sargeant. Turk broke the school scoring record against Kent in the last game of the season by netting seven goals, giving him thirty-eight goals and eighteen assists for the season.[462] The following year, midfieldman Frank Bice '77, newly elected lacrosse captain, would be elected "Athlete of the Month."[463]

Another first occurred at Canterbury on May 10, 1974, which would turn into a spring tradition: the staging of the school's first musical production, *Guys and Dolls*. Under the direction of Bill D'Alton and musical direction of Gerry Vanasse, the musical starred Rob Rigney '74 as Sky Masterson, Alex Guttieres '74 as Nicely Johnson, Martha Ayre '74 as Sarah Brown, and Nicole Vanasse '75 as Miss Adelaide.[464]

Community service remained a strong component of the School. Michael Conniff '72 and John Kiernan '72 founded Canterbury's summer camp for children, attended by approximately forty underprivileged children from the surrounding community. The camp ran for two weeks in the summer, and camper referrals were made by the New Milford Visiting Nurse Association and the Community Action Committee of Danbury. Funds raised from spring musical ticket sales offset the cost of running the summer camp, which was directed at this time by Mr. John Martiska, the school's business manager. Following the death of Robert Markey Steele '72 on June 7, 1973, Canterbury's summer camp was held in his memory, as he had served as a counselor at the first camp.[465]

In May 1975, the School's drama group gave four perform-

ances of *Flower Drum Song.* The proceeds from Friday's and
Saturday's shows (May 16 and 17) went to benefit the summer
camp. Sunday evening's proceeds supplemented the Canterbury
Dramatic Society. The money raised from the musical was close to
$5,000, and along with individual contributions totaling over
$3,600, the School raised enough to support the summer camp
with an excess of $2,000 for seed money for the following year.[466]

The drama group staged several smaller shows in addition to
the major fall and spring drama productions. Brian Meehan '78
directed a student Christmas production of *Our Town*.[467] After a
hiatus of some years, *Nine Lessons and Carols*, the beautiful
Christmas pageant, was performed in 1977.[468] To relieve the tedi-
um of the winter season, a combination talent show and Mardi
Gras was held on March 4, 1976. The idea for the Mardi Gras
came from Mrs. Gilda Martin, and her French III class provided
the decorations. Mr. and Mrs. Reydel attended dressed as a sailor
of the high seas and a coed. Best faculty outfit, however, went to
Mr. John Coffin for his authentic Asian costume.[469] The talent
show, which followed, featured Michael Burke '78 and his mari-
onette, "Mean Harry," and was a great success. Jed Coffin '72, son
of John and Mary Lou, came back from his junior year at
Hamilton to teach a month-long drama workshop.[470]

Brian Meehan acted as well as directed while at Canterbury,
playing the role of the shy salesman in the production of *Ah,
Wilderness*. He was ably assisted by Michael Kiernan '77 as the
father, Nat Miller. Mac Briggs '77 as Arthur and Steve Kiernan '78
as Richard were the two sons. Rounding out the cast were Denise
O'Connor '79 as a dizzy Irish maid and Michael Burke '78 as the
tough bartender.[471]

At the beginning of Jack Reydel's tenure, James Breene '74
and Casey Kiernan '74, the first female editor, were co-editors-in-
chief of *The Tabard*. Doug Pigott '74 served as one of the associate

editors.[472] During this time, *The Tabard* placed a heavier emphasis on sports reporting. Each issue usually contained at least one full page of sports photos and one or two pages of sports articles. On March 7, 1974, *The Tabard* published an all-sports extra. Shortly thereafter, *The Tabard* announced an overhaul of its format.[473] *The Tabard* staff wished to renew its commitment to serious reporting and articles of substance. The staff felt that too much of the paper was being taken up with humorous pieces, which had little to offer the community.

This time period was not without several tragedies. On September 11, 1974, Dr. James W. Colbert Jr. and sons Peter '75 and Paul '74 were killed in a plane crash while en route to the School.[474] Ed Perley '76 suffered a cerebral hemorrhage early Monday morning of the 1975 Winter Weekend break, which left him paralyzed from the left side of the neck down.[475] Ed was able to continue at Canterbury, and in fact, he and eight other students constituted one of the largest sacristan groups in recent years.[476]

With the increased enrollment of girls, the faculty in 1973–1974 saw the addition of four new faculty members, three of whom were female. Ellen Kristensen was hired to fill the position of nurse in the School's infirmary. Sylvia Lahvis came to work in the art department, and Betsy Conley, Vassar graduate, arrived to teach English. The lone man hired was Joe Fitzgerald. Four years later, on Saturday, October 29, 1977, Mr. Fitzgerald and Ms. Conley married in a service conducted in Canterbury's chapel.[477] Other new faculty to come on board during the Reydel years were Jack Karpoe, Peter O'Donnell '70, and. Betty Burke, wife of Walter Burke. Jack Karpoe arrived at Canterbury with twenty-nine years' teaching experience already under his belt, with two years at Lawrenceville Prep and the remaining years at football rival Trinity-Pawling. Jack would teach chemistry and algebra, and coach varsity football. Jack Karpoe raised a lot of eyebrows among the older faculty with his language, both on and off the field. Jean Hebert said Jack Karpoe could turn the air blue with the things he said.[478] Peter O'Donnell '70 came back to Canterbury after graduation from Tufts. Peter served initially as alumni secretary and assistant development officer, and also taught American history.[479]

Paul Cauchon was busy expanding computer services at Canterbury, focusing on using computers as an educational aid. During this time, Paul published two books: *Tutorial Exercises for Chemistry* (1973) and *Chemistry with the Computer* (1976). During the first week in December 1974, Paul attended the National Convention for Computers to demonstrate some of the programs in his first book.[480]

Jim Shea was honored to receive the Ryan Chair in history. Given by members of the Ryan family in memory of their father, Mr. Allan Ryan, one of the founding backers of Canterbury, this chair represented a portion of the fund drive campaign to raise one million dollars in endowment funds for faculty salaries and benefits.[481] Already a nineteen-year veteran, Mr. Shea taught such courses as the American Presidency, Twentieth-Century History, and American Foreign Policy.

The yearbook honored Peter Bordonaro with its dedication in 1974. Mr. Bordonaro originally came to Canterbury in 1967, but was drafted into the United States Army during the Vietnam War. After his years in the service, Mr. Bordonaro returned to Canterbury in 1970 and taught European history to Third and Fourth Formers.[482] In their 1978 senior superlatives, the graduating class voted John Coffin their favorite teacher, while they voted Messrs. Hebert, Burke, Mandler, and Cauchon best teachers.[483]

John Coffin began work at Canterbury in the same year as Paul Cauchon, in 1962. He lived in the faculty house at 5 Elkington Farm Road from 1966 until 1995. Based on his nine or so years' experience working for the Highway Department in New Haven, many members of the Canterbury faculty recognized Mr. Coffin as an expert in one-way streets.[484] Known for his desert-dry wit, timely delivery, and such sayings as "You guessed 'er, Chester," Mr. Coffin served Canterbury in a variety of areas. Over the years, he taught Algebra 2, Advanced Algebra, Physics, and Astronomy. For thirteen years, he coached varsity soccer, and he also coached varsity hockey for a number of years. As chair of the faculty committee on day-student affairs, John Coffin was in charge of the Brodie Room and snack bar. When commenting on Mr. Coffin's birthday one year, Mr. Clarke remarked, "Mr. Coffin's age—sixteen in athletic ability and hundreds in wisdom." Canterbury's yearbook listed Mr. Coffin as "favorite teacher" numerous times, as did several campus polls conducted by *The Tabard*.[486]

New in 1977 as a faculty member, Marc Vanasse '73 joined the ranks on a part-time basis. His duties included tutoring the international students, taking charge of the snack bar, running a film course for Sixth Formers, and directing the drama productions. The following year, as a full-time faculty member, Mr. Vanasse had additional duties as the assistant director of studies, faculty advisor to the yearbook, and teacher of English.[487]

Around this time, *The Tabard* occasionally ran faculty profiles. The first issue of *The Tabard* for the 1975–1976 school year included such a profile on faculty member Roderick Clarke '46. Mr. Clark, at this point a twenty-two-year veteran of Canterbury, graduated from Amherst and went on to complete graduate work at Georgetown University, where he received a master's degree in European history. When Rod returned to teach at Canterbury, the faculty only numbered eighteen; by 1975, this number had almost doubled. After Rod returned in 1953, the faculty joked that "Williams [College] wouldn't take him because he didn't care for American history."[488]

During the 1970s, the deaths of two of Canterbury's great men—Philip H. Brodie (1891–1975) and Edward F. Mack (1892–1977)—saddened the Canterbury community. *The Tabard* said this of Mr. Brodie:

> A diligent, sincere, and absolutely honest man he was, who did his duty as he saw it. He initiated no revolution, led no new movement in the field of education; but in his death he is a huge celebrity, mourned by more than the many we may know.[489]

A part of the fabric of Canterbury life since 1928, Ed Mack gave much to the School. Mr. Mack started the first choral club at Canterbury and became the School's "official carillonneur." It was Edward Mack who presided over the graduation mass when Nelson Hume was stricken with his heart attack. Ed Mack also wrote one of the school's early histories. Of course, Mr. Mack's best-known contribution to Canterbury remains the school song, *Cantuaria Floreat.*[490]

During the summer of 1978, Jack Reydel announced his resignation, effective August 9. In his short tenure, he presided over the increase in the female population at Canterbury, the institution of Saturday classes, wide swings in the dress code, and great achievements in interscholastic athletics. He greatly expanded the community service program, with students regularly visiting the local nursing home, day-care center, and Southbury Training School. Canterbury's finances were in the black, with enough excess to renovate North House and construct a new hockey rink. Although some of the turbulence of the 1960s and early '70s washed over the school, Canterbury, at the top of the hill, remained largely unscathed.

Jack Reydel, Canterbury's third headmaster, at the kickoff dinner of Canterbury's second major capital campaign. Lynn Sheehan, wife of second headmaster Walter Sheehan, is in the background. October 1973.

Vin Largay '49 at the capital campaign kickoff dinner. Lynn Sheehan and Headmaster Jack Reydel listen intently. October 1973.

Phil Brodie in retirement, the beloved "Mr. Chips" of Canterbury School.

Jack Karpoe giving a pep talk to an early 1980s football team.

Jim Shea and John Coffin, with over sixty years of teaching, coaching, and dorm experience between them.

Charlie Huntington during one of the annual alumni hockey games.

Second Headmaster Walter Sheehan standing next to Rod Clarke, who would go on to become the School's fourth headmaster.

President of the Sixth Form class during the winter term of the 1945–1946 school year, Rod Clarke became Canterbury's fourth headmaster in 1978. Yearbook 1946.

Celebrating the newly renovated Carter House, formerly South House, and May Hume's thirty-two years of service on the Board of Trustees. May Hume with son Stephen Hume. 1981.

JP and Lou Mandler, mid-1970s.

Rod Clarke, center, with Gerard C. Smith '31 (left) and Sargent Shriver '34 (right).

Two faculty workshops, one in December 1983 and one in March 1984, introduced the faculty to the School's Commodore PET computers. This classroom is now the theater green (ready) room.

5

THE CLARKE YEARS

Roderick Clarke, Fourth Headmaster

On being appointed acting headmaster, Roderick Clarke immediately "expressed Canterbury's commitment to the academic and spiritual growth of the students by instituting new programs and rules to provide the structure and atmosphere necessary to learn and grow both scholastically and spiritually."[491] When interviewed later by *The Pallium* on the uniqueness of the Canterbury experience, Rod responded:

> The commitment to being Catholic Christians comes before the commitment to success by worldly standards. Dedication to academic growth on the part of each student is regarded as a logical extension of his or her making the most of God-given talents. The school stresses that the worth of each individual lies in how he or she deals with the talents, limitations, and challenges found in his or her life. Counseling, effort grades, and written comments emphasize this viewpoint. We stress that the blessings of wealth and education require a large scale of generosity in dealing with others. Canterbury makes no place for cynicism or indifference.[492]

Rod's attack was threefold in that he fine-tuned academics, athletics, and spiritual life. The Curriculum Committee revised the grading system to bring it more in line with other schools. The Committee also abolished the system of class ranking.[493] Rod encouraged Catholic students to attend Mass and to participate in the social service programs offered by the School. The Board of Trustees issued a statement to the students at the first school meeting of the 1978 school year: Canterbury must become the best Catholic preparatory school in the country.[494] The hiring of two faculty in the theology department, Margaret Mitchell and Brendan McCormick, furthered the aim of enhancing the spiritual life at the School. Miss Mitchell and Mr. McCormick also assisted with the social services program. In addition, the school scheduled four or five retreats throughout the year.[495] In the words of Mr. Clarke, "We try to disturb the cocoon of adolescent self-absorption. Answers are sought within the structure of Christian morality . . . Individual growth is also encouraged through retreats, counseling, the social service program, and personal charity . . . Probably the most telling application of charity occurs in dormitory living where hard work and proximity put a challenge to the Golden Rule."[496]

Rod Clarke made participation in athletics mandatory. Miss Chirnside, originally from The Gunnery, where she had taught dance and coached an area women's hockey league, served as the new director of girls' athletics.[497] Mr. Clarke also brought back the practice of faculty evaluations. As reported in *The Tabard*, "Through these evaluations, suggestions can be made to the faculty for possible summer courses they can take to enhance their teaching skills and perhaps to familiarize themselves with new, current teaching ideas and methods."[498] Rod Clarke continued teaching history, for in his opinion, "it was important for the headmaster to be involved directly in the academic program which is the

chief focus of the school."[499] Changes in student life included the
initiation of hour-long detentions to combat absenteeism and the
requirement of attendance at mandatory workshop classes for
Sixth Form English students having difficulty.[500] The Board of
Trustees took steps to prepare for the future by establishing a long-
range planning committee and a corresponding faculty committee.
At a special school meeting on November 14, 1978, Vin Largay,
president of the trustees, announced the permanent appointment
of Mr. Clarke as Fourth Headmaster of Canterbury School.[501]

Vincent Brendon Largay graduated from Canterbury in 1949.
A native of Waterbury, Connecticut, Vin joined Canterbury's
Board of Trustees in 1976 and served as its president from 1978
until 1984. As the new headmaster, Rod found Vin to be an ideal
Board president. While Mr. Largay was very active in raising
money for the school, he took a hands-off approach to the aca-
demic program. If there was ever any complaint lodged against
Rod, Mr. Largay would respond, "We have every confidence in
Mr. Clarke, thank you."[502] Rod felt that his relationship with Mr.
Largay gave the school a wonderful balance. As early as 1949, Mr.
Largay had seemed destined for his position as president of the
Board of Trustees, as the 1949 yearbook notes in its "Superlatives"
section, *Biggest Politician—Largay* and also, in its "Imagine" section,
Imagine Largay without the angles.

Rod was an appealing choice for headmaster because he "did
a lot of talking up of the academic program."[503] While Walter
Sheehan and Jack Reydel were enthusiastic about the athletic program, and Walter Sheehan made English his specialty, Rod was an
enthusiastic promoter of the entire academic program. "Rod
Clarke, you might say, knew every blade of grass in the school . . .
Rod had been here. He knew what made the school tick. He had
been here a long time, he was a part of the school, and I think that
made a big difference," remarked Gilda Martin.[504] As director of

studies from 1957 through 1978, Rod had pressed for changes in the curriculum. His philosophy was "Build on what you have and don't worry about what you don't."[505] With only one science lab in the Old Schoolhouse, Rod pushed for physics and chemistry classes, as they seemed to demand less space than biology. Once Hume Hall was complete, there was more room for various science offerings. Hume Hall had one small lab and three larger science labs. With more faculty and more space, Canterbury was able to offer more courses.

Routine wear and tear had taken its toll on most of the campus buildings, and Rod's tenure marked a time of active maintenance and repair. The building most in need of attention was North House. In stage one of the renovation, Thomas Hume '46 (son of Raphael and nephew of Nelson) and his architectural firm of Kearin and Hume replaced the two ancient boilers, repaired window sashes, and insulated the building. The boilers and bathrooms were completed in 1977, and the old roof was rebuilt, complete with new roof drains and gutters. The second stage of the renovation was more extensive and more cosmetic. Workers gutted two dormitory floors and completely replaced the windows, ceilings, and walls. Other repairs included refurbishing the stairways and expanding the wiring throughout the dorm. Finally, the dorm rooms, corridors, and common room received wall-to-wall carpeting.[506]

The following school year, 1979–1980, South House, since 1998 known as Carter House, received similar treatment. The hallways and common room were carpeted and walls painted. Bathrooms were added, along with four washers and dryers. The common room received new couches, chairs, tables, and a soda machine. The piano was restrung and tuned.[507] To complement the newly renovated South House and to celebrate May Hume's thirty-two years of service on Canterbury's Board, a portrait of her was dedicated after Mass on Alumni Day.[508]

Renovations continued into the next school year with the repainting of dormitory rooms and common rooms in the upper dorms. The last major renovation done during this time period was during the 1981–1982 school year, when a great deal of work was done to Sheehan House (which was named during the 1978–1979 school year to honor Walter Sheehan), including some projects related to energy conservation.[509] New doors and locks were installed in all the rooms; the patio was made level and new tiles were laid; Thermopane windows and new exterior doors were installed; new partitions were constructed in the bathrooms; electrical wiring and fixtures were replaced; and exterior walls were patched and painted. To restore some of the common room's original beauty, the woodwork was replaced and stained a golden oak color. The lighting fixtures were cleaned and new track lighting was installed. The finishing touch was the installation of wallboard over the plaster.[510]

Faces familiar to many graced the faculty during this period. Fran Foley '64 returned to Canterbury as director of admissions. Walter Briggs '75, who brought along his dog, Frieda, returned to teach mathematics and coach Thirds football and varsity lacrosse. Lawrence Tallamy returned after a two-year absence to teach history and to take on responsibilities as college counselor, and JP Mandler returned to head the English Department after only one year away.[511] A regular column journalist for *The Tabard*, Mathew Davis, wrote in his "Parents' Day! A Viewpoint":

> Mr. O'Donnell was his usually dapper self; Mr. Lee put on his annual smile; Mr. Shea was mobbed again; and Mr. Coffin rehearsed a speech to the wall. There was the nonchalant character of Mr. Burke and then there was the iron-masked Mr. Cauchon.[512]

Mr. Clarke was very interested in restoring and expanding the various cultural events provided for the students. The special events committee, composed of several faculty members, planned a wide spectrum of events for the student body throughout the year, including educational films, guest speakers, and theater performances. In the fall of 1979, Quentin Keynes, grandson of Charles Darwin, spoke to the students. Two evening programs, a coffeehouse and a music series, further enlivened the campus.[513] Perhaps as a backlash to the activism of the 1970s and early '80s, participation in student government, the school newspaper, and the literary magazine were all down. To be sure, there were students eager to participate and contribute, but over the next ten years, both the literary magazine and the student government winked in and out of existence. The *Carillon* was reborn in 1982, with the addition of photography, artistic work, and interviews, although by 1984 the staff had shrunk from twelve students to six.[514]

The student government also reconvened in 1982. The last time a governing body had been in existence was in 1979 under the name of Student-Faculty Senate. The previous spring, a preliminary governing committee had organized some social events and had explored the possibility of expanding the role of the committee into a governing body, which finally happened.[515] By the mid-'80s, the student government had reestablished itself and won longer snack bar hours and more weekend activities.[516]

The Tabard spent some years on a reduced publication schedule before settling into a regular routine. Under the leadership of Joseph Viau '79 and Megan Shea '79, *The Tabard* presented a new, "meatier" look in 1979. Staff size increased, as well as the number of issues.[517] In a detailed report in 1979 on *The Tabard*, the Columbia Scholastic Press Association criticized the fact that, amongst other things, there seemed to be "little evidence of student opinion in the form of letters to the editor and guest columns.

In fact, student-written letters to the editor [were] about as rare as Mr. O'Donnell's smile."[518] The Columbia University competition eventually awarded Canterbury a third-place prize in 1982, but still noted a lack of in-depth articles. The Association did commend the inclusion of the "Inquiring Photographer" as a good feature because of its expression of student opinion.[519] Under the editorship of Jen Lee '84, daughter of Dr. Bev Lee and sister to Laura (Lee) Quirk '80 and Dr. Amy Lee '82, *The Tabard* won a first place in the American Scholastic Press Association competition. *The Tabard* earned a credible 450 points out of 500 for content and earned points for design, editing, art, and creativity, for a grand total of 910 points overall.[520]

Canterbury was still experiencing growing pains as it grappled with fully integrating the female population into the life of the school. Out of various small groups of girls voicing their concerns, the Girls' League (sometimes called the Women's League), under the auspices of Gilda Martin, was born.[521] Some girls felt that they were not well represented in the various clubs on campus, except for the Choral Club. Others objected to the gender-specific roles that seemed to be assigned to those students serving in the chapel.

At this time, the school had approximately fifty boarding girls enrolled, with a future goal of enrolling up to eighty.[522] Two female trustees had joined Canterbury's board in the fall of 1979: Mrs. Elizabeth Tucker and Mrs. Rosemary Sinnott. Elizabeth Tucker, of Pelham, New York, had enjoyed a long relationship with Canterbury. Mrs. Tucker's father was Professor Carlton Hayes, a historian and friend of Nelson Hume, who had played a prominent role in the founding of the school, serving as one of the members of the first Board of Trustees. Mrs. Tucker's four children were all Canterbury graduates: Peter '78, Libby '76, Carlton '73, and Paul '68 (author of *Monet at Argenteuil*).

Mrs. Rosemary Sinnott of Rye, New York, was the second new member. Her husband, Peter '59, served as class agent concurrently. The addition of Mrs. Sinnott and Mrs. Hayes to the Board helped foster a more responsive atmosphere for the girls. They kept the Board informed on the well-being of the female students at Canterbury. Special classes such as sewing or Women's Studies were discussed for the girls, underscoring how the School vacillated between traditional and modern views of women's roles in society.[523]

Another ongoing concern of the girls was the lack of parity in girls' athletics. A letter to the editor that appeared in *The Tabard* on November 20, 1981, aired several complaints. The author bemoaned the single practice time given to varsity and junior varsity girls' sports, the small size of the locker room, and difficult access to the training and weight rooms.[524] Through the Girls' League, several girls were able to instigate some changes. Sarah Lyons '82, president, and Sharon O'Connor '82, Sixth Form representative, won installation of a salad bar in the dining hall. "Jim Shea often jokingly [commented] that the salad bar in the dining room [was] the most significant change to occur at Canterbury since coeducation."[525] The girls organized dances, skating parties, and other events of particular interest to girls.[526]

The faculty also was concerned with the changes brought about by coeducation. In 1984, interested faculty formed a committee on coeducation, chaired by Mrs. Lou Mandler.[527] The purpose of the committee was to discuss gender issues and to promote a better climate for coeducation. The committee sponsored special issue days, speakers, and small discussion groups.[528] Coeducation received whole-hearted support from the headmaster. Mr. Clarke said, "Coeducation has been an incredible change for the better."[529] The *Pallium* reported that even Director of Development Peter O'Donnell '70, a man not given to liberated statements, agreed. O'Donnell added, "Boys have learned to cheer girls, compete with girls, and accept them as true friends."[530] From a start of nine girls and one female faculty member, Canterbury grew to seventeen female faculty members by 1985.[531] This same year, Ms. Bailey Breene Gendron '77, daughter of Mr. James Breene, joined Canterbury's Board of Trustees. Ms. Gendron was the first Canterbury alumna to serve on the Board.[532]

Several disciplinary issues marred this period in the school's history. The 1979 spring production of *Babes in Arms* almost didn't run when two members of the cast were expelled. The School placed three of the remaining five on expulsion probation.[533] The following season, *You Can't Take It With You* was canceled, probably due to illness among the cast and crew coupled with a general lack of organization in finding students to replace those ill. The first drama event of the 1979–1980 school year was a small production on Thursday, January 31, called "Drama Potpourri."[534] Not a play, "Drama Potpourri" was, as the name implies, selections from plays and dramatic readings. After eight consecutive years of large musicals, *You're a Good Man Charlie Brown* was the choice for the spring 1982 play. *Charlie Brown* had a small cast of six principals and no chorus. There was a return to a large musical the following year with the production of *Godspell*. The administration felt *Godspell* was a good choice because it involved many people and was spiritually uplifting.[535]

The Tabard devoted some space in its articles to wondering whether the class of 1981 would be allowed to have a prom after problems following other proms in recent years.[536] While drug and alcohol use increased on college campuses during the 1960s and early '70s, the late '70s and early '80s saw an increase in drug and alcohol use in secondary schools. Canterbury was not exempt from this trend, nor from some of the resulting behavioral issues. In late winter, Mr. Clarke announced that the prom would be given a second chance. *The Tabard* reported, "Even Mr. Burke thinks that the prom is a great idea."[537] The students canceled prom plans once again in 1983, however, after the School withdrew its sponsorship for a party to be held in New York City.

In May of 1982, Canterbury hosted a symposium, "Challenges to Leadership: Seeds which Produce Responsible Decision Makers." Well attended, the symposium featured some of the most important figures in education and politics of the time. The Honorable Gerard C. Smith '31 and The Honorable Sargent Shriver '34 were the symposium's chairmen.[538] Forty-sixth president of Georgetown University, President Timothy S. Healy, SJ, spoke on "The Religious Basis for Leadership." Dr. Robert Goheen, president emeritus of Princeton University, spoke on the "Importance of a Liberal Education." William R. Hearst III '67 introduced Mr. Clarke to speak on the role of a secondary school education in developing leadership, in one of the highlights of Rod's tenure. The symposium closed that evening with a speech on "Choices in Foreign Policy" given by Connecticut Senator Christopher Dodd.[539]

In 1983, enrollment increased to 290 students. The Third Form class, traditionally the smallest, increased by ten students (from fifty to sixty for the year). Conversely, the Sixth Form class, the largest, saw a decrease of fourteen students (from ninety to seventy-six). Fifth Form and Fourth Form enrollments were seventy-nine and seventy-five, respectively. Prospective students sent more than one thousand applications to the Admissions Office.[540]

The tradition of competing for the Sheehan Cup began in 1981. James Moore, formerly assistant headmaster under Walter Sheehan, had left Canterbury to become headmaster at Berkshire. Mr. Moore suggested the competition between the schools and offered a trophy named in honor of Mr. Sheehan.[541] With the exception of cross-country and football, sports overall were unremarkable during this time, although there were some great accomplishments by individual athletes, as noted in the "Athlete of the

Month" column in *The Tabard*. The cross-country team was able to stretch its record to sixty-five straight dual meet victories, led by co-captains Kevin Burke '79 and Tom McCormack '79.[542] The team recorded five unbeaten years in a row, before losing to Choate in the fall of 1979.

In 1980, Varsity football's record ended at 8-0-0, for the first time in twenty-one years. Canterbury's 7-0 victory over Wyoming Seminary ended Wyoming's five-year winning streak. Sarah Lyons '82 achieved individual recognition in cross-country by finishing first in every race she ran. The winter season saw accolades going to Ken Rigney in wrestling; he did not lose a match until the New England finals (1981). Volleyball captain Claire D'Alton and her spikers, Lydia Tenaglia and Debbie Smith, also were recognized.[543] The duo of Tenaglia and Smith would earn "Athletes of the Month" at least three more times, for accomplishments in field hockey, soccer, and, finally, as co-captains of the volleyball team.[544]

Sarah Lyons was back in the limelight in the spring for her accomplishments in track. The undefeated track team set several records in the spring of 1982. Co-captain Filippo Guerrini-Maraldi set a school record in the triple jump. Marcia Simpson set records for shot put and the discus, as well as sprinting in the 100-yard dash and 400-yard relay. Jen Lee[545] followed soccer captain Sharon O'Connor[546] as an acknowledged athlete, and would earn further recognition for her squash prowess.[547] Jen Lee (now Jen Chandler) returned to Canterbury as a faculty member in 1993. In addition to coaching girls' JV soccer, Jen has rebuilt the boys' squash program. By the end of the 2004–2005 squash season, boys' varsity squash had amassed an impressive 11-3 record, and placed tenth of seventeen teams in the B level at the New England Tournament at Choate.

Late in the summer of 1978, Canterbury lost one of its earliest students and greatest benefactors, Mr. James A. Farrell '19. Mr.

Farrell's father was one of the first members of Canterbury's Board of Trustees and financial backers. James continued this tradition, also becoming a member of Canterbury's Board. Among his many gifts to the school were four tennis courts and a physics laboratory dedicated in his name. In the early 1970s, when computers were an innovation, Mr. Farrell made it possible for Canterbury to have a computer system. *The Tabard* reported in 1978: "At the time of his death, it was made known that Mr. Farrell's legacy provided ongoing support for the Canterbury Idea."[548]

A full-page piece called "Mr. Cauchon and his Amazing Machines" appeared in *The Tabard* of October 27, 1978. The author noted that Mr. Cauchon's work with computer-assisted instruction over the years had drawn national recognition.[549] The Human Resource Research Organization reported that Canterbury's use of computers was among the best in the country.[550] Just a few years later, the American Chemical Society bestowed on Paul the honor of electing him National Coordinator for Workshops for High School Chemistry Teachers.[551] This was followed by Paul's appointment as chairman of the American Chemical Society's Committee on Computers in Chemical Education.[552] When Steele Hall opened in 1984 with its new computer lab, Paul received a grant to conduct computer workshops for the entire faculty during the winter intercession and March break. Faculty members learned the intricacies of word processing using the "Papermate" program on Commodore PETs.[553] Ever innovative, Canterbury was one of the first schools to purchase an Apple II computer, one of the few affordable computers available with graphics capabilities.

On Friday, December 11, 1981, Mr. Clarke unveiled plans for a new building on the vacant lot north of the Hume Building. The proposed building would become the most architecturally unique building on campus. The architectural firm of Daniel F. Tully Associates called it a "hyperbolic-parabolical structure." The building has also been compared to a series of saddles, or to a peaked tent.[554] Meant to bring the center of campus to the top of the hill, this building houses the library, computer center, dining hall, auditorium, and administrative offices within a 30,000-square-foot area. Harking back to the days of Nelson Hume, the headmaster would be able to enter one building and be able to get in touch with all the key centers of administration.[555] Tully Associates designed the building to be an oil and electricity con-servator, with a considerable portion of the building constructed below ground level.[556] Although the architect lobbied to have the library placed on the ground floor because of the weight of the books, Rod successfully petitioned for the upper floor with its inspiring views of the campus.[557] Through the generosity of the Copley family, especially David '70, the library was named the David Casey Copley Library.

The best location for this new building appeared to be the site occupied by the Cauchon house. When the green light came in the fall of 1982 for the new building, special trucks lifted and moved the Cauchon house to the north, and groundbreaking for the new building occurred in November. The building was named for Robert Markey Steele, 1954–1973. About one year after his grad-uation in 1972, Bob died in a tragic biking accident. His achieve-ments at Canterbury were many: as a student, as a sacristan, and as a golfer. Bob's friend and classmate, Mike Conniff '72, wrote in *The Tabard*:

> Often the most valuable and lasting lessons learned at Canterbury are taught not by the faculty, but by a single student . . . in the normal routine of daily life . . . such a person was Bob Steele . . . Bob was the Canterbury ideal perfected.

Robert Markey Steele Hall opened on January 8, 1984, although the official dedication did not take place until May of that year. Father Greenan, chaplain when Steele was a student, traveled from Ireland to bless the new building. The greatly expanded dining hall could hold 325 people, compared to 250 in the old dining hall in North House.

One of Mr. Clarke's most important goals was a richer connection between the school's library and the academic curriculum, with a focus on providing resources for more independent research. Knowing that the former library was inadequate to answer Canterbury's future needs,[558] he focused attention on creating an excellent new facility for the students. At least twice the size of the former library, which had been located in the Old Schoolhouse, the new facility would contain a variety of work and study areas. Mr. Clarke enlarged the book collection in scope and variety, and increased audiovisual equipment and other technology. Everything was done with one vision in mind: making the new Copley Library a central hub of the school. At the dedication, Mr. Clarke spoke "of how the Copley Library would hopefully lead to an important 'sense of independent, self-starting, self-learning process' for Canterbury students."[559]

With the opening of Steele Hall, Rod Clarke said it felt like the school had really gained two buildings. There was greater room for faculty apartments and for offices. Rod hoped that with the increase in space, the art and music programs could be expanded.[560] The air-conditioning in Steele Hall, particularly in the dining hall, enabled summer programs to go forward.[561] The former library rooms in the Old Schoolhouse were converted into classrooms, including music rooms. North and Sheehan Houses were further revamped, and the vacated offices were converted to faculty apartments.[563] Dr. Hume's apartment, used as the admissions office, became the residence of the Mandlers, and would remain so for many years.

Rod Clarke also promoted art exhibits around campus, including the display of students' artwork in the library and in the halls of the Hume Building. One such exhibit was a mural depicting numbers, created by students Brian Belvin '85, Tony Cassatt '84 (distant relation to the artist Mary Cassatt), Melissa Greene '83, and Craig Speight '83, painted outside Walter Burke's mathematics classroom.[564] Sylvia Hierro, then chair of the art department, best expressed the philosophy of the department regarding art education: "[T]o appreciate it, you must experience it; not just see it, but try it yourself."[565] The Duffy family, through a generous gift, granted the art department the space to expand in 1986. A ceramics room, painting area, teaching/lecture rooms, and a gallery, all dedicated to the Edward J. Duffy family, fill the 3,500 square feet of space formerly occupied by the dining hall.

The first piece of artwork given to the School after the opening of the new Duffy Art Gallery was Abe Echevarria's *Lazarus Effect*, originally commissioned by Putnam Publishers to serve as the cover art for a new book they were publishing, of the same name.[566] Alumni artists featured during the dedication ceremony included Terry O'Shea '59, Mark Garafalo '75, John Kernan '30, Regina O'Brien '78, Nancy Mygatt Martin '78, Mary Garafalo '79, Reed Armstrong '56, John Kernan Jr. '60, and Mike Berman '74.[567] The second show displayed works by the ISAIA (Independent School Art Instructors' Association). Art teachers Kim Tester and Sylvia Hierro exhibited some of their works in this show.[568] Favorite shows since then have included John Duffy's travel photographs and artwork by the children from the neighboring Children's Center.

Dust had barely settled from the groundbreaking of Steele Hall when ground was broken once again, this time for a new field house. Designed by architects Kearin and Hume, the field house contained two basketball courts and a volleyball court, all with electronic scoreboards.[569] Smaller projects were undertaken as well. The Sheehan House wall was rebuilt, and the outside of Sheehan House was painted.[570] The Reeds, Don V. '58 and son, Taylor '88, donated funds for new Sheehan House common room furniture.[571] The school store was revitalized under the management of Debbie Lyke Onorato. The new store offered a walk-around layout, expanded offerings, and increased hours.[572] The Haire brothers, Brett '67, Jack '70, and Paul '73, donated new chapel doors in honor of their father, Thomas '30. The four doors were constructed of heavy oak and specially carved.[573]

With a still-expanding enrollment of girls, Canterbury decided to purchase the Hickory Hearth property and building in July 1985, pressing it into service as an "outside house" for girls. The original house, once occupied by the mistress of Ingleside, burned down in 1937. The Taylor family rebuilt the house in 1945. Mrs. Jennifer Taylor lived there until her death in the spring of 1985, when Canterbury acquired the property.[574] The Hearth, situated on 8.5 acres and containing a barn, is located just south of South House (now called Carter House) on Aspetuck Avenue.[575] The Infirmary, built in 1951, became Ingleside House and Health Center in September 1988. Ingleside House provided housing for six students and three faculty members.[576]

After seventy-one years of acquiring land, Canterbury sold its first piece of land on September 30, 1986, selling 2.58 acres bordering Route 202 to the New Milford police department.[577]

Rod Clarke hired a graphic designer, Mr. Warren Smith, to work with the school to develop a fresh and updated look for the admissions publications in 1983. Part of this design package included the development of a school logo. Although Canterbury had long used an official seal for legal documents and diplomas, Canterbury did not have what could be called an official logo until this point. The original School seal was designed by Nelson Hume before Canterbury opened in 1915. Dr. Hume presented the seal at one of the organizational meetings of the Board of Trustees. Board member Mr. G. Robert Holmen '51 lobbied for the creation of a Canterbury School logo. Originally, Mr. Smith meant the design to have several separate parts, which could be used independently. Jack Burke '41 objected to this design. He felt that because a logo represents the School, there should be one design, which is never changed.[578]

The "guardian" of the logo was, and still is, Marc Vanasse. As director of publications, Marc makes sure that the logo is not corrupted or misused. The design consists of the pallium (vestment of a band of white wool, worn on the shoulders, with four purple crosses worked on it) over the chasuble as its central feature, with a dove above it symbolizing the Holy Spirit. To the left of the pallium is a lamb holding the pectoral cross, symbolizing the Lord the Savior, and peace; on the right is a lion holding a crozier, symbolizing the Lord as Shepherd and leadership.[579] The colors in the design are Columbian blue and white. The inspiration for the logo came from the big west window in the chapel, which depicts the Canterbury saints, and the symbols with which they are associated. There are many Canterbury graduates who would have preferred that the logo reproduce the seal exactly, instead of the updated version that Mr. Smith created.

About this same time, Mr. Smith created an admissions video for the school. Working with Fran Foley, then director of admissions, Warren Smith filmed approximately ten hours of School life to be distilled into a twenty-minute video.[580] The baby boom years were over, and from an enrollment high of 323 students in 1976, enrollment had declined to 299 students in 1986. According to demographic studies,[581] Canterbury and other secondary schools were in the midst of the post–baby boom years, or the years of Generation X. Indeed, Canterbury's enrollment would continue to decline through 1992, when, gradually, enrollment started to increase with the "echo baby boomers." Canterbury had to compete with other preparatory schools to attract students from a much smaller applicant pool. Board president John Duffy '59 and Rod Clarke both recognized the importance of aggressively promoting the school.[582]

The May 9, 1985, issue of *The Tabard* ran this short piece: "This year's senior class would like to extend its humble thanks to the English Department for creating one more obstacle which need be overcome on our road to graduation."[583] This obstacle was the Sixth Form paper, which Sixth Formers must still write today. Another cause for uproar among the students was the institution of a morning meeting, held each Tuesday at 7:40 A.M. Mr. Clarke announced that the purpose of the meeting was to inform and remind students of events during the week.[584] The Friday school meetings continued to provide entertainment and educational edification for the students by bringing in speakers, musical groups, and performing troupes.

In 1986, Marc Vanasse became the director of publications. As such, he served as faculty advisor to the *Cantuarian*, *The Tabard*, and the *Carillon*. It was his responsibility to also oversee production of the *Pallium*, the school's new alumni publication.[585] Steve Reynolds '78 aided Mr. Vanasse in his production of the *Pallium*, until 1988 when Mr. Vanasse became sole editor of the publication. After a brief hiatus, *The Tabard* brought back "Athlete of the Issue," and continued with its popular "Inquiring Photographer."[586] For a while, *The Tabard* settled into a five-issues-per-year publication schedule and routinely won first place in the Press Association contest for earning more than 800 points in the Association's 1,000-point scale. In 1989, *The Tabard* first used a computer and new desktop publishing software to experiment with layout. Comprising a Macintosh SE with a 40

MG hard drive and a two-page display monitor, the system ran MacWrite and PageMaker software. *Tabard* editors promised to experiment with a variety of formatting styles in the paper, as they continued to learn the new system.[587]

The *Carillon* was still struggling to make a comeback, but a small staff and general lack of interest made it difficult. Although two issues had been planned for the 1984–1985 school year, the editors announced that only one would be published. Despite these challenges, the *Carillon* persevered, and in 1987, under the leadership of Duchess Harris '87, the National Council of Teachers of English cited it as an outstanding art and literary magazine.[589]

In answer to a new generation of hazards to students' health and well-being, Canterbury continued its health education program. Added to the already-known dangers of alcohol and marijuana came a new threat—crack cocaine. Mr. Joseph Sullivan, a drug and alcohol counselor, appeared at a morning meeting to counsel students about the dangers of substance abuse.[590] Father Bruce Ritter of Covenant House spoke to the student body at least twice about the Covenant House program and what life was like for a runaway on the streets of New York City.[591] Phoenix House, a drug treatment and rehabilitation service run by ex-users, also made multiple appearances on campus. In the fall of 1984, Phoenix House presented an "Issues Day" for Canterbury students.[592] Among the recommendations made to the administration at the close of the program was for the school to sponsor more weekend activities. Additionally, the School restricted smoking to designated areas on campus, available only to Sixth Formers. Within a few years, student smoking was entirely banned on campus, and, shortly after that, smoking by faculty and staff was banned in buildings. By 1988, the student counseling program was revamped. Although a counseling program had existed on campus before, it was not well known, and had mostly been used on a "crisis" basis.[593]

Finally, in preparation for the ten-year evaluation by the New England Association of Schools and Colleges (NEASC)— which is the nation's oldest regional accrediting association, founded in 1885—a psychiatrist interviewed students about issues important to them. Students cited the discipline system, the food service, and the dress code as areas of concern.[594] Articles appearing in *The Tabard* around this time aptly demonstrated these concerns, especially with the discipline system.

To introduce some new life into the School, and to allow Mr. Clarke more time for fund-raising and student recruitment, the Board of Trustees hired William Burke as assistant headmaster in 1986. Declining enrollment and drastic budget cuts made attention to fund-raising imperative as never before.[595] Mr. Burke was a Middlebury graduate who had worked at Holderness for the last twelve years. Bill believed that Canterbury had gradually become isolated from the New Milford community and from the world at large. He issued a challenge to the Sixth Form to become leaders by example. At the Sixth Form retreat, Bill discussed the values that were important to create a better Canterbury. The Sixth Form picked respect as the value having the greatest impact on the campus community. Bill further emphasized that the most important part of having values was "being able to publicly affirm and practice them."[596]

With William Burke's help, Canterbury designed leadership workshops, held during the first weeks of school, and invited student leaders (sacristans, proctors, team captains, student representatives, and publication editors) to participate. The leadership workshops involved approximately forty students from the Sixth Form class. The two major themes were "Lead by example" and "With leadership comes responsibility."[597]

Around the same time that Mr. Burke was hired, Canterbury hired Bryan Kiefer to become the School's business manager. The

Pallium later reported, "His major goals at the start were to control costs, manage the plant effectively, and increase revenues."[598] Among other things, Bryan renegotiated the school's insurance contracts and updated the Canterbury fleet of vehicles. Bryan became instrumental in developing the first long-range plans for Canterbury, along with Mr. Clarke and Mr. Burke.

On Tuesday, February 11, 1986, the first Canterbury ring ceremony occurred in the chapel. Headmaster Clarke spoke of the significance and value of obtaining a Canterbury ring. The entire Fifth and Sixth Form classes assembled in the chapel after a sit-down dinner for the special ceremony. Sixty-three students from the classes of 1986 and 1987 purchased rings to participate in the ceremony.[599]

There were several other "firsts" inaugurated around this time. After discovering that public speaking was becoming a lost art in society, the English department initiated a public speaking program. Students had to present either a reading or an original speech in their respective English classes. The best speakers in each class presented their speech to the entire student body at one of the morning meetings.[600] Several faculty members acted as judges. The English department awarded graduation prizes for the best speaker in each form, and for the overall best public speaker in the school. The speech competitions were not exactly a first at Canterbury School, as founding Headmaster Nelson Hume had conducted speech classes in the 1930s. *The Tabard* , in a retrospective article looking at early speech classes reported, "The first classes [were] devoted largely to proper breathing, phonetics, tone production, and enunciation . . . The work will gradually develop into the giving of talks by the individual boys before the whole school."[601]

Late in 1989, the Canterbury Honor Society was founded. Conceived by then Director of Studies Mary Lou Coffin, the

Honor Society's aim was to recognize academic achievement in the student body. To become a member, students had to achieve grades within a particular GPA range, to demonstrate involvement in extracurricular areas of school life, and to model good citizenship. The Honor Society limited its inaugural membership to no more than 20 percent of the Sixth Form class, or, in 1989, a maximum of twelve students. The eight charter members inducted into the Canterbury Honor Society, all of the class of '90, were:

Brian O'Rourke	Sonya Hals
Jaime Martinez del Rio	Elizabeth Rubin
Marlene Schneider	Jacques Joubert
Madeleine Del Vicario	Daniel Bertram

Other programs designed to improve the academic life of Canterbury's students debuted during this time. Holly Hanes, college counselor, instituted the first College Night in 1987.[602] Representatives from more than 70 colleges arrived on campus to speak with students. The event was so successful that the following year, 105 schools attended.[603]

The Big Brother/Big Sister program also began in 1987. The coeducation committee had devised the Big Brother/Big Sister program as a way of making new students feel more comfortable when they first arrived on campus. Once assigned, a Big Brother or Big Sister would help new students through the registration process and assist in unpacking and setting up dorm rooms. Students played getting-to-know-you games in the evenings. The program culminated with a cookout at the Sheehan Terrace wall at the end of registration week. The Big Brother/Big Sister program is still in effect at Canterbury today, and enjoys the participation of many returning students. The current Assistant Dean of Students, Mary Holton, has extended the program to encourage students to communicate and bond with their assigned Little Brother/Little Sister all year, and not just during the first few weeks of school.[604]

Students also formed an Amnesty International chapter on campus. Amnesty International (AI) is a worldwide movement of people who campaign for internationally recognized human rights.[605] Still in existence on campus today, Amnesty International members organize letter-writing campaigns to support prisoners of conscience and to protest human rights violations.

In 1989, *The Tabard* reported on what was to become another well-loved tradition at the school: "On Thursday, January 26, 1989, after a sit-down dinner, the Canterbury community convened in the Duffy Art Gallery for dessert."[606] Thus began the Canterbury ritual of opening each new gallery show with a festive dessert and viewing. Today, there are approximately six gallery shows each year. One of the shows is a juried show of student work, while the others may feature the work of local artists, faculty, or Canterbury alumni. Sylvia Hierro has exhibited her raku pottery; there have been photographs by Marc Vanasse '73 and Hilary Duffy '87; and visiting artist Susan Moffett has displayed her digital imagery. The best-received exhibit, according to Kim Tester, has been Alexander Shundi's paintings, created from unusual angles and perspectives. A skilled draftsman, he incorporates the shape of the canvas into his work. Students were amazed both by how real the paintings appeared and by Mr. Shundi's imagination.[607]

The entertainment committee, led by chairman Bill Paxton '89, came up with the idea of enlivening the week preceding Parents' Weekend. The school held its first Spirit Week festivities with such events as "Nerd Day" and "Gender Opposite Day" in 1989. The committee planned to end the week with a bonfire and pep rally, which, unfortunately, had to be canceled due to bad weather. Spirit Week has persisted, however, and is still celebrated today. With today's politically correct climate, "Gender Opposite Day" is no longer included, but "Hat Day" and "Form Pride Day" have taken its place. Forms compete to accrue "spirit points." A special afternoon pep rally, with additional contests, is held in the gym, followed by a bonfire, weather permitting, in the old hockey rink below South House. Spirit Week had its desired effect, because in 1989, Canterbury won the coveted Sheehan Cup. At the end of the football game, Thomas Lord, headmaster of Berkshire, presented the cup to a beaming Rod Clarke.[608]

The final years of Rod's tenure as headmaster were transitional years for the faculty. Several longtime teachers retired, positions were changed, and the nucleus of today's faculty was hired. Mary Lou Coffin, wife of John Coffin, had joined the faculty in 1984. Mary Lou had run the gifted program in the New Milford schools and taught in the New Milford public school system for twenty years before coming to Canterbury as director of studies. Mary Lou dove right into her new duties, and took on the additional responsibility of teaching the Computer Literacy course. The chaplain honored Mary Lou by installing her as a Eucharistic minister, along with Gilda Martin and Marc Vanasse.[609]

Faculty members Sandra Behan, Bev Lee, Lou Mandler, and Guy Simonelli proved to be great additions to the departments of science, English, and theology. Some shifting of positions also occurred: Fran Foley, longtime director of admissions, tried his hand as dean of students; Pat Shea, wife of Jim, joined the development office; and Pat Finn, a newcomer from the Baltimore area, moved from the development office to admissions. Mr. Finn would become instrumental in developing a strong lacrosse program and fostering better ties between the New Milford athletic community and Canterbury.

Lou Mandler was notified that she had received a Klingenstein Fellowship for the 1990–1991 school year. Lou's proposed study was the American West through its history, literature, and art.[610] In 2000, the Women of Canterbury named Lou its Woman of the Year for her accomplishments as School registrar (1977–1978),

English teacher (1981–2000), Klingenstein Fellow (1990–1991), and director of studies. The previous year, Sandy Behan was the first recipient of the award.

Several "old masters" retired, although many maintained their connection with the School. Mr. William D'Alton and Mr. Jean Hebert retired, followed by Mr. Jack Karpoe and Mr. Gerry Vanasse. Jim Hayes '55, publisher of *Discover* magazine (and once a column writer for *The Tabard*), said that Mr. D'Alton had given him "a deep appreciation for good writing and a love of literature."[611] Paul Cauchon, John and Mary Lou Coffin, Jules Viau, Jim Shea, and Gilda Martin would follow into retirement a few years later. Until 2005, students could run into Mr. Shea running the track every afternoon; he still is a visible presence on campus almost every day. Jim and his wife, Pat, attend as many baseball and basketball home games as they can. Jim is always willing to pass the time of day and commiserate about the fortunes of the Red Sox. Mr. Jules Viau is a frequent visitor on campus, strolling up from his home on Aspetuck Avenue to enjoy a cigarette and to survey the playing fields.

The 1988–1989 school year opened to the sad news that May DesJardins Hume had passed away on August 8 at the age of 101. "On October 22, the ringing of the carillon called together not only May's family but members of the larger Canterbury family for a memorial service. In attendance were alumni who spanned the classes from 1920 to 1950, those who knew her best as the 'surrogate mother of lonely boys away from home' and 'the only woman who could keep the good doctor under control.' "[612]

This year also marked the passing of Peter D. Kiernan '40. Mr. Kiernan had served on the Board of Trustees from 1970–1978. His wife, Mary Agnes, also served on the Board from 1983–1988. All of the Kiernans' seven children are Canterbury graduates.[613]

Along with new members Donn Dolce '63, Jose Fanjul, and Charles Millard, Ms. Isabelle C. Reilly joined the Board in 1987.

Ms. Reilly formerly taught in the fine arts department at Canterbury, during the tenure of her husband, Gene. Three of their seven children, Kevin '68, Eugene '78, and Ellen '82, are Canterbury grads.

In a departure from the past several years of comedy, Director Marc Vanasse staged a thriller, *Night Watch*[614], for the fall show in 1985. Mr. Vanasse would soon pass the torch to Kevin Dearinger, but not before he directed his last show, *Joseph and the Amazing Technicolor Dreamcoat*, in the spring of 1986. This production featured Sixth Former Rachel Muszala as Joseph. Canterbury's drama department had come full circle from the days when boys had to play all the female parts.

Kevin Dearinger would produce his first Canterbury play the following fall, with a production of *Spoon River Anthology*. Mr. Dearinger maintained school tradition by producing a musical each spring, but he liked to challenge the students with different genres of theater in the fall. Kevin brought back comedy with *Brighton Beach Memoirs*, but experimented with straight drama, such as *Vanities*, as well as a one-woman show featuring Nicole Sidney '88 as Emily Dickinson. For this intimate performance, the audience was brought directly onto the stage, where Nicole delivered her lines as if she were speaking directly to each member of the audience.

In 1988, Canterbury theater received a wonderful gift from Arthur Halleran '65 to establish the Halleran Endowment for the Dramatic Arts. The income from this endowment helps fund the drama society's two major shows per year and also helps to maintain and improve the production facilities of Maguire Auditorium.[615] Although the gift had been made the previous spring, Arthur J. Halleran was honored in Maguire Auditorium on October 15, 1988.[616] Mr. Halleran had long ties with Canterbury. His father (Arthur '27) and two uncles (Thomas and Leo '34) attended Canterbury. Mr. Halleran's ties with Canterbury go even deeper; he graduated from St. David's School, of which David Hume '45, son of Nelson, was the headmaster for many years.[617]

The girls' athletic program continued to grow and achieve success during the 1980s, with some notable individual achievements. During her Sixth Form year, Marcia Simpson '85 captained three girls' teams—soccer, basketball, and lacrosse—and won the graduation prize for best all-around athlete. Marcia's accomplishments extended beyond the playing fields and courts. She worked for all three school publications, sang in the Choral Club, and was a North House proctor. Despite her busy schedule, she still found time to volunteer in the nursing home and hospital. As a true embodiment of Nelson Hume's ideals, Marcia was the sole winner of the Canterbury Award.[618]

Girls' teams continued to enjoy at success at Canterbury, and reached a high point in 1989. Under captains Cathy Brewer '90 and Megan McDonald '90, the girls' varsity soccer team won the division title against Governor Dummer. This game was special because the game was decided by a sudden-death penalty kick.[619] The same year that the girls won their title, the cross-country team topped a 14-0 season by also winning the New England championship. Adrian Dognin '90, undefeated all season, placed first to lead the Saints to victory and set a new course record.[620]

Some girls pushed the limit of sports at Canterbury, including Kim MacKenzie '91, who became the first girl in many years to earn a berth on the Thirds hockey team. In 1987, Michael Dunham arrived at Canterbury as a Third Former. As goalie for the Canterbury Saints, Mike became well known and respected for his strong defense. Now a professional NHL player, Mike has been tapped an unprecedented three times to represent the United States in the Olympics, including the 2002 Winter Games in Salt Lake City.[622] Walter Burke took some time to show his athletic prowess, but fulfilled a dream when he ran the New York City marathon in 3:51, and in his age group placed 456 out of 17,064.[623]

On the cusp of the school's seventy-fifth anniversary, Rod Clarke announced his impending retirement, and William Burke announced his move to become headmaster at St. Sebastian's in Needham, Massachusetts.[624] Although the School had weathered the politically turbulent 1960s and '70s, along with the accompanying social upheaval, the '80s had proven even more of a challenge with its economic uncertainty and dwindling secondary school population. Board presidents Vincent Largay and John Duffy, along with Headmaster Rod Clarke, had successfully kept the Canterbury ship afloat. The new headmaster would face some tough challenges in the next few years, but Canterbury School's mission remained intact and its spirit unbroken.

The Robert Markey Steele Hall, containing a new library, dining hall, and administrative offices, opened its doors in 1984.

Rod Clarke toasting David Casey Copley during the dedication of the library in May 1984.

A faculty meeting in the Steele Hall Lecture Room. Many familiar faculty faces from the 1950s through the 1980s can be seen. 1984.

Sargent Shriver '34 meets with students in Headmaster Rod Clarke's dining room. Mid-1980s.

Rod Clarke presenting Jack Karpoe with a gift during Alumni Day. 1981.

Opening of the Duffy Art Gallery, located in the former North House dining hall. To Rod's left is Sylvia Hierro, then chair of the Art Department, and Kim Tester, current chair. 1986.

Students, with Sylvia Hierro, working on a project in one of the Duffy art rooms.

Although Dr. Hume wanted to purchase Hickory Hearth, part of the old Ingleside School for Girls, it did not become part of the Canterbury campus until 1985.

Supercertari semel a traditae sanctis fidei. The school motto of Canterbury School, "to fight valiantly for the faith once delivered to the saints."

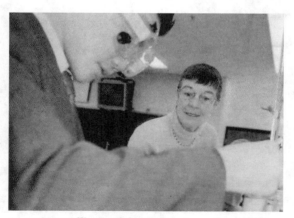

In a 2001 *Pallium* article, Dr. Bev Lee compared herself to the element potassium because, she said, "It is highly reactive."

Science chair Sandy Behan watches as students complete a laboratory exercise. Sandy is also the faculty advisor to Women of Canterbury and the Environmental Club.

Paul Cauchon conducts a chemistry experiment.

Vous ne me comprenez pas, vous?

Bill D'Alton with May Hume in the Old Schoolhouse library.

Faculty members lining up for the graduation procession. Faces of Bill D'Alton, Jules Viau, Don Roberts, Jim Shea, and John Coffin are visible

The graduation procession from Sheehan House to the Chapel is one of Canterbury's best-loved traditions.

Fifth Headmaster Tom Sheehy and wife, Betsy, during Tom's first year at Canterbury School. 1990.

Math teacher Walter Burke makes a point.

Among the Canterbury Medal recipients are several of Canterbury's Old Guard. Seated: Rod Clarke '46; Middle row: Jean Hebert, Hope Carter, Jules Viau, and Gilda Martin; Back row: Don Reed '58, John Duffy '59, Steve Hume '43, and Jim Shea. This picture was taken at the medal dinner in the fall of 2001.

Madeleine Dreeke gives stage direction to Katie Heidbreder '07 and Joe Lapke '07 in their roles as King Ferdinand and the Princess of France in the Fall 2005 production of Love's Labour's Lost.

The Old Schoolhouse was completed in three stages. The main part was finished in 1938 and the north wing a year later. The Old Schoolhouse was last renovated in the late 1990s.

In 1999, the new athletic facility opened, connecting the rink and the field house and adding five new squash courts, a wrestling/multipurpose room, and a weight room.

One of Canterbury's many community service projects is an annual pilgrimage to assist the malades at the Lourdes shrine. Front row: Viv Simonelli, Hope Carter, Mark Simonelli '99, and Marc Vanasse '73. Back row: Jean Francois Montaine (not of Canterbury), Guy Simonelli, Rich Carter '95, and Yves Rounazeilles (not of Canterbury).

The fields in back of Sheehan House. Duffy House, formerly North House, is in the background. This photo was taken from a window in Carter (South) House

6

THE SHEEHY YEARS

Thomas J. Sheehy III, Fifth Headmaster

On December 18, 1989, after a six-month nationwide search, the Board of Trustees voted unanimously to appoint Thomas J. Sheehy III as Canterbury's fifth headmaster. As reported in *The Tabard*, "Mr. Sheehy grew up on Long Island and comes from a large family. He graduated from the Loyola School in 1965 and Bowdoin College (BA, Classics) in 1969, and received a Master of Arts degree from Penn State."[625]

Tom arrived at Canterbury with considerable boarding school experience, having served for six years at Cranwell School and eight years at Tabor. Mr. Sheehy taught American history, chaired the classics department, served as dorm head, coached sports teams, and served on committees such as the executive and faculty affairs committees. Just prior to his appointment as the fifth headmaster of Canterbury, Tom had served as headmaster of the Old Westbury School of the Holy Child in Old Westbury, New York.[626]

From his first days at Canterbury, faculty, students, parents, and trustees all recognized that Tom had a strong vision for

Canterbury School and its mission. John Duffy, finishing his tenure as board president, explained some of the reasons why Mr. Sheehy was selected: "[For] his interest in young people, [his] appreciation for a talented faculty, [his] commitment to high educational standards, and a life informed by the teachings of the Catholic Church."[627]

Mr. Sheehy began his tenure during the School's seventy-fifth anniversary year. The School planned a convocation to be held in October. Sargent Shriver '34 and Tom Gerety '64, president of Trinity College, were among the honored guests and participants.[628] The convocation opened with *Cantuaria Floreat* played by a brass quartet. Patricia Sardoni '92 read a letter from President George Herbert Walker Bush congratulating the School on its accomplishments. As president of the Student Council, Brian Delaney '91 delivered a speech on behalf of the student body. Stephen '43 and David '45 Hume presented the school with the papal certificate Nelson Hume had received. Peter Tacy, head of the Connecticut Association of Independent Schools (CAIS), spoke about how Walter Sheehan had been instrumental in creating CAIS. Sargent Shriver acted as master of ceremonies, while Tom Gerety delivered the keynote address.[629]

The School held its inaugural Canterbury Medal Dinner on Friday, September 16, 1994, in the Brodie Room on campus. Wishing to honor those individuals who had given so much to benefit the School, Mr. Sheehy had a plaque and medal designed by Tricia Barry, graphic designer and parent of Jackson Barry '98. The award recognizes and honors individuals for their service, loyalty, and dedication to Canterbury School.[630] Board member John O'Neil '57 acted as the master of ceremonies, while Tom Sheehy and Board President Hope Carter presented the medals. Within two years, the dinner had expanded beyond the Brodie Room and had to be moved to the David Casey Copley Library.[631] Today, the medal dinner is held in Canterbury's dining hall in order to accommodate all the recipients, their families, and invited guests. It was at the medal dinner on October 2, 1998, that incoming president of the Board of Trustees, William O'Connor '57, announced that South House would be renamed to honor Hope Carter for her years of service to Canterbury School, including eleven years on Canterbury's Board of Trustees.[632]

Low enrollment continued to be a pressing concern for Mr. Sheehy and the Board. Post–baby boom demographics limited the preparatory school applicant pool, exacerbated by the economic recession of the early 1990s, which limited the number of families who could afford a private school education.[633] By the mid-'90s, enrollment had recovered to around 330 students per year, where it stayed until 2001. In the past three years, there has been a ten-student increase each year, until Canterbury opened with 366 students in the 2004–2005 school year. The target goal for 2005–2006 was 360 students,[634] which the School hopes to maintain for the next several years.[635]

With enrollment down in the early '90s, Business Manager Bryan Kiefer instituted immediate measures to conserve resources and to save money. The School re-bid its liability insurance, changed its health insurance, and eliminated some staff positions. The School also instituted several smaller money-saving measures, such as changing its security system and deciding to show videos in the Steele Hall Lecture Room rather than renting the large film reels to show movies in the auditorium.[636] A fund-raiser headed by D. V. Reed '58 raised money to renovate two of the tennis courts. The School also replaced the hockey rink bed and installed new insulation and piping. Workers replaced the tiles in the pool, emptying and cleaning it.[637] Although ever mindful of the economy and the need to spend wisely, Canterbury applied for and received a substantial grant from the Wiegand Foundation to build a science

232

lab in the Hume Building. The E. L. Wiegand lab was ready for the 1993–1994 school year and is home to the four sections of biology Canterbury now offers.

Recognizing the need to move forward and to plan for the future, the Board and Mr. Sheehy embarked on the formulation of a long-range plan for the school. After meetings with Board members, parents, students, faculty, and others, Mr. Sheehy unveiled the plan in 1997. The plan listed three core goals, which focused on dealing with faculty, facilities, and the non-physical environment of the school.[638] Broadly outlined, the plan sought ways to ensure a qualified, happy faculty, with adequate facilities for promoting the School's mission in an environment conducive to the moral and spiritual health of the school.[639] Canterbury would aim to meet the goals in the long-range plan in conjunction with the goals outlined in the master facilities plan. Some of the concrete recommendations in the long-range plan included renovation of the Old Schoolhouse; construction of a new athletic center; expanded parking; and the construction of non-dormitory faculty housing on campus. Other recommendations included ideas for faculty enrichment, Board evaluation, and an action plan to keep Canterbury's finances healthy, especially by increasing Canterbury's endowment and by developing foundation support for capital projects.[640]

Two of the projects outlined in the long-range plan had already been completed by the time Tom Sheehy made the announcement. A sixty-space parking lot now occupies land between the headmaster's residence and the maintenance shed. This lot is used by students and the many area residents who use the rink and athletic facilities at Canterbury. The School extended the road just beyond Steele Hall and built three houses for faculty families. The former Cauchon house, located on the corner of what is now called Circle Drive, became the new home of the development office.

The Old Schoolhouse renovation project was another component of the school's long-range plan. Built over the course of seventeen years, the Old Schoolhouse had served Canterbury School for decades, providing classroom and study hall space. The original middle section was constructed in 1938, followed the next year by the north wing. Slightly over a dozen years later, the south wing, containing physics and chemistry laboratories, was finally added.

In planning the renovation, architects made every effort to maintain the traditional feel of the Old Schoolhouse, while still updating the building's features. English and history classes, in recent years taught in both the Hume Building and in the Old Schoolhouse, were consolidated now in the Old Schoolhouse. The north wing downstairs became the offices of the English department, with working space for all department faculty members. The Old Schoolhouse also houses the foreign language department. Part of the original study hall, which had served as the school's library for many years, now serves as a seminar room for some honors and advanced placement classes.[641] The rededication and blessing of the Old Schoolhouse took place on a rainy October 8, 1998, and the entire school was invited to participate. The drizzle falling from the sky could not dampen the spirits of those in attendance.

Even before the ribbon-cutting ceremony proclaimed the completion of this phase of the long-range plan, excavators broke ground for the new athletic facility. In addition to connecting the existing field house and hockey rink, the 24,000-square-foot stone structure would house a fitness center, an expanded trainer's room, five squash courts, and an open lobby to watch the activity inside the rink and the field house. The school store and snack bar open directly onto the lobby, which has become a favorite gathering place for students in the afternoon.

The oldest building on campus, once used for the staff of Weantinaug Hall, became the chaplain's residence after extensive renovation transformed it into a two-bedroom cottage with a small kitchen, funded by Jim Briggs, Joe Wheelock, and other members of the class of 1956. As reported in a 1999 issue of *The Tabard*, the chaplain "will now be able to live and meditate in peace without any of the distractions that come with living in a dorm. In addition, the Bishop will now have a place to stay overnight when he comes for confirmation and various other occasions."[642]

During the same year that his residence was being remodeled, Father Sebastian Leonard OSB celebrated Mass, during which seven stained-glass windows were rededicated. Over the years, the windows had suffered damage due to extremes in weather, especially the windows on the south side of the chapel. The restoration would not have been possible without the generosity of several benefactors: Hendrik Vietor, husband of the late Miep Vietor; Walter Burke and family, in memory of his wife Betty; Mr. and Mrs. William DiTullio, parents of Nicholas '01; Mr. and Mrs. John Nelson, parents of Vincent '00 and John '90; Hope E. Carter; and Jim Rowland and Steve Hume, members of the class of 1943.[643]

Thanks to fund-raising efforts and major contributions from L. Michael Sheehy '56, William B. O'Connor '57, and Stephen Hume '43, the School was able to refurbish the old squash courts into a new choral classroom. The project began in early spring of 2001 and was completed by late August of the same year. Named the L. Michael Sheehy '56 Music Classroom, the new space has a 24-foot-high ceiling, oak floors, and acoustic baffles. The music classroom provides a place for voice and instrumental lessons, recitals, and the Chorale and Octet classes. Chorale, as a class taken for credit, replaced the older Choral Club. Canterbury's Octet, also a course for credit, is the equivalent of an academic honors section. Mr. Robert M. Birmingham '62, owner of the

Steinway company from the late 1980s through the mid-'90s, donated a Model B Steinway grand piano for the room.[644] Several years earlier, Stephen Hume and his wife, Lacey, had donated funds to establish The Stephen and Lacey Hume Music Center. The Music Center occupies the space formerly occupied by the weight room and coaches' locker room. In addition to his outright gift, Steve has established a permanent endowment in his and Lacey's name to support the music program.

In 2002, an anonymous donor provided funds for the construction of a new student center. The center is located near the snack bar area of the dining hall, providing easy access to the snack bar while still being separated from the dining hall. The room contains a 43-inch television with cable hookup, an iMac for Internet access, and a Ping-Pong table.[645]

A $50,000 grant from the Ford Foundation combined with a matching 2:1 gift from the James S. Copley Foundation enabled the School to go ahead with some needed additions to the David Casey Copley Library. In addition to fresh paint and new carpeting, the library gained a newly furnished periodicals and reading room. Eight computer stations positioned throughout the library provide access to the computerized card catalog, and a new computer lab with space for multimedia work provides needed computer classroom space.[646]

Canterbury was honored to be named a major beneficiary under the will of Byron King '41 in 2002. Mr. King had arrived at Canterbury as a Second Former in 1937, and won several photographic awards while at the school. Mr. King attended Dartmouth, but left college to serve as a naval officer in WWII. In a pattern of service to his country, he left his business again to serve during the Korean conflict.[647]

While only time will tell which of the current faculty will become school "personalities," several new faces have appeared on

Canterbury's campus in recent years. Madeleine Dreeke joined the faculty the same year Tom Sheehy became headmaster. In addition to teaching Third and Fourth Form English, Madeleine assumed the responsibilities of the theater department. Canterbury alumni Amy McKenna Omaña '86, Frank Bice '77, Diane Parese Haggard '91, and Paddy McCarthy '94 returned to their alma mater to work in admissions, theology, language, and history respectively.

These names represent only some of the alumni who have returned to give years of service to their school. "It is amazing how many alums come back to teach," says Caroline Foley '99, daughter of Fran Foley. "It tells students that they enjoyed their time here, that they agree with and support the School and its values, and that they want to be a part of the experience for future students."[648] After graduating from Canterbury in 1970, Peter O'Donnell returned to Canterbury for eleven years, including three years as director of development. Jules Viau, Jim Shea, and Gilda Martin all have bid Canterbury farewell, but all have maintained almost a daily presence on campus. Gilda has since returned to tutor and to conduct a minor language course called Spanish Study. Although retired from teaching in 1990, Gerry Vanasse continued as the School's organist until 1998, for a total of thirty-eight years of service to Canterbury School.

The Canterbury community must hold considerable attraction, as Math Department Chairman Jack McCabe announced his departure from Canterbury in 1999, only to return several years later. The School is grateful to have "Uncle Jack," southern gentleman and poet, back at the helm. Kim Tester returned in 1995, while Steve Abbott returned in 1996. Steve taught Latin and Art History from 1969 to 1972 before leaving for South Kent. After a fourteen-year hiatus, Steve returned to Canterbury as director of the Annual Fund.

Campus personalities and self-proclaimed "science nuts" John Coffin, Paul Cauchon, and Bev Lee helped former student Keith Choate, now a PhD and MD, to realize his interest in science and medicine, and taught him "a great deal about how to think scientifically."

> On the day Keith Choate graduated from Canterbury, his name was announced so many times as he took home academic prize after academic prize that his full name, Keith Adam Choate, became the day's mantra. Even graduation speaker Dominick Dunne '44 couldn't resist leading off his commencement remarks with one of the day's most humorous and memorable lines, "When I was a student at Canterbury School, I was certainly no Keith Adam Choate."[649]

Keith credits his success in part to the encouragement and support he received while at Canterbury. These faculty "personalities," and many other faculty members past and present, provide mentoring that goes beyond the students' years at Canterbury.

The last fifteen years have also been memorable for those the school has lost. Paul Cauchon and John Coffin retired in 1992 and 1995, respectively. After serving for one year as temporary headmaster at St. Gregory's in Loudonville, New York, Fran Foley announced his permanent appointment in that position. The *Cantuarian* honored Mr. Foley with the yearbook dedication in 1999. Early in 1991, Lillian Fontaine Sheehan, wife of former Headmaster Walter Sheehan, passed away.[650] Not quite three years later, on October 23, 1993, Walter Sheehan, second headmaster of Canterbury School, also passed away, while living at the Candlewood Valley Care Center. On January 2, 1992, Canterbury lost retired faculty member Jack Karpoe, who died unexpectedly. Jules Viau, in presenting this tribute to Jack, said, "He will be missed in the classroom where his strident voice served to lash the reluctant student into activity. Yet there was always the underlying kindness and great solicitude for the student's welfare that could not be hidden even behind his sometimes forbidding exterior."[651] Betty Burke, who had served for twenty-one years as the School's nurse before retiring in 1995, passed away at the beginning of the school year in 1997.

Canterbury School lost two other longtime faculty members in 2000, Charlie Huntington and John Martiska. Since arriving from Storm King School in 1969, Mr. Huntington "contributed to Canterbury in a quiet, laid-back, and completely devoted way; he was always loyal to the school's tradition."[652] Generations of soccer and hockey players, both at Canterbury and in the town, owe their thanks to Charlie, since he was responsible for establishing both youth programs in New Milford. Due to his great contribution to school athletics, the Canterbury Girls' Athlete Award is named after Charlie.[653] With the death of John Martiska, his wife Virginia retired his sit-down dinner bell. The call for quiet at dinner for countless numbers of Canterbury students, the bell was too special a memento to Mrs. Martiska to give up. Mr. Stankus-Saulaitis, school librarian and sit-down dinner administrator, replaced Mr. Martiska's bell with a schoolyard-type bell. The bell is engraved THE JOHN MARTISKA SIT-DOWN DINNER BELL and still announces the beginning of each Thursday night's sit-down dinner.[654]

In 1991, the PET computers were laid to rest and replaced by the short-lived Apple IIc clones, the Laser 128s.[655] Unable to equip an entire lab with the more expensive Apple IIc computers, Paul Cauchon had to decide whether to purchase enough Laser 128 computers for a classroom, or only half as many Apple IIc computers. Hoping that within several years the school would be able to provide better state-of-the-art technology, Paul opted for the less-expensive computers; after all, the vTech Laser 128 had been in existence since 1984.[656] Unfortunately, although the Lasers were relatively stable with only one person using them, they did not do well in a classroom setting. The disk drives were especially quirky, and sometimes Paul could only get them to work by turning the whole unit on its side. After establishing a strong computer department at Canterbury, Paul retired in June 1992.

Although for some years e-mail and Internet access had been available on a limited basis to faculty, it wasn't until the school year of 1997–1998, under Rob Roffe, that e-mail and voice mail became available to students, along with the development of a Canterbury Web presence. Rob and his wife Cammy, daughter of former teacher and current trustee Jim Briggs '56, had arrived in the fall of 1995. There was a lab of Apple PowerMac 7200s on the first floor of Hume, and a lab of Windows 3.1 computers in the library.[657] Under Rob's stewardship, outside contractors dug 4-foot-deep trenches around campus in the summer of 1998 in preparation for wiring the campus. The trenches carried fiber-optic and voice wire to all the buildings on campus, including dormitory common rooms, faculty apartments, and each classroom in the Old Schoolhouse.[658]

With the reconstruction of the library in the summer of 2004, a library reading room replaced the drop-in computer lab, and the drop-in lab moved to a larger space along the north portion of the library. The new lab is equipped with a special area for multimedia editing and production. With the wiring of the campus buildings, Canterbury was in a good position to install wireless service as soon as pricing made it economically feasible. Students may now access the Internet or their own network storage area from any class or dorm building.

The curriculum continued to expand throughout the 1990s. By 1998–1999, Canterbury offered advanced placement courses in English language, English literature, calculus, American history, biology, chemistry, studio art, music theory, French, and Spanish.[659]

Departments offered more electives based on the interests and expertise of the faculty. Some of the electives reflected a renewed emphasis on spiritual growth as outlined in the school's mission statement, such as Sports Ethics and Ethics in Fiction, a course detailing how readers view characters and make judgments about them.

The history department recognized the growing global community by offering electives in The History of Asia and The History of Africa.[660] The science department offered Anthropology, Oceanography, and minor courses in Western African Civilization and Historical Debate. Dave Overthrow, a part-time member of the Canterbury community who had given music lessons and conducted the ensemble, joined the faculty full-time in 1996. Mr. Sheehy wished to develop the music program and expand the offerings in the fine arts department. Today, students may take classes such as Music Theory, Improvisation, The History of Rock, and Computer Music, as well as strictly performance classes such as the Jazz Chamber class. In addition, there are numerous performing instrumental and vocal groups.

It quickly became apparent that with expanded offerings and a growing fine arts program, it was necessary to find more time in the daily schedule. At the request of Lou Mandler, director of studies, Jen Chandler attended a weeklong summer institute in 1997, "Scheduling Without Conflict," sponsored by ism®, (Independent School Management). Canterbury incorporated many of the scheduling ideas Jen brought back from the institute. The new class schedule, introduced at the beginning of the 1997–1998 school year, eliminated the five minutes of passing time between classes. With an earlier start to the day at 7:45 A.M., the schedule also eliminated the need for separate winter and spring schedules and built in more time for students to seek and receive extra help.[661]

Mrs. Mandler revamped the senior project application process by "enlarging the role the curriculum committee plays in advising seniors who undertake projects."[662] Sixth Form students interested in completing a Senior Project must submit a proposal, which is then refined through the input of the curriculum committee. Each student finds a faculty sponsor to oversee his or her project and must also have an off-campus sponsor willing to report on the student's work. At the conclusion of the project, students make presentations to the curriculum committee and interested guests, at which time the students also defend their work.

Headmaster Sheehy's second year at Canterbury, 1991–1992, marked the twentieth anniversary of coeducation at the School. A special winter drama production consisting of excerpts from *The Diary of Anne Frank*, *Joan of Lorraine*, and *The Heiress* celebrated the anniversary of coeducation.[663] The Girls' League, which had slowly become inactive over the years, was replaced by the Women of Canterbury. Women of Canterbury offered an educational forum to female students and planned programs to deal with contemporary issues of concern to the girls, such as date rape and gender discrimination.[664] Ultimately, the League merged with the Mission Society and became a coeducational group. Newly named the Canterbury League, this club organized social events and fundraisers for charitable groups.[665]

Just two short years later, Canterbury appointed its first female dean of students, Margie Jenkins. Working together, Sandy Behan and Lou Mandler created an independent-study course called Women's Studies.[666] It didn't take very long for the course to grow into a regular elective, which is still offered today. Mrs. Sandy Behan earned the yearbook dedication in 1998 in recognition of the impact she had had not only on all the girls attending Canterbury, but also on the entire student body. In addition to teaching AP Biology and many upper-form science electives,

Sandy also was—and still is—the faculty advisor to Women of Canterbury, the Environmental Club, and SADD (founded as Students Against Driving Drunk, and today known as Students Against Destructive Decisions).

Sandy would earn another honor in April of 1999, when Women of Canterbury sponsored their first Mother-Daughter Dinner. The members chose Sandy as Woman of the Year for all of her contributions to the Canterbury community.[667] This yearly dinner has become a highly anticipated event among the girls, and has featured such speakers as actress Mia Farrow and author Patrice Gaines.[668]

Today, Canterbury's girls represent almost half of the School's enrollment, and a high percentage of the students in Honors and AP classes. They are also active participants in Chorale, the theater, and other clubs.[669] "A truly coeducational school does not serve just girls and women better. It also serves boys and men better . . . The goal of Canterbury continues to be to provide an excellent education for all, and we believe coeducation plays an integral part in such an education."[670]

In October of 1993,[671] several interested faculty and students formed the Canterbury Association for Racial Equality (C.A.R.E. Club). Members hoped to establish cultural awareness, to act as a support group for diversity on campus, and to foster an open-door policy toward all students.[672] In its early years, CARE raised money to sponsor children in different parts of the world through organizations such as Save the Children. The club invited speakers to the school, including alumnus Tracy Simms '86. In 1998, the club broadened its scope and became CARES, the Canterbury Association for Racial and Social Equality. Within the past two years, CARES has changed its name to the Diversity Committee, but its mission of promoting tolerance and acceptance remains strong.

An overall commitment to community service is a cornerstone at Canterbury School. Although already involved with several existing projects, the students and faculty are always looking for new ways to promote service. The town cleanup day began in 1995, with volunteers from the School raking leaves on the town green as well as at the Children's Center and Richmond Center. The Sixth Form adopted this project when the School decided that each form would participate in a community service class project.[673] Form projects have included such diverse activities as blood drives, fund-raising for Jump Rope and Hoops for Heart, and pulling weeds on the varsity baseball field. Jump Rope and Hoops for Heart are national educational fund-raising programs that are sponsored by the American Heart Association (AHA) and the American Alliance for Health, Physical Education, Recreation and Dance (AAHPERD). The goal of these two programs is to educate kids about health, fitness, and the importance of a regular exercise program while simultaneously instilling values such as community involvement, leadership, and altruism.[674] Librarian Algis Stankus-Saulaitis revived the School's Amnesty International chapter in 1998. The student members of Amnesty sponsor petition-signing events in the dining hall and write "letters of conscience" to help political prisoners.

Each year since Rod Clarke's headmastership, just prior to Thanksgiving break, the Canterbury community participates in an Oxfam Fast Day, originally run by Guy Simonelli, but now supervised by the dean of students' office. Students and faculty may sign up to fast during breakfast and/or lunch, with the money contributed to fight world hunger. Rather than conducting a more traditional fund-raising event, participating in the Fast Day enables the students to experience firsthand, albeit only for one day, what it feels like to be hungry. School participation in Oxfam has reached a high of 90 percent. The Fast Day always ends with an expression of gratitude for all that the Canterbury community has, as expressed with a Thanksgiving sit-down dinner.[675]

All of Canterbury's community service since 2003 has been under the umbrella of the assistant to the dean of students, currently Mary Holton. Mary is the faculty advisor to the Canterbury League, often referred to as the community service committee. Along with various faculty members who organize and encourage support for different service organizations, the students of the League meet and coordinate events. In the spirit of outreach, students during the March 2005 spring break could choose between two service trips, one to Haiti and the other to Nicaragua.[676] On the trip to Nicaragua, students helped paint and repair a school for young children. In Haiti, students assisted at Project Pierre Toussaint in Cap Haitian, a school and residential village helping the poorest of the poor children in Haiti get off the street.

Sometimes tragedies happen in the world at large that unite the entire Canterbury community with a singleness of purpose. Two such events have already happened in this new millennium: the September 11 terrorist attacks against the World Trade Center and Pentagon, and the tsunami of 2004 off the coast of Indonesia. The shock and enormity of these events bonded the School, as students, staff, and faculty found comfort in attending Mass, in fund-raising efforts both organized and impromptu, and in each other.

One other project has arisen from tragedy, this time a tragedy within the community that was deeply felt by everyone. In July 1999, Guiseppe "Joe" Leto '97 succumbed to heat exhaustion and died during basic training maneuvers with the United States Marine Corps. His commanding officer was charged with improperly marching his charges. Joe had been an active participant on the football, wrestling, and lacrosse teams, and he had captained the wrestling team. Through the inception and generosity of the

Leto family, the "Run for Joe" raises money to award to a Canterbury student in need of financial aid. In its first two years, the run was able to raise $35,000 to donate to the scholarship fund.[677] Current students participate in the run and are joined by many faculty and former classmates who remember Joe.

After several years' absence, the Student Council returned in 1993.[678] In an effort to give student leaders greater visibility, Mr. Sheehy conducts morning meetings jointly with the student government president. Sacristans open the meeting with a prayer, followed by faculty announcements and any business Mr. Sheehy needs to conduct. When faculty announcements conclude, Mr. Sheehy turns the floor over to the student government president, who presides over student announcements. The student government sometimes works in conjunction with the Community Service Committee to organize events, and it has largely been this student committee, along with a volunteer parents' group, that has been responsible for bringing back and organizing the prom.

The Tabard continued to win awards from the American School Press Association in the early 1990s.[679] However, throughout most of the recent decade, *The Tabard* has only been published a maximum of four times per year. In the late '90s, the future of *The Tabard* seemed uncertain as publication dropped to only two times per year, and, in the 2000–2001 school year, no *Tabards* were published at all. The next year, *The Tabard* resumed publishing four issues a year. A second death knell almost tolled when the first issue of the 2003–2004 *Tabard* appeared as a stapled newsletter sheet instead of the regular newspaper format. The editors rectified the formatting for the second issue, and in 2004–2005, *The Tabard* editors endeavored to increase the publication schedule. For future generations of Cantuarians, *The Tabard* remains the single best source of information, documenting the history of the school.

After disappearing for at least two years, the *Carillon* made an end-of-the-year appearance in 1992.[680] Over the next five years, the *Carillon* published at least one issue per year. Recently, the *Carillon* has published two issues per year. In 2003–2004, the *Carillon* came full circle, back to its roots, by announcing that the spring issue would dedicate itself to works of short fiction. This harks back to the *Carillon's* immediate predecessor, *The Canterbury Quarterly*, which produced student literature, and its ancestor, *The Quill*, which published news, essays, and literature, primarily from Dr. Hume's classes. At least since 2000, the editors of the *Carillon* have celebrated the publication of each of the magazine's issues with an evening of poetry reading by contributors and other volunteers.

The same year that Tom Sheehy became headmaster, Madeleine Dreeke took over the theater department. Madeleine brought a combination of many years of classroom teaching along with an equal number of years' acting experience. Mrs. Dreeke had appeared in the original versions of *Sweet Charity* and *Marathon 33* on Broadway, and had also done a great deal of regional and summer stock work.[681] Working alongside Mattie is her husband, Robin, who oversees the technical end of each production, such as lighting, sound, and set construction and design. *Noises Off*, which Mrs. Dreeke directed in 1997, has earned its place as one of the most memorable theater productions at Canterbury. The most technically challenging of all the plays Mrs. Dreeke has directed at Canterbury, *Noises Off* also had the best ensemble work, with a seasoned and dedicated cast and crew.[682]

With each subsequent production, the Dreekes have encouraged their cast and crew to greater heights. Robin and Madeleine Dreeke were the second recipients, in 1998, of the Duffy Travel Award. John Duffy and his wife, Anne, established the John P. and Anne Duffy Faculty Travel and Teaching Award to promote travel among the faculty. On their grant, the Dreekes traveled to

London and investigated the many acting schools and theater programs there. Since March 2000, the Dreekes have sponsored a theater trip to London during each March break. Limited to no more than a dozen serious students of theater, students take classes at The Globe Theatre in London and other acting schools, such as LAPA (London Academy of the Performing Arts) or East 15 Acting School.

Mr. and Mrs. Dreeke have also implemented their plan of bringing Shakespeare to the whole community. Each fall since 2000, they have produced one of Shakespeare's plays. All English classes, no matter which form, study the play at approximately the same time it's produced. Actors and crew visit classes to answer questions about plot and production techniques. Mrs. Dreeke has even provided study guides and children's versions for the many faculty children.

The Pirates of Penzance was the spring 2005 musical production. The centerpiece of the stage was the pirate ship, constructed in two pieces and hinged, so the ship could be moved throughout the play.

The school year of 1990–1991 marked the beginning of a new girls' athletic program at Canterbury—ice hockey. Girls' ice hockey didn't appear in the *Cantuarian*, however, until the 1992 book, when the team posted a record of two wins and three losses. Today, approximately twenty girls play at the varsity level, with another twenty playing at the junior varsity level. During the 2003–2004 winter season, the girls played twenty-four regular season and tournament games, finishing with a record of 16-7-1.[683]

In 1991, the Canterbury lacrosse team made its debut in the Division I League. Under the leadership of Captain Brian Whalen, Canterbury not only won the championship, but had an undefeated season with a record of 14-0. In the final game of the championship, the score seesawed until late in the fourth quarter, when the Saints were down by four goals. A supreme effort on the part of the Saints tied the score, and the game went into "sudden death," with Canterbury winning.[684] The girls' varsity basketball team also had a good winter season that year. They went on to win the New England small schools tournament.[685]

Other notable athletic accomplishments in the past fifteen years have included the boys' varsity hockey win over Avon in the New England tournament in 1993,[686] as well as twice winning the New England hockey tournament, in 1994 and 1997. In addition, the boys' varsity football team twice won the Class B New England Championship. In what was billed by *The Tabard* as "Canterbury Football's Miracle Season," the Saints scored a 28–20 win over Salisbury in 1995.[687] In 2003, the Saints, with an 8-1 record, defeated New Hampton 9–7 for the championship. A last-minute sack saved the day. The School demonstrated a tremendous out-pouring of support for the team with transportation and food pro-vided by the athletic department for the game's spectators.[688] And, for only the sixth time in the nineteen years of its existence, Canterbury regained the Sheehan Cup on October 23, 1993. The Sheehan Trophy is an annual all-school athletic competition between Canterbury and Berkshire School named in honor of Mr. Sheehan. Coincidentally, this was the very morning that former headmaster Walter Sheehan, the man for whom the cup was named, left this world. What a fitting honor to bestow upon this great Canterbury man.

7

A LOOK FORWARD[686]

In the past ten years, Canterbury School has achieved many of the goals set forth in the 1996 Long-Range Plan. The total student population has increased, and the percentage of female students has increased from 34 percent to 42 percent. The School has built a new athletic center and extensively renovated the Old Schoolhouse. Faculty have three new houses on Circle Drive and new apartment space in the dormitories. Through the generosity of many, Canterbury now has the Hume Music Center, the Sheehy Choral Classroom, and the E. L. Wiegand Science Lecture Room. There also are newly installed sidewalks for student safety, and an additional student parking lot.

At the opening school meeting of 2005–2006, Headmaster Sheehy announced that the Board of Trustees had given him the green light to embark on the School's next major capital campaign. Based on a projected $30-million-plus price tag, the next phase of the long-range plan includes renovations to almost all the current buildings on campus, with special plans to expand Steele

Hall, Carmody House, Havemeyer House, and the Art Center. The addition of a sixth dormitory for girls is also part of the plan.

Canterbury continues in its efforts to attract a seasoned, loyal faculty by providing better housing, increasing compensation, and focusing each teacher's workload into two or three main areas. At least for the next few years, the School hopes to maintain its current enrollment, but wishes to increase female enrollment so Canterbury can become fully coeducational. Along with improved facilities, Canterbury hopes to offer quality programs in the arts and drama to continue to attract a greater variety of students.

Canterbury's updated 2002 Long-Range Plan never loses sight of Canterbury's mission statement of "a broad and challenging program in a small school setting. The School's educational environment fosters academic rigor, athletic development, artistic enrichment, and spiritual growth."

Addressing the Canterbury community via a letter in the *Pallium* in 1996, Hope Carter wrote the following words, whose spirit is still true today:

> Canterbury owes its progress to a succession of outstanding headmasters, superb teachers, and generous benefactors. In 82 years, the School has grown from four teachers instructing 16 boys in three buildings on eleven rented acres to a faculty of 50 men and women who teach 335 boys and girls in 26 buildings on a campus of 150 acres. From founding headmaster Nelson Hume to present headmaster Tom Sheehy, from teachers Phil Brodie to Jim Shea, and from benefactors Henry O. Havemeyer to John Duffy '59, an unbroken line of individuals faithful to the Canterbury ideal has built the school that exists today.[690]

Just as we included words from Edward Mack's history between sections detailing the old and the new, it seems appropriate to turn once again to Mr. Mack to close this history:

It would seem that to a school it is proper to propose: What can be done for the individual soul and the individual mind notwithstanding, whatever handicaps may encumber it? What that school has been able to do within the framework of its possibilities would be a fair measuring-rod of success. The vision, the courage, and the faith of Nelson Hume and his co-founders have been justified and their efforts happily achieved to be passed on to hopeful and capable successors.

For if "A boy's will is the wind's will, And the thoughts of youth are long, long thoughts,"[691] then the wind was captured and the long, long thoughts were close to his heart in a mystic world wherein God was his Friend and his enriched faith the inviolable sanctuary of those long, long thoughts.

And with the support of all the Canterbury family, the future will be as bright as the past has been glorious. [692]

Cantuaria floreat.

252

PART I: *The Hume Years*

1 "America's Richest." *The First Rich List – Forbes.com* [http://www.forbes.com/2002/09/27/0927richest_9.html]. March 20, 2006. The humble job of a dry goods clerk in Baltimore did not suit Thomas Fortune Ryan, so he migrated to Wall Street. He made enough to buy a seat on the New York Stock Exchange... The Street has known few speculators as daring and as successful financially as Ryan.

2 *Danbury News Times* Thursday, June 17, 1948.

3 Letter. Henry O. Havemeyer to Clarence Mackay. March 25, 1915.

4 Letter. Henry O. Havemeyer to Clarence Mackay. March 25, 1915.

5 *NY Herald.* Wed., November 3, 1915 and *The Evening World.* Wed., November 3, 1915. See also Letter. Clarence Mackay to Henry O. Havemeyer, September 28, 1915.

6 Letter. Nelson Hume to Henry O. Havemeyer. November 25, 1914 (written on WP Nelson Company letterhead).

7 Letter. Nelson Hume to His Eminence John Cardinal Farley. June 17, 1915. "Dr. Carroll's letter written June 13th did not reach me until yesterday afternoon June 16th upon my return from Washington where I had been spending several days at Georgetown University for the purpose of receiving the degree of Doctor of Philosophy."

8 Letter. Nelson Hume to Henry O. Havemeyer. January 2, 1915; Letter. Henry O. Havemeyer to Nelson Hume. January 4, 1915.

9 Prospectus. [n.d.] in correspondence file w/ January 1915 letters.

10 Letter. Nelson Hume to Henry O. Havemeyer. January 28, 1915.

11 Letter. Nelson Hume to Henry O. Havemeyer. February 17, 1915.

12 Letter. Nelson Hume to Henry O. Havemeyer. February 17, 1915.

13 Letter. Clarence Mackay to Henry O. Havemeyer. March 18, 1915.

14 Letter. Nelson Hume to Henry O. Havemeyer. December 28, 1916. ". . . the certificate be made out leaving out the name 'George,' because he had discontinued the use of 'George' in his name, although it was by this name that he was put down as one of our directors by Mr. Mackay."

15 Minutes. Board of Directors of Canterbury School, Inc. December

1915.

16 *New York Times* article on 25th anniversary. [nd]

17 "St. Dunstan." *Catholic Encyclopedia.*
http://www.newadvent.org/cathen/05199a.htm; *New York Herald Tribune.* Thurs., October 25, 1956.

18 Letter. Nelson Hume to Henry O. Havemeyer. August 1915.

19 Letter. Henry O. Havemeyer to Nelson Hume. August 26, 1915.

20 This quote came from *Memorandum on the Admission of Boys* written by Nelson Hume and given to the Board of Directors sometime during the summer of 1915.

21 Ibid..

22 Letter. Nelson Hume to Henry O. Havemeyer. March 7, 1915.

23 Letter. Henry O. Havemeyer to Nelson Hume. July 12, 1915.

24 Six 1/4 page ads appeared in America; a 1/4 page ad appeared in *Catholic World,* and once in *Lamp.* Minutes. Board of Directors of the Canterbury School. July 7, 1915.

25 Letter. Nelson Hume to Henry O. Havemeyer. September 16, 1915.

26 In my photocopied papers, I have the English II Form examination 1917, gift of Cyril Clemens.

27 Thomas J. and Harriet K. Hume had nine children: John K. 1877, Marie 1879, Nelson 1881, Alexander 1882, Madeline (died as a child), Constance 1886, Raphael 1888, Dorothy 1892, and Cyril 1900.

28 *The Tabard.* April 16, 1935. 1st Head-Boy dies of pneumonia at the age of 37.

29 Letter. Nelson Hume to Henry O. Havemeyer. September 16, 1915. As late as this, Hume notes that the Ryans are not going to be enrolled in Canterbury for this year.

30 Letter. Henry O. Havemeyer to Allen A. Ryan. October 20, 1914. Letter of introduction for Nelson Hume, with proposition with regard to the founding of a school for boys . . . Letter. Alec Hume to Henry O. Havemeyer, October 17, 1915.

31 A nephew of Havemeyer.

32 Letter. Nelson Hume to Henry O. Havemeyer. September 26, 1916. Grosvenor Fessenden had to drop out because his father died about Easter time, which made a difference in the family's finances.

33 http://www.hvceo.org/luchange_newmilford.php?print=yes "In 1819, when the Town's population was about 3,800 persons, the Gazetteer of Connecticut and Rhode Island described New Milford as a 'flourishing post-town' with three bridges across the Housatonic and 'numerous sites for mills.'"

34 "84 miles from New York – 1 mile from New Milford: Erected by Zachariah Sanford, 1788."

35 "1910 U.S. Federal Census – CT- Litchfield – Other towns . . ." [http://content.ancestry.com/Browse/list.aspx?dbid=7884&path=Connecticut.Litchfield.New+milford]

36 *The Tabard.* January 15, 1935.

34 Letter. Mr. Charles Barlow. August 5, 2005.

38 Executive Committee Minutes. Board of Directors of Canterbury School. Wed., June 23, 1915.

39 Carmody, Ed. *Letter to May Hume.* February 2, 1979. p. 27. "The Sixth Form House" was the official name of the Bungalow, but it was not commonly used.

40 Alec Hume was known variously as Al or Alex, although he always signed his letters Alexander.

41 Letter. Alexander Hume to Henry O. Havemeyer. April 10, 1917.

42 Letter. Alexander H to Henry O. Havemeyer. January 22, 1918.

43 Minutes. Board of Directors of Canterbury School. July 10, 1918. Board accepts his resignation and replaces Alex with Mr. John T. King. King gives graduation speech 1919.

44 Carmody, Ed. *Letter to May Hume.* February 2, 1979. p. 28.

45 Letter. Nelson Hume to Henry O. Havemeyer. April 19, 1917.

46 *The Tabard.* November 30, 1926.

47 Ben Halsey was a student in the early 1930s. *The Tabard.* January 24, 1933. Captain of championship swim team in March 1934. The great-

nephews of Ben Halsey are Mark Nailor '05 and Tom Nailor '08.

48 Letter. Nelson Hume to Henry O. Havemeyer. August 4, 1931.

49 Letter. Nelson Hume to Henry O. Havemeyer. August 4, 1931. During the Depression, Canterbury's average cost of food per boy was approximately 32¢. Nelson relates to Mr. Havemeyer that at one large girls' boarding school, "where they do not eat a great deal and where they are not accustomed to a high standard," their food cost is as low as 19¢.

50 Lessing, Lawrence. "Changing Tables." *The Canterbury Quarterly*. Vol. 11, no. 1. December 1926. p. 42.

51 Additional information from Letter. Nelson Hume to Henry O. Havemeyer. October 29, 1930.

52 Letter. Nelson Hume to Henry O. Havemeyer. September 24, 1941.

53 Letter. Nelson Hume to Henry O. Havemeyer. October 29, 1930.

54 Ibid. As a matter of fact, Hume says, "From the outset, the meats and vegetables were first-class, but the soups were very poor. However, by keeping after it, Mr. MacDermott has got the chef to make pretty good soups, so that question has been settled. The desserts are not particularly attractive or well made, but there again he is working on his second cook, who is also the baker, and his work is improving."

55 Letter. Henry O. Havemeyer to Nelson Hume. September 7, 1915.

56 Letter. Nelson Hume to Henry O. Havemeyer. July 15, 1919. "In having colors made we have found that the most understandable way to describe our colors is to say they are a combination of navy blue and Columbia blue. Navy blue gets us away from what is called royal blue or Yale blue, which does not combine well with light blue because it makes light blue look gray, and Columbia blue is a particular shade of light blue not inclining towards the greenish tinge usually known as robin's egg blue."

57 Jude 1:3. This is the way the passage appears in the King James version of the Bible. However, the wording is different in each different edition of the Bible.

58 Executive Committee Minutes. Board of Directors of Canterbury School. July 21, 1915.

59 Letter. Clarence Mackay to Nelson Hume. May 25, 1917.

60 Executive Committee Minutes. Board of Directors of Canterbury School. July 21, 1915.

61 Letter. Henry O. Havemeyer to Nelson Hume. August 11, 1915.

62 Letter. Nelson Hume to Henry O. Havemeyer. March 5, 1929. Earlier letter NH to Henry O. Havemeyer. December 26, 1916. "Just a word about the Tiffany paper . . . Once the die is made we get our paper at Tiffany's commercial rates for practically the same price charged by inferior stationers for inferior goods . . . [I] use this paper only in correspondence with the parents of boys and people inquiring about the school . . . it gives an indication at the very outset that everything else in connection with the school is of a high quality, which is the impression we want to create."

63 *The Tabard*. March 11, 1924.

64 A poll in *The Tabard* in the early 1920s indicated that the boys' favorite author was Robert Louis Stevenson.

65 "Canterbury Tales." *The Quill*. Vol. 1, no. 1. December 1916. p. 13.

66 *The Tabard*. October 21, 1930. Mr. Meehan also gave the school its pipe organ.

67 Miller, Theron B. Jr. "Crossing their tees." *The Canterbury Quarterly*. Vol. 9, no. 3. June 1925, p. 260.

68 Carmody, Ed. *Letter to May Hume*. February 2, 1979. p. 32.

69 Series of letters between Nelson Hume and Peter Maloney, Jan.–Feb. 1916.

70 Compare with Wife of the Centaur by Cyril Hume. [http://www.iofferstores.com/bi/sandsbooks--MYSELF-YOUNG-BOWMAN-Cyril-Hume-Lm-Signed--1.2-0.88-2012957] Cyril Hume, born March 16, 1900 at New Rochelle, New York, was the younger brother of Nelson Hume. He left Yale before getting a degree. His first book, *Wife of the Centaur* (1923), became a successful movie. He wrote screenplay adapta-

tions and occasionally appeared in magazines.

71 [http://www.hvceo.org/luchange_newmilford.php?print=yes] West of Lake Candlewood and the Housatonic River high ridges extend along the border of Sherman, the principal ridge lines consisting of Green Pond Mountain, Candlewood Mountain, Stillson Hill, Barnes Hill and Boardman Mountain.

72 "Canterbury Tales." *The Quill*. Vol. 1, no. 1. December 1916. p. 14.

73 Letter. Nelson Hume to Henry O. Havemeyer. January 8, 1916.

74 *The Tabard*. April 15, 1924. It may seem early for raspberries, but if we are to believe the members of the baseball team, there is already a crop in full bloom. – Francis T. Carmody.

75 Carmody, Ed. *Letter to May Hume*. February 2, 1979. p. 43.

76 Ibid.

77 Ibid. p. 26.

78 Letter. Nelson Hume to Henry O. Havemeyer. August 23, 1916.

79 Letter. Nelson Hume to Henry O. Havemeyer. February 20, 1917. There will be a special parlor-car on the train, reserved for the guests of Canterbury School. Seats for this car should be purchased from the Pullman conductor on the train, not at the ticket office in the station.

80 *The Tabard*. December 15, 1919. Juniors' Joy and The Searchlight were two such publications.

81 *The Tabard*. May 8, 1923 and *The Tabard*. November 27, 1923. Within three weeks of publication, the movie rights were sold for $25,000, one of the largest sums ever paid at this time.

82 *The Canterbury Quarterly*. Vol 8, no. 1. December 1923. Formerly *The Quill*.

83 *The Tabard*. October 25, 1986. Original story in *The Tabard*. March 13, 1923.

84 *The Tabard*. October 11, 1921.

85 Ryan, Leicester Y. "First Assignment." *The Canterbury Quarterly*. Vol. 11, no. 3. June 1927. p. 214.

86 *The Tabard*. October 27, 1936.

87 Some *Tabards*, personal copies of Nelson Hume, show his editing marks (particularly those in 1934–1936).

88 Letter. Nelson Hume to Henry O. Havemeyer. April 18, 1918 and *The Quill*. Vol. 3, no. 1. December 1918.

89 *New York Times* article on 25th anniversary. [nd]

90 Letter. Nelson Hume to Henry O. Havemeyer, Clarence Mackay, etc. [May 1917?]

91 Letter. Parsons to Henry O. Havemeyer. May 22, 1917.

92 Letter. Nelson Hume to Henry O. Havemeyer. April 25, 1917.

93 Minutes. Board of Directors of Canterbury School. 1919. Havemeyer wished Hume to receive salary of stock or share of profits. A compromise was reached, but over the year letters indicated different ideas of when exactly NH's school year began. In August of 1919, they are still wrangling over salaries.

94 Folder for April 1919 has organization plans as drawn by Carmody.

95 Letter. Nelson Hume to Henry O. Havemeyer. August 12, 1943.

96 Letter. Alexander Hume to Henry O. Havemeyer. September 18, 1920 and [http://hearth.com/questions/qa1888.html] After being wrested from the ground, the coal was generally graded into four differing grades . . . pea coal was less than less than 3/8 inch . . . some stove's shaker systems burn pea very well, but for others it's too small—too dense.

97 Letter. Nelson Hume to Henry O. Havemeyer. August 29, 1921.

98 "Canterbury Tales." *The Quill*. Vol. 1, no. 3. June 1917. p. 17.

99 *The Tabard*. February 17, 1925.

100 Letter. Henry O. Havemeyer to Nelson Hume. November 27, 1918.

101 "Canterbury Tales." *The Quill*. Vol. 3, no.1. December 1918. p. 20.

102 Letter. Nelson Hume to Henry O. Havemeyer. November 20, 1918.

103 *The Tabard*. April 7, 1919.

104 *The Tabard*. October 11, 1921.

105 Interview. Jean Hebert. August 2004.

106 *The Tabard*. May 27, 1986.

107 Vanasse, Marc. "The 'Bear' Essentials: A Conversation with Jean Hebert." *Pallium*. Vol 5, no. 2. Fall 1988. p. 4.

108 *The Tabard*. November 21, 1975

109 "Canterbury and the Peace Corps: 25 Years of Shared Service." *Pallium*. Vol. 2, no. 4. Spring 1986. p. 5.

110 *The Tabard*. November 21, 1975.

111 David Hume suggests Keyser Island. No evidence to verify one way or the other, but Canterbury did have ties with Keyser.

112 In the archives there is a little pamphlet containing "school prayers."

113 Letter. Nelson Hume to Henry O. Havemeyer. January 6, 1920. Gift $4,000. Rink cost $3,552.41.

114 Carmody, Francis T. "Scorn not the shovel." *The Canterbury Quarterly*. Vol. 9, no. 2. March, 1925. p. 130.

115 Interview. Stephen Hume. July 15, 2004.

116 This story could not be verified.

117 *The Tabard*. October 8, 1935. The parent was Mr. Charles C. Pettijohn. Several of the masters took out Motion Picture Operators' Licenses, so they could operate the machine during performances.

118 From an unpublished history of the school written by Andrew Smith.

119 Letter. Nelson Hume to Henry O. Havemeyer. February 23, 1928. *The Plan*. Trustee circular to parents and interested parties. [n.d.] The Collegiate Gothic style of architecture will be followed. Correspondence file February 1921.

120 *Report of the Headmaster to the Board of Trustees*. Nelson Hume. March 5, 1920.

121 Letter. Nelson Hume to Henry O. Havemeyer. July 13, 1917 and Letter. Raphael Hume to Nelson Hume. May 10, 1920.

122 Letter. Nelson Hume to Henry O. Havemeyer. April 17, 1920.

123 *Memorandum by the Headmaster on the Development of the School*. Nelson Hume. December 3, 1920 and *The Quill*. Vol. 4, no. 3. June 1920. p. 5.

124 Letter. Henry O. Havemeyer to Mr. Philip Scheuerman. May 9,

1939.

125 *The Tabard*. February 21, 1921.

126   [http://www.hvceo.org/luchange_newmilford.php?print=yes] Route 7 was completed through the town as a paved two-lane road by 1920, and Routes 25 (now 67 and 202) and 37 were completed a few years later.

127 *The Tabard*. March 7, 1922.

128 *The Tabard*. November 28, 1922.

129 Letter. Nelson Hume to Henry O. Havemeyer. February 20, 1923.

130 Dr. Hume's outline for the town meeting is in the archives.

131 Located on Terrace Place.

132 "Records of the retreat." *The Quill*. Vol. 2, no. 2. March 1918. p. 25.

133 *The Quill*. Vol. 3, no. 1. December 1918. p. 34. Picture of John McCormack.

134 In Vanasse, Marc. "Canterbury Drama Center Stage: A History in Five Acts." *Pallium*. Vol. 4, no. 4. Spring 1988. p. 3. Marc cites 1919.

135 At least one parent withdrew her son in 1918 after an outbreak of the measles, and Mrs. Havemeyer reprimands Dr. Hume after her son, Frederick, develops a cough after the measles in 1920. In defending his care of Freddy, Dr. Hume responds by saying that it was Frederick who brought the measles onto campus this time.

136 *The Tabard*. March 22, 1920.

137 *The Tabard*. February 17, 1925.

138 *The Tabard*. June 13, 1920.

139 *The Tabard*. April 28, 1925.

140 *The Tabard*. October 13, 1925.

141 *The Tabard*. May 28, 1925.

142 Hume, David, '45. "May Hume: A Canterbury Original." *Pallium*. Vol. 3, no 4. Spring 1987. p. 12.

143 *The Tabard*. December 11, 1923.

144 F. Scott Fitzgerald attended the Newman School ca. 1911.

145 Interview. Stephen Hume, Tuesday, September 14, 2004.

146 Hume, David, '45. "May Hume: A Canterbury Original." *Pallium*. Vol. 3, no 4. Spring 1987. p. 12.

147 E-mail. David Hume. Feb. 15, 2006.

148 E-mail. Stephen Hume. Feb. 15, 2006.

149 Hume, David, '45. "May Hume: A Canterbury Original." *Pallium*. Vol. 3, no 4. Spring 1987. p. 12.

150 Carmody, Ed. *Letter to May Hume*. February 2, 1979. p. 59.

151 Letter. Nelson Hume to Clarence Mackay. January 15, 1923.

152 *The Tabard*. December 8, 1925.

153 Ibid.

154 Ibid.

155 Carmody, Guerin. "The new old house." *The Canterbury Quarterly*. Vol. 11, no. 1. December 1926. p. 40.

156 *The Tabard*. March 2, 1926. "The exact location [of the dormitory] was determined by the position of the Chapel. The building would begin at the west side of the chapel and go north so that the chapel would become a subsidiary wing to the building."

157 "From old neighbor to new addition." *Pallium*. Vol. 2, no. 2. Fall 1985. p. 15.

158 *The Tabard*. February 2, 1926.

159 Letter. Nelson Hume to Henry O. Havemeyer. May 21, 1928. Mr. Smith also assumed the overrun on the chapel amounting to an additional $1,724.64.

160 Ibid.

161 *The Tabard*. December 6, 1927.

162 Letter. Nelson Hume to Henry O. Havemeyer. June 16, 1928. Dedication occurred on June 10 over graduation weekend.

163 Letter. Nelson Hume toHenry O. Havemeyer. May 25, 1928. Blessing of the Chapel, Sunday, June 10.

164 *The Tabard*. March 5, 1929. First three windows to be dedicated to Our Lady; these are the windows on the south aisle between tower and porch.

165 Ibid.

166 *The Tabard.* April 9, 1929. Work of Nicola d'Ascenzo of Philadelphia.

167 *The Tabard.* January 12, 1937. Placed in Chapel. Fourth from sanctuary on left-hand side.

168 *The Tabard.* May 14, 1929.

169 Letter. Nelson Hume to Henry O. Havemeyer. May 17, 1929.

170 Pages 24–25 of Mack's history elaborates on various chapel gifts.

171 *The Tabard.* December 9, 1930. In an article written by Nelson Hume, he explains the difference between a carillon and chimes.

172 Letter. Nelson Hume to Henry O. Havemeyer. April 30, 1931. Nelson took lessons in carillon playing from Lefevere.

173 Letter. Nelson Hume to Henry O. Havemeyer. May 11, 1931.

174 *The Tabard.* April 28, 1931.

175 *The Tabard.* May 5, 1931.

176 *The Tabard.* May 12, 1931.

177 Letter. Nelson Hume to Henry O. Havemeyer. June 8, 1931. *The Tabard* article Nelson Hume refers to is May 5, 1931, and *The Tabard* author is actually quoting from the *Waterbury Republican.* However, in *The Tabard.* December 9, 1930, Nelson Hume says, "It is like a giant harp made not of wire strings, but of bells, and it sings from a tower in the open air."

178 *The Tabard.* June 28, 1937. Georgetown University, A.B., A.M., L.L.B.

179 *The Tabard.* February 27, 1934.

180 Letter. Nelson Hume to Henry O. Havemeyer. April 39, 1931. Cost of window $7,500, bells $8,500.

181 Letter. Nelson Hume to Henry O. Havemeyer. July 29, 1931.

182 Letter. Nelson Hume to Mackay. April 4, 1928. "If we do not start the building without further delay, we can not enroll boys to occupy it for the coming year." There is a subscription list available, which went out in letter to Henry O. Havemeyer April 4, 1928.

183 *The Tabard.* October 25, 1932.

184 Interview. Jean Hebert. August 2004.

185 Letter. Nelson Hume to Henry O. Havemeyer. September 2, 1931.

186 Mack writes on page 60 of his history that a musical club was formed in 1919.

187 *The Tabard.* November 26, 1929.

188 Letter. Nelson Hume to Henry O. Havemeyer. June 18, 1929.

189 Letter. Nelson Hume to Henry O. Havemeyer. July 26, 1929.

190 "Canterbury Appeal is Dismissed." [*New Milford paper* (name?)]. [n.d.] [n.p.]

191 Letter. Nelson Hume to Henry O. Havemeyer. April 4, 1930. Lien placed on property for taxes of 1927.

192 Letter. Nelson Hume to Henry O. Havemeyer. June 26, 1929.

193 Letter. Nelson Hume to Henry O. Havemeyer. September 28, 1929.

194 Letter. Nelson Hume to Henry O. Havemeyer. September 30, 1930.

195 Letter. Nelson Hume to Henry O. Havemeyer. November 11, 1929.

196 Letter. Nelson Hume to Henry O. Havemeyer. February 24, 1930.

197 Letter. Nelson Hume to Henry O. Havemeyer. April 30, 1931.

198 As reported in the Smith history.

199 Letter. Nelson Hume to Henry O. Havemeyer. September 24, 1931.

200 Letter. Nelson Hume to Henry O. Havemeyer. December 5, 1931

201 *The Tabard.* December 5, 1933.

202 *The Tabard.* November 28, 1933.

203 *The Tabard.* October 11, 1932.

204 "Joseph Campbell '21, Expert on Mythology, Remembered: The *New York Times* obituary and personal tributes." *Pallium.* Vol. 4, no. 3. Winter 1988. p. 4.

205 Ibid.

206 *The Quill.* Vol. 4, no.1. December 1919. p. 1.

207 *The Tabard.* November 11, 1930. Joe was to hold the record at Columbia for the half-mile for a number of years.

208 *The Tabard.* June 13, 1921.

209 *The Tabard.* January 31, 1922.

210 *The Tabard.* May 3, 1927.

211 *The Tabard.* November 11, 1930.

212 Ibid. The Krugs had the highest averages in school. Paul had 85.20 and was also hockey captain. Thomas followed with an 84.40. In school year 1930–1931, Thomas was editor of *The Tabard* and of *The Quarterly.*

213 *The Tabard.* May 10, 1932.

214 *The Tabard.* June 25, 1938.

215 *The Tabard.* January 20, 1931.

216 *The Tabard.* February 26, 1935. Alec was born in 1882; he was only 53 when he died.

217 From Smith history.

218 *The Tabard.* April 14, 1936.

219 *The Tabard.* February 11, 1936.

220 *The Tabard.* January 21, 1936 and *The Tabard.* October 6, 1936. Gregory Smith '30 donates over fifty books to library in the first gift since the fire.

221 *The Tabard.* April 14, 1936.

222 From page 30 of Mack's unpublished history.

223 *The Tabard.* April 21, 1936.

224 There is more to the description of the building found on page 71 of the Smith history, which is omitted here.

225 Which was the alumni room when Smith wrote his history.

226 *The Tabard.* January 26, 1937.

227 *The Tabard.* February 14, 1933. The idea may have germinated as a result of a letter to the editor in this issue. "There is one element that is lacking at Canterbury . . . It is something which we can refer to in case of an actual victory . . . and is also something which leaves with the boy a lasting remembrance of his school. That one item is a school song."

228 *The Tabard.* October 25, 1935.

229 *The Tabard.* October 14, 1943.

230 Leonard, Fr. Sebastian, O.S.B. "A Restoration Story." *Pallium.* Vol.

20, no. 1. Fall 2003. p. 38.

231 *The Tabard*. October 5, 1937.

232 *The Tabard*. December 7, 1937.

233 *The Tabard*. October 5, 1937.

234 *The Tabard*. November 2, 1937. Ad in later *Tabard*: Timber Trails Inn was located on Route 37, Sherman, CT.

235 Letter. Nelson Hume to Henry O. Havemeyer. November 29, 1941.

236 Letter. Nelson Hume to Henry O. Havemeyer. June 20, 1938.

237 Letter. Nelson Hume to Henry O. Havemeyer. August 12, 1939.

238 Letter. HMcD to Henry O. Havemeyer. July 29, 1938.

239 *The Tabard*. June 7, 1931. Gerard Coad Smith, architect of the first SALT talks and recipient of a Canterbury medal.

240 Letter. HMcD to Henry O. Havemeyer. August 2, 1938.

241 Minutes. Board of Trustees meeting. June 10, 1938.

242 Letter. Nelson Hume to Henry O. Havemeyer. August 27, 1938. Includes architect's drawing and floor plan.

243 Letter. Nelson Hume to Henry O. Havemeyer. November 26, 1938.

244 Minutes. Board of Trustees meeting. Tuesday, June 1939.

245 *The Tabard*. April 26, 1946. Awarded Laetare Medal for the "brilliant discharge of a wartime diplomatic mission;" Ambassador to Spain in 1942.

246 Letter. Nelson Hume to Henry O. Havemeyer. September 15, 1938.

247 Notification of Trustee Meeting. May 31, 1941. T. F. Carmody. In this notification, John Burke's name is typed as Charles S Burke.

248 Letter. Nelson Hume to Henry O. Havemeyer. February 16, 1939.

249 Letter. Nelson Hume to Henry O. Havemeyer. February 2, 1939.

250 Andrew Smith in his unpublished history makes reference to the First Form being eliminated years ago and the Second Form being continued intermittently and *The Tabard*. October 9, 1934, "Canterbury Opens 20th Year With 35 New Boys" "First Form Again Added to Lower School with Seven Younger Fellows."

251 Letter. Nelson Hume to Henry O. Havemeyer. February 2, 1939.

252 Letter. Nelson Hume to Henry O. Havemeyer. October 24, 1939.

253 Letter. Henry O. Havemeyer to Nelson Hume. October 31, 1939. Havemeyer goes on to say, "I do wish you would let this star shine brighter than the others that come to your immediate vision from time to time."

254 Letter. Nelson Hume to Henry O. Havemeyer. November 1, 1939.

255   [http://www.catholicliturgy.com/index.cfm/FuseAction/ PartEssay/Index/100/SubIndex/0/ContentIndex/11/Start/8] "The recitation with the celebrant of all the prayers which are sung by the people at Missa Cantata, the Gloria (Et in terra, etc.), the Credo (Patrem omnipotentem, etc.), the Sanctus, and the Agnus Dei."

256 *The Tabard.* November 11, 1930. "The largest one [bell] will be rung every evening at nine o'clock. The latter will be a revival of a custom common in Catholic countries, when at the time of curfew, a bell known as the De Profundis bell is rung to call the people to pray for the dead."

257 *The Tabard.* November 30, 1937.

258 *The Tabard.* January 25, 1938.

The   Tabard.   February   8,   1938   and [http://www.georgeglazer.com/prints/nathist/marine/liedl.html] Charles Liedl was a renowned and prolific illustrator of hunting, fishing, and wildlife scenes.

260 Ibid.

261 Fullan, Robert, '39. "Reflections of a *Tabard* Editor." *Pallium* Vol. 4, no. 2. Fall 1987. p. 11. This *Pallium* article lists all *The Tabard.* editors from 1919–1988.

262 Letter. Nelson Hume to Henry O. Havemeyer. February 16, 1939.

263 In a telegram September 27, 1940, Nelson Hume writes, "There will be nothing out of the ordinary except a feast for the boys." *The Tabard.* October 2, 1940.

264 Telegram Nelson Hume to Henry O. Havemeyer. September 27, 1940.

265 Letter. Nelson Hume to Henry O. Havemeyer. September 30, 1939.

266 Letter. Nelson Hume to Henry O. Havemeyer. October 2, 1940.

267 1940–1966.

268 Interview. Jules Viau. Wed., August 25, 2004.

269 *The Tabard*. February 19, 1941.

270 *The Tabard*. March 8, 1938. "Originally it was a Chevrolet truck of some antiquity. The body of an old Studebaker Farm Truck replaced the existing one. From this point to the present, the number of changes made has been lost track of, but as a monument to almost every make and model of the horseless buggy yet made there remains the present contraption."

271 David Hume, son of Nelson, now has possession of the cigarette case.

272 Even from Canterbury's earliest days (Letter. Nelson Hume to Henry O. Havemeyer. April 29, 1916) NH is constantly beseeching Havemeyer to come and visit the school. "The small boys are playing a base ball game this morning, and the weather is fine and warm . . . Mr. Ryan and Mr. Ward motored out to see both games. I wish you could come out occasionally so as to get first hand impressions as to what is being done."

273 Letter. Henry O. Havemeyer to Nelson Hume. December 27, 1940.

274 *The Tabard*. April 24, 1928.

275 Letter. Nelson Hume to Henry O. Havemeyer. April 8, 1942.

276 Letter. Nelson Hume to Henry O. Havemeyer. June 7, 1941.

277 *The Tabard*. April 23, 1941. This firm also did the chapel organ front and some work in St. Patrick's Cathedral in New York City.

278 *The Tabard*. March 5, 1941.

279 *The Tabard*. May 7, 1941.

280 Graduation program. June 6, 1942. In Hume correspondence file.

281 This is interesting because Gilbert's father resigned from the board in 1919. However, John retained close ties with the school. He met his wife, Miss Salembier (sister to Dick and Junie) at one of the Canterbury school dances.

282 *The Tabard*. October 1, 1941 and *The Tabard*. October 8, 1942. Miss Feeley replaced Miss Walsh the following year.

283 Letter. Nelson Hume to Henry O. Havemeyer. August 29, 1942.

284 *The Tabard*. February 11, 1942 prints a summary of the report Doctor Hume wrote for the March issue of *The Independent School Bulletin*.

285 "Homecoming Day 1942" in Hume correspondence files.

286 Ltrs. 1942.

287 *The Tabard*. January 21, 1942.

288 *The Tabard*. January 14, 1942.

289 *The Tabard*. November 8, 1945.

290 *The Tabard*. February 8, 1945. Two boys also graduated midyear in 1945, James Couzens and George Hamilton. They completed a program of acceleration during the summer. There was a small farewell party in Middle House prior to their leaving. *The Tabard*. October 19, 1945. This issue of the paper notes that Charles Kipp also left early for the Army Air Force.

291 *The Tabard*. March 4, 1942. The remainder of this story is apocryphal.

292 *The Tabard*. February 4, 1943.

293 *The Tabard*. April 29, 1943.

294 *The Tabard*. June 15, 1944. The Roll of Honor was published in the Graduation Issue, p. 10.

295 *The Tabard*. April 23, 1942.

296 *The Tabard*. December 3, 1942. Steve Hume, Tony Cudahy, and Tom Murray were on duty in North House.

297 *The Tabard*. October 22, 1942. Stirnweiss started as basketball coach in the fall of 1942. At the time he was second baseman for the Newark Bears of the International League. On March 15, he was scheduled to go into spring training with the Yankees. As assistant coach in football, Stirnweiss took over when Thesing was called into the service.

298 *The Tabard*. September 30, 1943.

299 *The Tabard*. December 4, 1946.

300 Letter. Nelson Hume to Henry O. Havemeyer, June 5, 1941.
301 Vanasse, Marc. "The 'Bear' Essentials: A Conversation with Jean Hebert." *Pallium*. Vol 5, no. 2. Fall 1988. p. 4.
302 Interview. Jean Hebert. August 2004.

PART II: The Sheehan Years

303 Interview. Roderick Clarke. October 28, 2004. Mr. Carmody assumed the responsibilities as President of the Board of Trustees in 1949, a position that he held until 1959.
304 *Time*. July 19, [1948].
305 Viau, Jules. "A Tribute." *Pallium*. Vol 10, no. 1. Fall 1993. p. 1.
306 *The Tabard*. October 6, 1948.
307 Interview. Jean Hebert. August 2004.
308 Moore, James R. "Remembering Walter Sheehan." *Pallium*. Vol. 10, no. 1. Fall 1993. p. 5.
309 Viau, Jules, "A Tribute," *Pallium*. Vol. 10, no. 1. Fall 1993. p. 1; Letters, Walter Sheehan, various years; Moore, James R., "Remembering Walter Sheehan," *Pallium*. Vol. 10, no. 1. Fall 1993. p. 5.
310 *LaLumiere School Online*: Home/Index [http://www.lalumiere.org/]
311 In the interim, Mr. Moore served as the eighth headmaster of Berkshire School (1979 to 1987). Berkshire School What's Up [http://www.berkshireschool.org/goingon/archives/2004/120604-moore.htm]
312 *Minutes of the La Lumiere School for Boys Board Meeting*. December 13, 1967.
313 Moore, James R. "Remembering Walter Sheehan." *Pallium*. Vol. 10, no 1. Fall 1993. p. 5.
314 Interview. Gilda Martin. August 23, 2004. Confirmed in interview with Jules Viau, Wed., August 25, 2004.
315 Letter. Jim Wickenden, Headmaster, Tabor to Walter Sheehan, et. al. "Re: Frank Boyden dinner." January 16, 1968.

316 Moore, James R. "Remembering Walter Sheehan." *Pallium.* Vol. 10, no. 1. Fall 1993. p. 5.

317 Interview. Jean Hebert. August 2004.

318 Interview. Gilda Martin. Mon., August 23, 2004.

319 Interview. Jules Viau. Wed., August 25, 2004.

320 *The Tabard.* October 6, 1948.

321 Friend of Bill D'Alton and a Canterbury alumnus, Howard Junker '57 returned to Canterbury around this time to teach Latin. He published his first free-lance piece, "Ice Fishing on the Housatonic," for the *New Milford Times.* "*Tabard* Ties." *Pallium.* Vol. 4, no. 3. Winter 1988. p. 2.

322 Vanasse, Marc. "Canterbury Drama Center Stage: A History in Five Acts." *Pallium.* Vol. 4, no. 4. Spring 1988. pp. 3–4.

323 Ibid.

324 *The Tabard.* October 12, 1959.

325 Letter. Nelson Hume to Henry O. Havemeyer. August 12, 1939.

326 Letter. Walter Sheehan to Francis X. Maguire. December 20, 1967.

327 Letter. Walter Sheehan to Peter D. Kiernan. September 19, 1973.

328 Letter. Walter Sheehan to Mr./Mrs. John O. Teeter. June 11, 1969.

329 Moore, James R. "Remembering Walter Sheehan." *Pallium.* Vol. 10, no. 1. Fall 1993. p. 5.

330 Letter. Nelson Hume to Henry O. Havemeyer. June 24, 1931.

331 Hierro, Sylvia. "The Agony and The Ecstasy: The Development of A Fine Arts Program." *Pallium.* Vol. 4, no. 3. Winter 1988. p. 6.

332 *The Tabard.* October 30, 1982.

333 *The Tabard.* March 2, 1984.

334 Although as early as 1920, a librarian did come in part-time each school day. *The Tabard.* October 18, 1920.

335 *The Tabard.* October 17, 1969.

336 Interview. Jean Hebert. August 2004.

337 In an interview with Rod Clarke, October 28, 2004, Rod made mention that Francis Carmody approached his old roommate from Yale, Paul Mellon, to fund this. It was Paul's donation that created the faculty

retirement endowment.

338 Marc Vanasse says the houses purchased were 16 Treadwell Avenue and 29 Summit Street.

339 Remarks of Trustee President Francis Carmody Honoring Philip H. Brodie at Commencement can be found in *The Tabard* October 15, 1956.

340 *The Tabard*. February 19, 1980.

341 *The Tabard*. May 26, 1973.

342 Ibid.

343 *The Tabard*. January 12, 1937. Alumnus Wisner Miller '30 offered post as business aide to headmaster.

344 *The Tabard*. October 23, 1993.

345 *The Tabard*. December 16, 1980.

346 Author's personal reminiscences.

347 Letter. Nelson Hume to Henry O. Havemeyer. April 12, 1916.

348 Leonard, Fr. Sebastian, O.S.B. "A Restoration Story." *Pallium*. Vol. 20, no. 1. Fall 2003. p. 38.

349 "The Extraordinary Synod: Diversity Within Union." *Pallium*. Vol. 2, no. 3. Winter 1986. p. 2.

350 Ibid. p. 3.

351 As Executive Director of the International Physicians for the Prevention of Nuclear War, Conn Nugent won the Nobel Peace Prize in 1985.

352 "Canterbury's Agents of Peace." *Pallium*. Vol. 2, no. 3. Winter 1986. p. 8.

353 *Cantuarian*, 1956.

354 *The Tabard*. November 9, 1944. The Trapp Family Chorus performed at Canterbury on Monday, November 20, 1944.

355 Interview. Jean Hebert. August 2004.

356 *The Tabard*. October 10, 1960.

357 *The Tabard*. November 16, 1962.

358 Interview. Roderick Clarke. October 28, 2004.

359 Hierro, Sylvia. "The Agony and The Ecstasy: The Development of

A Fine Arts Program." *Pallium*. Vol. 4, no. 3. Winter 1988. p. 6.

360 The day was made doubly exciting by victories by both the varsity football and soccer teams. In fact, soccer would go on to have its best record, 5-2-1, since 1961. *The Tabard*. November 21, 1967.

361 Fr. Quinn returned to Canterbury again in February of 1968 to deliver a speech on the subject of change in relation to the unchanging God. *The Tabard*. February 22, 1968.

362 Interview. Roderick Clarke. October 28, 2004.

363 *The Tabard*. October 17, 1968.

364 Ibid.

365 *The Tabard*. October 26, 1926 and *The Tabard*. October 25, 1935. By 1935, over three hundred bushels produced; cider served to boys at the afternoon tea at 5:00.

366 *The Tabard*. April 26, 1966.

367 Son of Hubert McDonnell.

368 Letter. January 16, 1968. "Twit" Sheehan would return the favor two years later, by serving as toastmaster at a dinner honoring Frank Boyden.

369 *The Tabard*. May 13, 1966.

370 *The Tabard*. June 1, 1966.

371 Interview. Gilda Martin. August 23, 2004.

372 *The Tabard*. October 27, 1978.

373 *The Tabard*. May 27, 1972.

374 *The Tabard*. March 4, 1982.

375 *The Tabard*. October 25, 1966.

376 *The Tabard*. April 26, 1972.

377 *The Tabard*. October 13, 1967; *The Tabard*. January 20, 1968; *The Tabard* April 1, 1968; *The Tabard* June 10, 1968.

378 *The Tabard*. October 13, 1967.

379 *The Tabard*. June 26, 1969.

380 *Shriver, Robert Sargent* on encyclopedia.com [http://www.encyclopedia.com/html/S/Shriver.asp] Feb. 2006.

381 *The Tabard.* May 8, 1969.

382 *The Tabard.* October 17, 1969.

383 *The Tabard.* October 10, 1970.

384 Ibid.

385 *The Tabard.* February 27, 1970.

386 *The Tabard.* June 13, 1970.

387 *The Tabard.* November 25, 1970.

388 *The Tabard.* June 13, 1970.

389 *The Tabard.* February 28, 1971; March 23, 1971; April 26, 1972; May 27, 1972.

390 Mandler, Lou. "Not for Women Only: Issues and Trends in Coeducation." *Pallium.* Vol. 8, no. 1. Fall 1991. p. 2.

391 *The Tabard.* November 26, 1968.

392 *The Tabard.* November 12, 1970.

393 Gumpper, Valerie, '74. "I Remember." *Pallium.* Vol. 8, no. 1. Fall 1991. p. 4.

394 Mandler, Lou. "Not for Women Only: Issues and Trends in Coeducation." *Pallium.* Vol. 8, no. 1. Fall 1991. p. 2.

395 "The Canterbury Observer." *Pallium.* Vol. 8, no. 1. Fall 1991. p. 10.

396 *The Tabard.* October 21, 1972.

397 *The Tabard.* May 27, 1971.

398 *The Tabard.* October 21, 1972.

399 *The Tabard.* February 28, 1973.

400 *The Tabard.* May 17, 1973.

401 *The Tabard.* May 27, 1972 and *The Tabard.* January 3, 1973.

402 *The Tabard.* May 26, 1973.

403 *The Tabard.* December 20, 1969.

404 "A Life in Review: Walter F. Sheehan 1910 – 1993." *Pallium.* Vol. 10, no. 1. Fall 1993. p. 4.

405 Ibid. p. 3

406 Viau, Jules. "A Tribute." *Pallium* Vol. 10, no. 1. Fall 1993. p. 1.

PART III: The Long Look Backward

407 Final chapter of Mack history

PART IV: The Reydel Years

408 Letter. Walter Sheehan to Mr. Franklyn E. Learned, State of CT, State Dept. of Education. February 14, 1973.
409 Interview. Gilda Martin. August 23, 2004.
410 Interview. Jean Hebert. August 2004.
411 Letter. Jack Reydel to Peter L. Cashman. September 27, 1973.
412 *Philosophy of Education* [September 4, 1973].
413 Letter. Jack Reydel to James M. Mead. October 24, 1973 and Headmaster's Report to the Trustees [n.d.].
414 Interview. Roderick Clarke. October 28, 2004.
415 *The Tabard.* October 26, 1973.
416 Letter. Jack Reydel to Gordon Lawson. December 21, 1973.
417 *The Tabard.* November 28, 1973.
418 Letter. Frank Cavanagh (Trustee) to Jack Reydel. October 15, 1973.
419 *The Tabard.* May 12, 1975.
420 *The Tabard.* October 11, 1975.
421 Letter. Jack Reydel to Thomas F. Gilbane. November 30, 1973.
422 *The Tabard.* November 21, 1975.
423 *The Tabard.* November 28, 1973.
424 Vanasse, Marc. "The 'Bear' Essentials: A Conversation with Jean Hebert." *Pallium.* Vol 5, no. 2. Fall 1988. p. 5.
425 *The Tabard.* November 20, 1976.
426 *The Tabard.* April 29, 1977.
427 *The Tabard.* October 21, 1977.
428 Ibid.
429 *The Tabard.* October 5, 1974.
430 *The Tabard.* May 12, 1975.

431 Letter. John J. Reydel to Parents. December 6, 1973.

432 Ibid.

433 *The Tabard*. November 28, 1973.

434 *The Tabard*. May 11, 1974.

435 *The Tabard*. February 6, 1975.

436 *The Tabard*. November 21, 1975.

437 *The Tabard*. October 11, 1975.

438 *Philosophy of Education* [September 4, 1973].

439 *The Tabard*. October 5, 1974.

440 *The Tabard*. November 28, 1974.

441 *The Tabard*. October 5, 1974.

442 *The Tabard*. November 20, 1976.

443 *The Tabard*. June 2, 1977.

444 *The Tabard*. April 29, 1977.

445 *Welcome to A Better Chance* [http://www.abetterchance.org/] March 20, 2006.

446 Canterbury School. Admissions Office. Statistics provided by Erin Deshaies.

447 *The Tabard*. May 12, 1975.

448 *The Tabard*. October 5, 1974.

449 *The Tabard*. November 28, 1974.

450 *The Tabard*. October 21, 1977.

451 *The Tabard*. October 11, 1975.

452 *The Tabard*. November 21, 1975.

453 *The Tabard*. October 26, 1973.

454 *The Tabard*. November 28, 1974.

455 *The Tabard*. February 6, 1975.

456 *The Tabard*. May 5, 1975.

457 *The Tabard*. November 21, 1975.

458 *The Tabard*. November 20, 1976.

459 *The Tabard*. February 9, 1977.

460 *The Tabard*. May 11, 1974.

461 *The Tabard.* April 29, 1976.

462 *The Tabard.* June 5, 1975.

463 *The Tabard.* June 2, 1977.

464 *The Tabard.* May 11, 1974.

465 *The Tabard.* February 9, 1977.

466 *The Tabard.* June 5, 1975.

467 *The Tabard.* November 21, 1975.

468 *The Tabard.* February 25, 1978.

469 *The Tabard.* April 29, 1976.

470 *The Tabard.* February 6, 1975.

471 *The Tabard.* November 20, 1976.

472 *The Tabard.* September 29, 1973.

473 *The Tabard.* March 30, 1978.

474 *The Tabard.* October 5, 1974.

475 *The Tabard.* May 5, 1975.

476 *The Tabard.* October 11, 1975.

477 *The Tabard.* October 21, 1977.

478 Interview. Jean Hebert. August 2004.

479 *The Tabard.* October 11, 1975.

480 *The Tabard.* March 1, 1974.

481 *The Tabard.* June 8, 1974.

482 Ibid.

483 *The Tabard.* May 30, 1978.

484 *The Tabard.* November 20, 1981.

485 *The Tabard.* June 3, 1980.

486 Ibid.

487 *The Tabard.* October 1, 1980.

488 *The Tabard.* October 11, 1975.

489 *The Tabard.* November 21, 1975.

490 *The Tabard.* April 29, 1977.

PART V: The Clarke Years

491 *The Tabard.* September 27, 1978.

492 "Why Canterbury." *Pallium* Vol. 3, no. 3. Winter 1987. p. 2.

493 *The Tabard.* December 17, 1986.

494 *The Tabard.* October 27, 1978.

495 *The Tabard.* September 27, 1978.

496 "Why Canterbury?" *Pallium.* Vol 3, no 3. Winter 1987. p. 3.

497 *The Tabard.* October 27, 1978.

498 *The Tabard.* December 12, 1978.

499 Ibid.

500 *The Tabard.* September 27, 1978.

501 *The Tabard.* December 12, 1978.

502 Interview. Roderick Clarke. October 28, 2004.

503 Ibid.

504 Interview. Gilda Martin. August 23, 2004.

505 Interview. Roderick Clarke. October 28, 2004.

506 *The Tabard.* September 27, 1978.

507 *The Tabard.* October 20, 1979.

508 *The Tabard.* October 25, 1980.

509 *The Tabard.* October 1, 1980.

510 *The Tabard.* October 24, 1981.

511 *The Tabard.* October 20, 1979.

512 *The Tabard.* October 27, 1978.

513 *The Tabard.* September 27, 1978.

514 *The Tabard.* March 2, 1984.

515 *The Tabard.* October 30, 1982.

516 *The Tabard.* December 14, 1983.

517 *The Tabard.* September 27, 1978.

518 *The Tabard.* May 9, 1981.

519 *The Tabard.* October 30, 1982.

520 *The Tabard.* May 11, 1984.

521 *The Tabard.* October 27, 1978.

522 *The Tabard.* December 12, 1978.

523 *The Tabard.* April 20, 1979.

524 *The Tabard.* November 20, 1981.

525 Mandler, Lou. "Not for Women Only: Issues and Trends in Coeducation." *Pallium.* Vol. 8, no. 1. Fall 1991. p. 3.

526 *The Tabard.* December 16, 1981.

527 "The Girls Are Doing it for Themselves." *Pallium.* Vol. 2, no. 2. Fall 1985. p. 5.

528 Mandler, Lou. "Not for Women Only: Issues and Trends in Coeducation." *Pallium.* Vol. 8, no. 1. Fall 1991. p. 3.

529 "The Girls Are Doing it for Themselves." *Pallium.* Vol. 2, no. 2. Fall 1985. p. 5.

530 Ibid.

531 Ibid. p. 6.

532 "New Trustees Join Board." *Pallium.* Vol. 2, no. 2. Fall 1985. p. 8

533 *The Tabard.* May 12, 1979.

534 *The Tabard.* February 29, 1980.

535 *The Tabard.* February 3, 1983.

536 *The Tabard.* October 1, 1980.

537 *The Tabard.* February 17, 1982.

538 "The Presidential Medal of Freedom." *Pallium.* Vol. 11, no. 1. Fall 1994. p. 6.Gerard C. Smith received the Presidential Medal of Freedom from Jimmy Carter in 1981; Sargent Shriver from Bill Clinton in 1994. The third Canterbury graduate to receive the Presidential Medal was James Burnham '23, founding editor of the *National Review*. He received the medal from Ronald Reagan in 1983.

539 *The Tabard.* May 12, 1982 and *The Tabard.* June 1, 1982.

540 *The Tabard.* October 21, 1983.

541 *The Tabard.* December 5, 1989.

542 *The Tabard.* October 27, 1978.

543 *The Tabard.* November 20, 1981; February 17, 1982; May 12, 1982.

544 *The Tabard.* October 30, 1982; December 2, 1983; February 10,

1984.

545 *The Tabard*. October 21, 1983.

546 *The Tabard*. October 30, 1982.

547 *The Tabard*. February 3, 1983.

548 *The Tabard*. October 27, 1978.

549 Ibid.

550 *The Tabard*. November 19, 1980.

551 *The Tabard*. March 4, 1982.

552 *The Tabard*. May 29, 1984.

553 *The Tabard*. February 10, 1984.

554 *The Tabard*. October 30, 1982. Original plans called for two dining halls and student lounge.

555 Interview. Roderick Clarke. October 28, 2004.

556 Ibid.

557 Ibid.

558 *The Tabard*. February 17, 1982.

559 *The Tabard*. May 29, 1984.

560 *The Tabard*. October 30, 1982.

561 Interview. Roderick Clarke. October 28, 2004.

562 *The Tabard*. October 25, 1984.

563 Ibid.

564 *The Tabard*. March 3, 1983.

565 *The Tabard*. October 30, 1982.

566 *The Tabard*. May 27, 1986. This piece now hangs in the Academic Office.

567 "Same Place, New Space." *Pallium*. Vol. 2, no. 4. Spring 1986. p. 12.

568 Interview. Kim Tester and Sylvia Hierro. March 18, 2005.

569 *The Tabard*. October 25, 1984.

570 *The Tabard*. October 21, 1989.

571 *The Tabard*. May 27, 1990.

572 *The Tabard*. December 17, 1987.

573 *The Tabard*. May 26, 1987.

574 *The Tabard.* November 22, 1985.

575 From old neighbor to new addition." *Pallium.* Vol. 2, no. 2. Fall 1985. p. 15.

576 *The Tabard.* October 29, 1988.

577 *The Tabard.* December 17, 1986. The school received $150,000 for the land.

578 Interview. Roderick Clarke. October 28, 2004.

579 *The Tabard.* March 2, 1984.

580 *The Tabard.* November 16, 1984.

581 "The labor force and unemployment: three generations of change – Gen X, Baby Boomers, and Echo Boomers." *Monthly Labor Review*, June 2004, pp. 34–41.

582 Elderhostel speech. Roderick Clarke. 1990.

583 *The Tabard.* May 9, 1985.

584 *The Tabard.* October 25, 1984.

585 *The Tabard.* May 27, 1986.

586 *The Tabard.* October 29, 1988.

587 *The Tabard.* October 21, 1989.

588 *The Tabard.* November 16, 1984.

589 *The Tabard.* May 31, 1988.

590 *The Tabard.* October 25, 1986.

591 *The Tabard.* November 16, 1984.

592 *The Tabard.* November 16, 1984.

593 *The Tabard.* October 29, 1988.

594 *The Tabard.* November 22, 1985.

595 Ibid.

596 *The Tabard.* October 25, 1986.

597 *The Tabard.* October 29, 1988.

598 "Tangible Assets: Bryan Kiefer and Company." *Pallium.* Vol. 4, no. 2. Fall 1987. p. 4.

599 *The Tabard.* February 28, 1986.

600 *The Tabard.* March 10, 1988.

601 *The Tabard.* December 14, 1990.

602 *The Tabard.* October 24, 1987.

603 *The Tabard.* December 13, 1988.

604 Big brother/big sister letter. Mary Holton, Assistant Dean of Students, Summer 2004.

605 *About Amnesty International – Amnesty International.* [http://web.amnesty.org/pages/aboutai-index-eng]

606 *The Tabard.* March 1, 1989.

607 Interview. Kim Tester and Sylvia Hierro. March 18, 2005.

608 *The Tabard.* December 15, 1989.

609 *The Tabard.* December 17, 1986.

610 *The Tabard.* May 27, 1990.

611 *The Tabard.* February 28, 1986.

612 "Bright Smile, Gentle Ways." *Pallium.* Vol. 5, no. 2. Fall 1988. p. 3.

613 *The Tabard.* October 29, 1988. Peter III '71, John '72, Mary Carroll '74, Gregory '75, Michael '77, Stephen '78, and Anne '81.

614 *The Tabard.* November 22, 1985. Reported in *The Tabard* as Deathwatch.

615 Vanasse, Marc. "Canterbury Drama Center Stage: A History in Five Acts." *Pallium.* Vol. 4, no. 4. Spring 1988. p. 6.

616 *The Tabard.* December 13, 1988.

614 Kiefer, Bryan. "The Show Must Go On." *Pallium.* Vol. 11,no. 1. Fall 1994. p. 14.

618 *The Tabard.* May 28, 1985.

619 *The Tabard.* December 15, 1989.

620 Ibid.

621 *The Tabard.* December 13, 1988.

622 Vanasse, Marc. "America's Goalie." *Pallium.* Vol. 18, no. 2. Winter 2002. p. 3.

623 *The Tabard.* December 17, 1987.

624 Interview. Roderick Clarke. October 28, 2004.

PART VI: The Sheehy Years

625 *The Tabard*. March 2, 1990.

626 "Thomas J. Sheehy, III: Canterbury's Fifth Headmaster." *Pallium*. Vol. 6, no. 3. Winter 1990. p. 2.

627 *The Tabard*. March 2, 1990.

628 *The Tabard*. October 27, 1990.

629 Ibid.

630 *The Tabard*. October 24, 1994.

631 *The Tabard*. November 15, 1996.

632 *The Tabard*. October 30, 1998.

633 EconEdLink: Economics Minutes: A Case Study: United States International Trade in Goods and Services. [http://www.econedlink.org/lessons/index.cfm?lesson=EM224] Accessed March 23, 2005.

634 Canterbury School opened on September 10, 2005 with 365 students.

635 Interview. Keith Holton, director of admissions. April 7, 2005.

636 *The Tabard*. March 8, 1991.

637 *The Tabard*. October 23, 1993.

638 "A Vision For The Future: The Long-Range Plan of Canterbury School." *Pallium*. Vol. 13, no. 2. Winter 1997. pp. 2-9.

639 Ibid.

640 Ibid.

641 "Old Schoolhouse Renovated." *Pallium*. Vol. 15, no. 1. Fall 1998. p. 1.

642 *The Tabard*. October 22, 1999.

643 "Restored Chapel Windows Dedicated in Ceremony." *Pallium*. Vol. 15, no. 1. Fall 1998. p. 20.

644 *The Tabard*. October 19, 2001.

645 *The Tabard*. May 10, 2002.

646 *The Tabard*. [nd] 2003.

647 "A King-Size Gift." *Pallium*. Vol. 19, no. 2. Winter 2003. p. 3.

648 *Canterbury School View Book* 1998–1999.

649 Vanasse, Marc. "Gene Whiz." *Pallium.* Vol. 13,no. 1. Fall 1996. p. 6.

650 *The Tabard.* March 8, 1991.

651 *The Tabard.* March 2, 1992.

652 Sheehy, Tom, *The Tabard.* May 30, 2000.

653 *The Tabard.* May 30, 2000.

654 E-mail. Algis Stankus-Saulaitis. Mon., March 28 and Tues., March 29, 2006. Ms. Sara Steiger is now in charge of organizing sit-down dinners.

655 *The Tabard.* October 19, 1991.

656 *Apple II Family: Information From Answers.com.* [http://www.answers.com/topic/apple-ii-family] March 31, 2005.

657 E-mail. Rob Roffe. March 31, 2005.

658 *The Tabard.* March 30, 1998.

659 A Guide to Canterbury School 1998–1999.

660 *The Tabard.* December 17, 1992.

661 *The Tabard.* October 17, 1997.

662 *The Tabard.* May 7, 1999.

663 *The Tabard.* March 2, 1992.

664 *The Tabard.* October 19, 1991.

665 *The Tabard.* December 19, 1991.

666 *The Tabard.* March 7, 1994.

667 *The Tabard.* May 7, 1999.

668 Gaines, Patrice. Laughing in the Dark: : From Colored Girl to Woman of Color. NY: Crown, 1994.

669 *The Tabard.* May 10, 2002.

670 Mandler, Lou. "Not for Women Only: Issues and Trends in Coeducation." *Pallium.* Vol. 8, no. 1. Fall 1991. p. 3.

671 C.A.R.E. may have been in existence as early as 1991.

672 *The Tabard.* October 23, 1993.

673 *The Tabard.* October 30, 1998.

674 *Jump rope and hoops for heart.* [http://www.ncaahperd.org/4heart/]

Jan. 2006.

675 E-mail. Guy Simonelli. Tues., March 29, 2005.

676 E-mail. Mary Holton. Tues., April 5, 2005.

677 *The Tabard*. December 10, 2001.

678 *The Tabard*. October 23, 1993.

679 *The Tabard*. May 26, 1992.

680 Ibid.

681 Interview. Madeleine Dreeke. Tues., March 29, 2005.

682 E-mail. Madeleine Dreeke, Thurs., March 31, 2005.

683 *Remedy* database [accessed Sept. 2005] Results for 2004–2005 not posted in Remedy.

684 *The Tabard*. May 28, 1991.

685 *The Tabard*. May 11, 1991.

686 *The Tabard*. March 7, 1994.

687 *The Tabard*. January 1996.

688 *The Tabard*. December 16, 2003.

PART VII: A Look Forward

689 *Canterbury School 2002 Long-Range Plan.*

690 Carter, Hope. "A Letter from the President of the Board of Trustees." *Pallium*. Vol. 13, no. 2. Winter 1997. p. 1.

691 Longfellow, Henry Wadsworth. "My Lost Youth." *The Oxford Book of English Verse*. [http://www.bartleby.com/101/689.html]. Jan. 2006.

692 Final chapter of Mack history.